KATHARINE GRAHAM

The Leadership Journey of
an American Icon

Robin Gerber

PORTFOLIO

PORTFOLIO
Published by the Penguin Group
Penguin Group (USA) Inc., 375 Hudson Street, New York, New York 10014, U.S.A.
Penguin Group (Canada), 90 Eglinton Avenue East, Suite 700, Toronto, Ontario,
Canada M4P 2Y3 (a division of Pearson Penguin Canada Inc.)
Penguin Books Ltd, 80 Strand, London WC2R 0RL, England
Penguin Ireland, 25 St. Stephen's Green, Dublin 2, Ireland (a division of Penguin Books Ltd)
Penguin Books Australia Ltd, 250 Camberwell Road, Camberwell, Victoria 3124, Australia
(a division of Pearson Australia Group Pty Ltd)
Penguin Books India Pvt Ltd, 11 Community Centre, Panchsheel Park,
New Delhi–110 017, India
Penguin Books (NZ), Cnr Airborne and Rosedale Roads, Albany,
Auckland 1310, New Zealand (a division of Pearson New Zealand Ltd)
Penguin Books (South Africa) (Pty) Ltd, 24 Sturdee Avenue, Rosebank,
Johannesburg 2196, South Africa

Penguin Books Ltd, Registered Offices: 80 Strand, London WC2R 0RL, England

First published in 2005 by Portfolio, a member of Penguin Group (USA) Inc.

1 3 5 7 9 10 8 6 4 2

PHOTOGRAPH CREDITS: Insert page 1 (two photos), 2 (top), 3 (bottom): Library of
Congress; 2 (bottom): Image courtesy of the Kathleen Galvin Johnson '53 Archives
of The Madeira School; 3 (top), 6: Copyright *Washington Post,* reproduced by permission
of the DC Public Library; 4 (top), 5 (two), 7 (bottom), 8 (bottom): AP/Wide World Photos;
4 (bottom): Bill Fulton; 7 (top): *The Washington Post,* photo courtesy of Mary Beckner;
8 (top): Copyright *Washington Post,* reproduced by permission of the DC Public
Library, photographer Ray Lustig, *The Washington Star*

LIBRARY OF CONGRESS CATALOGING IN PUBLICATION DATA
Gerber, Robin.
Katharine Graham : the leadership journey of an American icon / Robin Gerber.
p. cm.
ISBN 1-59184-104-6
1. Graham, Katharine, 1917– 2. Publishers and publishing—United States—
Biography. 3. Washington Post (Washington, D.C. : 1974)—History. 4. Newspaper
publishing—Washington (D.C.)—History—20th century. I. Title.
Z473.G7G47 2005
070.5'092—dc22
[B]   2005047655

Printed in the United States of America

For Tony

FOREWORD

Courage, it's said, is not the absence of fear, but the ability to act in the presence of fear, and by that definition Katharine Graham stands as one of the most courageous CEOs of the twentieth century. For this reason, among others, she earned a spot in an article written for *Fortune* magazine highlighting ten of the greatest chief executives in American business history. There stands Graham alongside the corporate icons Sam Walton (founder of Wal-Mart), James Burke (CEO of Johnson & Johnson during the Tylenol crisis), Bill Allen (the man who led the world into the jet age with the Boeing 707 and 747), and the most important leaders in the history of companies like Merck, 3M, and General Electric. To make the list, a leader had to accomplish four tasks. First, the leader had to deliver exceptional results during his or her tenure. Second, the leader had to bring about a distinctive impact on the world, in part by creating a role model that others follow. Third, the leader had to preside over a significant crisis or renewal, making the company even stronger than before the struggle. And finally, the leader had to leave a legacy that transcends his or her own tenure, and ultimately beyond his or her own life. Katharine Graham accomplished all four objectives, becoming a role model not only for women, but for anyone—male or female—who aspires to effective leadership.

Yet she was an accidental CEO, thrust into the role by personal tragedy. On August 3, 1963, Graham heard the crack of a gunshot within her house. She ran downstairs to discover that her husband, Philip, lay dead by his own hand.

On top of the shock and grief, Graham faced another burden. Her father had put the Washington Post Company in her husband's hands with the idea that he'd pass it along to their children. What would become of it now? Graham laid the issue to rest immediately: The company would not be sold, she informed the board. She would assume stewardship.

"Steward," however, would not describe Graham's approach to her new role. At the time, the *Washington Post* was an undistinguished regional paper; Graham aimed for people to speak of it in the same breath as the *New York Times*. A crucial decision point came in 1971, when she confronted what to do with the Pentagon Papers—a leaked Defense Department study that revealed government deceptions about the Vietnam War. The *Times* had already incurred a court injunction for publishing excerpts. If the *Post* published, it risked prosecution under the Espionage Act. That, in turn, could jeopardize the company's pending public stock offering and lucrative television licenses. "I would be risking the whole company on this decision," Graham wrote in her memoir, *Personal History*. Yet to opt for assured survival at the cost of the company's soul, she concluded, would be worse than not surviving. The *Post* published.

Eventually vindicated by the Supreme Court, it was a remarkable decision for an accidental CEO who suffered from lifelong feelings of insecurity; phrases like "I was terrified" and "I was quaking in my boots" pepper her memoir. That anxiety would soon reach a crescendo as *Post* reporters Bob Woodward and Carl Bernstein doggedly investigated what became known as Watergate. Today we take that story's outcome for granted. But at the time, the *Post* was largely alone in pursuing it. In choosing to publish, Graham built a great paper and, in turn, a great company—one that ranks among the fifty best-performing IPOs of the past quarter-century and earned the investment of Warren Buffett. Graham never awarded herself much credit, insisting that, with Watergate, "I never felt there was much choice." But, of course, there was a choice, and many executives would have lacked Graham's stoic will to make the right choice.

If I were forced to pick only one business leader from whom to draw professional learning and personal inspiration, that one leader would very likely be Katharine Graham. She is the consummate example of a Level 5 leader. Most corporate CEOs barely make it to Level 4; few make it to Level 5—the highest level we discovered in our research into what separates great companies (and their leaders) from merely good ones. These leaders distinguish themselves not by their towering personalities—indeed, most had a "charisma bypass"—but by something quite surprising: their humility. But it is humility of a special type: the leader is ambitious first and foremost for the cause, the company, and its core values, not himself or herself. When you combine this beyond-self ambition with the ferocious will to do whatever it takes (*whatever* it takes) to make good on that ambition, you have the makings of a truly great leader.

People often ask, "What does it take to become such a leader?" That is the very point of this book: to help the rest of us learn from this remarkable person, her life, and her executive process. Robin Gerber has dedicated herself to answering this question, and by picking Katharine Graham as her focal point, she has done us all a great service.

Jim Collins
Author of *Good to Great*

CONTENTS

INTRODUCTION: TWICE-BORN

"I'd led what I thought of as two separate lives. Wife and mother for twenty-three years, and then working person for thirty."

—Katharine Graham

The occasion was a much anticipated dinner party just after the end of World War II. Katharine Graham, wife of Major Phil Graham, fussed over the plans for the evening. Her husband had just returned from his post in the Pacific as an intelligence officer in the Army Air Corps. Four years earlier, on December 7, 1941, just eighteen months after their wedding, the United States had entered the war. Like Americans in every part of the country, with Phil's return the couple were working out their postwar plans. Phil was torn between his father's entreaties to return to his home state of Florida and his father-in-law's offer to become heir apparent at the *Washington Post* as associate publisher.

The young couple were also getting reacquainted, adjusting to the demands of two young children, and creating a social life. After their whirlwind courtship and marriage, the war had fragmented their time together. The last time Phil had been home on a short leave, Katharine had been near to term with their second child. The visit had been frantic and strained, reflecting slowly emerging marital problems.

The war's end marked a new beginning for Phil and Katharine's domestic life. Because his postings had kept him from meeting some of Katharine's best friends, she looked forward to hosting an intimate evening of introductions. She had invited June Bingham and her husband, Jonathon, to dinner, along with two other couples. Katharine and June had been pregnant at the same time during the war. They often lunched together, did support work for the troops, and shared stories of the men they loved and missed. June was looking forward to meeting Phil after all she had heard from Katharine. "I love her, so I'm sure I'll love him," she thought.

As the evening approached, Katharine worried about the menu, about the seating, and about how everyone would get along. Her first dinner party during the war, when Phil was away, had been a disaster. A political disagreement had broken out between her friends and they left in fury. How had her mother carried off such flawless evenings of good food and sparkling conversation? she wondered.

Katharine's house also presented challenges. She had bought it in haste, after driving Phil to the airport for his final tour overseas. He told her during the car ride that a house she planned to buy was suddenly unavailable. The real estate agent told him that the property had a restrictive covenant against Jews and Negroes. Katharine's father, Eugene Meyer, millionaire financier, former head of the Federal Reserve, adviser to presidents, and owner of the *Washington Post* was Jewish. With her second baby soon to be born and Phil leaving, Katharine decided to renew her search rather than sue over the incident. Dispirited, she bought the first house she could, writing her husband that it didn't suit her at all, and no wonder. Built in nondescript gray stone, the ground floor had two living rooms, but the kitchen and dining area were in the basement.

Katharine greeted her guests with a mixture of delight and anxiety. Phil seemed in sparkling form. Historian Arthur Schlesinger Jr. would say of Phil, "Only John Kennedy among my contemporaries had comparable gifts of intelligence and charm." The menu was simple, but Katharine's liquor cabinet held good whiskey from her father's supply, which was a treat for the small gathering. Phil began drinking early and heavily. Before long he was drunk, stumbling out to the backyard, where he passed out on the grass. Katharine acted as if nothing was amiss. She carried on gamely, despite the turmoil she must have been feeling inside. When it came time for the guests to leave, Katharine disappeared, then returned with Phil, who managed a tepid good-bye to his guests.

Katharine and June never discussed the embarrassing evening, but June had begun to form her opinion of the man her friend so adored. The two couples would spend other times together, playing tennis, having dinner, attending the same parties, and the pattern was the same. "He wasn't nice to her," June said.

As the years passed, after Phil became the powerful head of the *Washington Post*, others would say worse—that he called her names in front of people, even in front of the children. That he belittled her intellect, her looks, her Jewish heritage. That he physically abused her. That years of marriage to Phil ate away at Katharine's self-confidence, which had been undermined years earlier by her overbearing mother. Then, eighteen years after the harbinger that was an embarrassing evening with friends, everything changed in an instant.

On August 3, 1963, Phil Graham, publisher of the *Washington Post*, head of a growing media empire, adviser to presidents, traveled to his country home with his wife. As Katharine napped, he took a 28-gauge shotgun and loaded it with one cartridge of bird shot. Taking the gun into a downstairs bathroom, he shut the door, sat on the edge of the tub, and propped the weapon against his temple. Katharine woke to the deafening explosion. She raced to find Phil, but grief and horror sent her running from the scene.

Katharine's years of marital turmoil ended with Phil's death, but scars remained. Despite their difficulties, he had been her greatest love; she would never find another. His violent end shattered the fragile facade of normalcy she had maintained for years. She had children to comfort, her own emotions to master, and a sudden void in the company now solely in her control.

Katharine felt "paralyzed . . . in a state of absolute terror," and outsiders thought they could take advantage of her shock. Other publishers told her they wanted to help, but she knew they wanted to take the paper, figuring the "poor widow" would want to sell. She saw them as "vultures and hawks circling around [her] head . . . asking and asking and asking." She had other ideas.

Just two days after Phil's death, Katharine decided to take the advice of Fritz Beebe, chairman of the Post Company board of directors, who would prove to be a sympathetic and supportive mentor. She asked to speak at a meeting of the board. She was beyond nervous, having lived for so many years in her husband's larger-than-life shadow, without the barest preparation for speaking to men of power and importance about business matters. Her twenty-year-old daughter, Lally, had come home from college to help. Lally drafted some notes for her mother, tried to reassure her, and finally hopped in the car, still clad in her pajamas, to go along for the drive to the meeting. Katharine, dressed in black, entered the room with her eyes downcast, her face gray and solemn. She sat down and straightened her back, while the room full of anxious men listened intently.

Speaking in a low but even voice, Katharine started by thanking them for their work and their loyalty during Phil's illness. She said nothing of her own pain, and she shed no tears but rather concentrated on telling them what they most wanted to hear. "This has been, this is, and this will continue to be a family operation," she said. "There is another generation coming, and we intend to turn the paper over to them." She let them know that she would be stepping into the place Phil had held, and her steadiness steadied them. Whatever happened next, at least they knew the paper wouldn't be sold. On September 9, 1963, the new president of the Washington Post Company walked into her husband's old office and her own new life.

As Phil's wife, Katharine had been a timid, matronly woman, her talent and vision largely hidden for more than twenty years as she fulfilled her duties as wife and mother. Insecure and downtrodden, she seemed to lack either business experience or ambition. How did she find the courage and confidence to take the helm of a multi-million-dollar corporation? This is the central question of Katharine Graham's life, and the answer lies in a multiplicity of factors. As historian Michael Beschloss writes, "In real life there is usually not one single clue to what motivates people." In Katharine's case there were many clues, some conflicting and some in concert, so that those who knew her often had varying interpretations of her behavior.

Phil's death allowed Katharine's mature and long-concealed self to emerge. As her friend June Bingham put it, "The mantle had fallen on her, and in some ways, it must have been an enormous relief." With Phil gone, the pent-up energy of Katharine's unrealized desires and ambitions began to drive her actions. That energy combined with a deep sense of duty to the enterprise her husband and father had built. Her father intended the paper to pass down through generations of his family, and Katharine wanted to fulfill his dream. To do so, she would have to overcome the inner voices from a life in which she had been a powerless observer, denying much of who she had been to fill an overwhelming new role. According to psychologist and philosopher William James, "Emotional events, especially violent ones, are a potent force in altering our plans and vision for the future." Katharine had to end her first life after the shattering death of her husband. Her understanding of her place in the world collapsed and reformed. She became, in James's words, "twice-born"— a leader whose future was forged from the fires of personal trial.

James believed that people who are twice-born could reach a "heroic level" of performance "in which impossible things . . . become possible, and new energies and endurances are shown." Katharine, whose heroic leadership would be recognized in time, experienced a rare but not unique conversion. She joined the company of other great leaders whose transformation came as a result of intense distress or life-altering challenges.

In 1893, twenty-four-year-old Mohandas Gandhi came to a turning point in his life when he encountered ferocious racism in South Africa. Trained as a lawyer in London, he went to South Africa to practice law but found himself threatened and humiliated as a "coolie barrister." He "experienced his moment of truth" when on a train bound for Pretoria he was ejected for asserting his right to sit in the first-class compartment, for which he'd held a ticket. Shivering in the station, he thought about duty, about giving up and about returning to India or staying to change racist conditions in South Africa. "I decided," he wrote, "to take the next available train to Pretoria." He remained in South Africa for more than twenty years, leading protests and developing his creed of nonviolent resistance, before returning to his native India.

In 1921, Franklin Roosevelt, a vigorous thirty-eight-year-old husband and father, lost the use of his legs to polio one night while vacationing on Campobello. He reemerged in public life seven years later, a resilient, compassionate, and optimistic leader. Eleanor Roosevelt believed that her husband's suffering gave him "a greater sympathy and understanding of the problems of mankind." His subsequent leadership through the Great Depression and World War II made him one of America's greatest presidents.

Eleanor was herself transformed after discovering her husband's infidelity in 1918. Like Katharine, Eleanor had sacrificed her deep desire to work for change to become a wife and mother. Her conversion came when she found Franklin's love letters to another woman. "The bottom dropped out of my own particular world," she said, "and I faced myself, my surroundings, my world, honestly for the first time." Nearly twenty years before, Eleanor had abandoned an active and growing interest in social reform. After discovering the affair, she reignited her leadership passion, starting a new life in which she changed her country and the world through her work for civil and human rights.

Katharine would show an Eleanorean ability to learn and change. She had to be proactive in her quest to become a successful leader. She needed new skills. She had leadership traits to refine and habits of mind and heart to employ to achieve her new purpose. She discovered, as James wrote, that feelings and ideas that have grown cold and dead can be reborn into something "hot and alive within us [and] everything has to re-crystallize about it." To begin, Katharine drew on the lessons of her past: the influences of her family, the guidance of her schooling, and the experiences of her early career in journalism.

Katharine's journey to leadership, full of life's exhilaration, tragedy, and continuing challenge, is the focus of this book. Late in her life, Katharine offered the world her inner thoughts, and a detailed personal view of those around her, through an intimate memoir. Her book is the starting point for this book's focused view of her leadership. Through her story we can deepen our understanding of how people transform themselves. We can be reminded that the redemption of our best selves is never out of reach. We can learn that leadership is a human trait called forth as circumstance demands, refined and strengthened by our choices and our determination.

KATHARINE GRAHAM

CHAPTER ONE

THE AMBIGUOUS ROOTS
OF LEADERSHIP

"The nuclear family is a tiny political system—a small Leviathan, *Hobbes called it—and a primitive leadership system."*

—James MacGregor Burns

Katharine was the child of leaders. Their traits—sharp, restless, and inquisitive minds, courage, resilience—were her inheritance. Their style—setting and achieving grand goals, cultivating powerful networks, holding values close and family distant—set up a model of leadership for Katharine, as well as leaving her with deep personal insecurities. As Katharine's character develops, it's easy to spot the unstoppable childhood drive to satisfy her parents no matter the cost or difficulty. But could she ever satisfy her mother's demands for excellence in the face of the unrelenting criticism that accompanied those demands? If leadership was in her blood, could Katharine overcome the opposing expectations that came along with being female? Her father, who alternately encouraged her leadership and denied it, had not had to face that issue as he built an empire in his parents' adopted land.

Eugene Meyer, Katharine's father, considered leadership a birth-right. Born in 1875, he was his parents' first son, descended from a long line of rabbis and civic leaders. In the tradition of his forebears, Eugene decided at an early age to make public service part of his life's plan. With characteristic self-confidence, he intended to make history. He wanted to discover and invest in new industries and be part of the birth of new ideas. But to accomplish this goal, he felt he would first need to establish himself, find a wife, and become a father.

Establishing himself meant achieving financial success. Eugene broke away from his father's plan to follow in the elder Meyer's foot-steps and join the financial firm Lazard Frères. Instead, Eugene par-layed the six hundred dollars his father gave him as a reward for not smoking into the $50,000 needed to get a seat on the New York Stock Exchange. In much the same way that Katharine's great friend and mentor Warren Buffett would make his fortune more than a half century later, Eugene invested other people's money. He was tough and a risk taker. When he couldn't reach his family after the San Francisco earthquake in 1906, he set out from New York with $30,000 in his money belt and a pistol in his pocket. Finding his family safe, he decided to stay and use the opportunity of San Francisco's rede-velopment to build his fortune. He became a millionaire the next year, at the age of thirty-one. He had conquered the world of high fi-nance, and with success in hand, he took the next step in his plan.

Eugene met Katharine's mother, Agnes Ernst, the year after he reached the ranks of millionaires. He spied the self-confident twenty-one-year-old woman at an art museum he happened into with a friend. Blond and blue-eyed, wearing a gray tweed suit and a squirrel-fur hat atop her tall, slim frame, Agnes was used to attracting male attention. In a case of kismet meets the Kabbalah, Eugene told his friend, "That's the girl I'm going to marry," but he refused to speak to her or even try to learn her name. Leaving the museum, however, he felt confident of his destiny. It was an astounding act from the hard-nosed, practical businessman, yet it worked. Little more than a week later his friend met Agnes again at a party. Soon after, Eugene and his mystery girl were having their first lunch together.

Agnes had German-born Lutheran parents and a penchant for defying convention and challenging their traditional views. Following her Barnard education, she became the first woman reporter on the *New York Sun*. Her parents were scandalized that she had not pursued teaching or clerical work, which were the only occupations that they considered acceptable for an educated woman. Their daughter also combined an astute eye and a passionate love of art with an enthusiastic, somewhat narcissistic sense of confidence. And no wonder, having been described by the photographer Edward Steichen's wife as "the girl from the sun . . . because of her Valkyrean beauty, her intellect and her . . . job with the *New York Sun*." Eugene, short and broad shouldered, with brown eyes so dark they appeared black, stood in sharp physical contrast to Agnes. But something about this powerful, vibrant woman led him into romantic fantasy. The young couple were married in a small Lutheran ceremony on February 12, 1910, and settled in New York.

And what did Agnes see in Eugene, a man who, though comfortably assimilated into her upper-class world, shared neither her culture nor her religion and was clearly not the handsomest suitor she could have chosen? Agnes carried grand dreams of a glamorous career, but she had also carried the burden of supporting her debt-ridden family. Her adored father, a lawyer, was a frequent drunk as well as a womanizer. Agnes opted for marriage to a man who could save her financially destitute family. Her new husband offered her security, tolerated a surprising degree of freedom, and showed devoted love. In return Agnes gave up her job and took on the role of wife and mother.

For women in the first years of the twentieth century, marriage and a profession were incompatible. Agnes, in character, longed to have it all. All around her, as the nineteenth century moved into the twentieth, the first generation of graduates from women's colleges such as Vassar, Bryn Mawr, Mt. Holyoke, and Wellesley were making their mark. Agnes's contemporaries took the lead on a number of impressive projects, laying the groundwork for social change. Jane Addams started the American settlement house movement in the late 1880s. At the beginning of the new century, Florence Kelley led the National Consumers League's investigation of the treatment of women and children at work. Her protégée Frances Perkins became the first woman cabinet member, as secretary of labor in President Franklin D. Roosevelt's administration. Anarchist Emma Goldman wrote and spoke about women's need to have sexual freedom. Margaret Sanger battled for birth control.

The New York of Agnes's youth was a hotbed of women activists, and Agnes, with her vibrant and wide-ranging mind, absorbed their influence. Her ambition grew out of her times. Katharine describes her as not sympathizing with her era's political radicals, yet Agnes developed a personal radicalism of her own. When educated women were still straining to "fill a place that did not yet exist" for them, she wrote serious freelance newspaper articles, as opposed to the sentimental pieces often written by the few women reporters at the time. One article led Agnes to the world of avant-garde artists, where she befriended the painter Georgia O'Keeffe and photographer Edward Steichen. She reveled in this group of artists and unconventional thinkers. For Agnes, Katharine wrote later, "art dominated all."

Her marriage to Eugene led to a lifetime of ambivalence, shifting between creating a family that fit her enormous expectations and clinging to the world of art and ideas that she loved. In her memoir she wrote, "I wanted a big family but I also wanted to continue my life as an individual." She returned from her honeymoon pregnant with her first child. Two more children were born within the first six years of their marriage.

Meyer Exceptionalism

In early 1917, Eugene decided to start the public service portion of his life plan. Believing the United States' entry into World War I was inevitable, Eugene went to Washington, D.C., to offer his services to President Wilson and his friend Justice Louis Brandeis. He left the three children and his wife, then pregnant with Katharine, on the seven hundred isolated acres of their farm in Mt. Kisco, New York.

Katharine was born on June 16, 1917. In October, Agnes joined her husband in the capital. She was anxious to discover the intellectual and artistic life there, and so she left her children at her and Eugene's Fifth Avenue apartment in New York. A trusted nanny, nicknamed "Powelly," became the children's surrogate parent. Agnes did her duty, bearing Eugene's children and managing the households, but she refused to abandon the bohemian life she so enjoyed before her marriage. "She provided a great nurse who gave us the warm and cuddly stuff," Katharine wrote. "My mother's maternal instincts were less well developed than her artistic ones."

The Meyers lived in Washington without their children until 1921. Katharine was four years old, with a younger sister, before she and her siblings moved to a grand mansion in the heart of Washington, D.C.

Eugene had taken an appointment to the Council of National Defense and then moved to the War Industries Board, where he found his niche as a dollar-a-year man during the First World War. After the Armistice in 1918, he turned his business acumen and large vision into what he called "the work of peace." He wrote that the government must take the helm to "save life and to reestablish the production of the material wealth of the peoples of the whole world." In his role as an adviser to a Senate committee on reconstruction, he called for strength and leadership, and offered his advice with calm self-assurance.

Eugene also maintained his optimism despite the crises of the 1920s, and he maintained his fortune as well. He liked to wisecrack, stayed calm when others flailed, and had a reputation for being open-minded. *Business Week* magazine wrote that he appeared to be having "the time of his life" as an adviser to the president and Congress. In 1931, President Hoover appointed him as governor of the Federal Reserve. From that lofty perch he worked on America's economic future, viewing his options through the smoke of fine and large cigars.

When they were reunited in 1921, the Meyer family moved in and out of several city mansions. Unfortunately, being in the same home as her parents did not assure Katharine of their attention. Eugene's responsibilities and reputation left little time for family. He did, however, make keen observations about his children with his eye characteristically focused on the future. He saw great potential in his third daughter when she was only in grade school. Remarking to the famous gossip and presidential daughter Alice Roosevelt Longworth, Eugene said, "You watch my little Kate; she'll surprise you." Katharine would remember a strong sense of having her father's support, though not a great deal of his time. "Nobody knew him. I knew him best of all and I liked him a lot, but I was never intimate with him," she told an interviewer. Despite his distance, time would show that Eugene had picked Katharine as his favorite child, and Katharine would derive much of her unshakable motivation to fulfill his legacy from his early faith in her.

Eugene's preoccupation with public service and business did not encourage Agnes to pick up the parental slack. Katharine's encounters with her mother were often marked by indifference and even disdain. The Meyer matriarch made no secret that, with four daughters and a son, she would have preferred more boys. Her diary makes scant reference to her children and no mention of Katharine until she was two and a half years old.

Agnes seemed to give little thought to the effect of her maternal behavior on her children. She had a nonstop schedule and went out for dinner most evenings with Eugene while the children stayed home. In the mornings, he brought her breakfast in bed and sat eating beside her at the bedside table. Katharine decided on a plan. "Could the children make appointments to see her?" she asked her mother, who did not find the suggestion amusing. The little girl was left to make her own efforts to be around as her mother dressed or had a massage. Opportunities were fleeting. I'm a "conscientious but scarcely a loving mother," Agnes admitted. Katharine shared the assessment, saying her mother "came on so strong you wilted." The pattern of Katharine's childhood was woven from the strong threads of Agnes as a powerful, intelligent role model and the thin, sharp strands of her criticism. Katharine would wear this childhood mantle her entire life, often appearing strong on the outside but feeling small within.

For Agnes, being a loving mother simply paled beside the psychological rewards of continuing her artistic and intellectual interests, especially with the opportunities presented by her husband's wealth and position. The era's most stimulating people—Charles Lang Freer, Leo and Gertrude Stein, and the sculptors Rodin and Brancusi—became her friends. Marriage to Eugene gave Agnes the freedom to take graduate courses at Columbia University, sail off to Europe on her own, and study Chinese art. When Katharine was six, Agnes published her first book, *Chinese Painting as Reflected in the Thought and Art of Li Lung-mien*. She traveled with Freer, whose gallery in Washington, D.C., would display many of the treasures they found together.

Agnes's friendships and interests developed at a frenetic pace. She not only became interested in an idea, she devoured it, along with the great minds she encountered. This was especially true with men. She had intense, passionate obsessions, most notably with Thomas Mann. She translated his work from German, put him up in her home, and drove him to impatience with her demands. Were her interests in men also intimate? Most were reputedly platonic or unrequited. Whatever the case, she went on inhaling life.

If, as *Time* magazine reported, Eugene had the energy of a "fast-feeding geyser," Agnes fit that description equally well. But as a woman, she could not embrace this energy or live at her peak. She had a household to keep and children to raise. She strained against the confining role and condescended to everyone, even her children. She wrote in her memoir that she felt as if "the whole world were in a conspiracy to flatten out my personality and cast me into a universal mold called 'woman.'" Her five children bore the weight of being both their mother's grandest accomplishment and her greatest frustration. The shadow of Agnes's discontent would follow them for years.

Reconciling the inner conflicts of intellectual and home life led Agnes to create an idealized world. If family was to be her central "profession," it had to be extraordinary. Agnes valued "brilliant eccentrics" over "normal or average" people. She proclaimed and demanded that her family meet her standard of Meyer exceptionalism. Being smarter or more able didn't suffice. She prodded her children toward perfection. She insisted on it in every arena, from sports to academics to social life. After Katharine told her mother that she had read *The Three Musketeers,* Agnes replied, "Undoubtedly a waste of time my dear, unless you read it in the original French."

When "Ma" and "Pa," as the children called them, managed to be around, "discussions" were the order of the day. The children learned that they were expected to make a difference in the world, not simply enjoy their wealth. Agnes said that she and Eugene taught the children that "it was fatal to depend on money for the quality and content of your life." Discussions were about issues and ideas, about being citizens of the world. As Katharine wrote in her autobiography, "In proportion to our lack of experience we of the younger generation contributed heat and dogmatic assertions to these discussions, whatever the topic. The noise at our table was often such that nervous indigestion and sometimes a manifest tremor were the unhappy fate of the timid guest who took things too seriously." Years later, at her own dinner parties, Katharine re-created the intellectual ferment of those family meals, giving a new generation of guests a glimpse into the challenges and pleasures of a Meyer upbringing.

Such fascinating, often famous, people as politician and diplomat Adlai Stevenson, French poet and playwright Paul Claudel, and American photographer Edward Steichen came through the Meyer house. Katharine even met Albert Einstein on a trip to Europe when she was fourteen, declaring him, "simply grand!" "Katharine had hobnobbed with the great from her early years," her friend June Bingham recalls, "so later in her life she wasn't intimidated." She grew into a person who seemed most comfortable with people of accomplishment and some fame, a style that would serve her well when she became head of a media company where interaction with the famous and powerful was a frequent part of the job.

Reaching for excellence was also part of Katharine's future, and in this Agnes played a strong role. Shortly after Katharine married Phil Graham, Agnes wrote to Phil of the bond she felt they shared as people who had made their own way during their most formative years. She wrote of driving herself "mercilessly" rather than resting on the comfort of her wealth. "This has been so intense an obsession," she wrote her new son-in-law, "that I fear it affected Eugene and the children almost too much and created an almost restless ambition in everybody." She had, with narcissistic flair, set expectations that only she could meet. Preserving her inflated sense of self meant viewing all but a few exceptional people as failures, and she never changed. Late in life she heard Katharine give an inspired speech introducing John Gardner, the secretary of Health, Education and Welfare in the Johnson administration. As the crowd broke into an ovation, Agnes beamed. Later she told Katharine, "You reminded me of myself." On another occasion Katharine introduced her mother to the architect I. M. Pei. As Katharine chatted with Pei, she responded to a point he made by saying, "I didn't know that." Agnes quickly interjected, saying, "What's surprising about that? You've never known anything." The drumbeat of Agnes's comments over the decades of Katharine's life did more than damage her self-image. Their mother-daughter relationship seemed to color Katharine's ability to trust other women, an emotional block that affected her later behavior as company president.

Even as Agnes belittled her children, she refused to cede an inch in her vision of the family's importance. In her autobiography, Katharine recounts the story of a lavish children's birthday party given by the McLeans, who owned the *Washington Post* at the time. Agnes wouldn't allow her daughters to go, explaining that the McLeans' ostentation was in poor taste. Responding to a friend who suggested that the party was an important place to be seen, Agnes replied, "I want my children to be the ones to want to be with." Ironically, it would be Katharine, the child whose inferiority Agnes seemed to cultivate, who was destined to fulfill her mother's wish.

Festina Lente

Katharine began kindergarten in 1922 at one of the first Montessori schools in Washington, D.C., where she discovered principles of learning she would use her whole life. The founder of this type of school was Maria Montessori, the first female physician in Italy, who developed nontraditional ideas of independent learning that she brought to America in 1915. Katharine could stand on her head and turn cartwheels with tie-dyed scarves, part of the school's unconventional and active approach. Forty years later, Katharine relied on Montessori concepts of "learning by doing" as she grappled with her new role at the *Post*. Even more powerful in Katharine's leadership development were her formative teenage years spent at Madeira, the exclusive girls' school in nearby Virginia.

Madeira held a special place in the Meyer family. Eugene admired Lucy Madeira Wing, the founder, and sent all of his daughters to her school. He and Agnes took a deep and active interest in the school. When Lucy had the vision to move the in-town school to the country, it was Eugene who secured the $300,000 loan to make it happen. He and Agnes also donated 178 acres to expand the property.

The new campus was christened "Greenway." "It is a place of rare beauty," Lucy wrote in the *Alumnae Bulletin* of 1929, with "a long ridge, the highest land along the Potomac for many miles, ending in a promontory, which extends into the river." Madeira's founder had discovered the perfect location to complement her mission—festina lente—a Latin adage translated as "make haste slowly." The Renaissance scholar Erasmus had explained its meaning, "the right timing and the right degree, governed alike by vigilance and patience, so that nothing regrettable is done through haste, and nothing left undone through sloth." Madeira girls were encouraged to be thoughtful and decisive leaders, committed to a Fabian vision of social reform.

Eugene also contributed $25,000 to establish the Harriet Meyer Scholarships, in honor of his mother, at the school. He contributed to furnishings for the library until as late as 1956. Lucy wrote to him with familiarity, addressing him as "Eugene," and thanking him "again and again from the bottom of [her] heart," claiming he had saved her when she was down and out. She also traveled to New York City with Agnes, who introduced Lucy to some of her prominent friends.

Katharine entered Madeira with a class of twenty other girls, in the year of the great stock market crash, 1929. She came to more than a school, however. She came to a family legacy. Two sisters had preceded her, and when the school moved to the country in her second year, she was fully aware that her father had made possible the impressive grounds she walked on. She commuted for two years, sneaking on the lipstick her mother forbade. Later, she boarded in the square redbrick dormitories at the heart of a sheltered world. While a "Poverty Party" provided the chance to raise money for the Social Welfare Fund, the girls' education suffered little from the economic devastation sweeping the country.

Having already had two daughters at Madeira before Katharine, her parents must have been aware of the school's philosophical bent. Madeira girls were headed for a life of marriage and children, but they would carry with them the founder's belief that God was a woman. Lucy offered nontraditional ideas under a traditional umbrella. She wrote to the alumnae of the importance of women's education but tied it tightly to the accepted sphere. "[T]he pivot of civilization is the home," Lucy wrote, "which in every instance must be made by a woman . . . who makes these homes beautiful, gay, charming, sober, earnest, serious, and the quality of our personal culture is the index of the culture of the home." Madeira girls were destined for a proscribed greatness.

In her commencement speech at the end of Katharine's first year, the headmistress struck an Emersonian note, speaking with passion of the American struggle between "tradition and progress." She encouraged the girls to look toward the latter, to show "self-control, imagination and energy" to push "further and faster into the future." She called on them to help create a just and equitable distribution of wealth. In Lucy's vision, parents and teachers held the future of the world in their hands far more than "great men of affairs." Lucy's students would lead the nation from their kitchens and nurseries following her oft-repeated admonition: "Function in disaster. Finish in style."

In addition to spirited leadership, Madeira also had a traditional and rigorous course of study. Top grades were difficult to achieve. Katharine managed A's in history and French, solid grades in her other classes, and A+'s in "order, conduct and punctuality." She carried a heavy schedule in addition to her class work, taking piano lessons; playing hockey, baseball, and tennis; running track; and swimming. She was also a proctor and fire captain in student government, a member of the Glee Club, Camera Club, and Dramatic Association, and a writer and business manager of the school paper, *The Tatler*. She enjoyed the demanding schedule and thrived on the competition. The school's pace would serve Katharine well in the leadership years to come.

Katharine's first piece for *The Tatler*, written in February 1933, was titled "How to Think and Be Successful: By One Who Doesn't and Isn't." The comic self-deprecation of the title didn't match the serious intent of its sixteen-year-old author. Literally a "think" piece, Katharine had taken the festina lente motto to heart. To become independent people, Madeira girls must think matters out "ahead of time, formulating opinions and developing ideas." Well ahead of her time, Katharine slammed women's tendency to ruminate, writing that "it does no good to brood . . . this is nothing but a form of feminine egotism." These words would ring with irony when, as an adult, she had a notorious tendency to rehash every misstep in agonizing and prolonged detail.

Katharine also called on the girls to be thinkers, to see the larger world beyond boarding school. "The business of keeping our minds awake and moving," Katharine wrote, "is not only vital, but necessary for an interesting life." She also showed a comic touch later that year in her junior class report: "Since after numerous efforts we have now all succeeded in passing 'choral,'" she wrote, "we will try to be seniors of some note, and will do our best to make life next year just a song."

A year later, Katharine became business manager of the school newspaper and wrote another clever piece. In a breezy and confident voice, Katharine penned "From the Diary of a Sub-Deb" for *The Tatler*. The sub-deb of the title is a silly and shallow girl. Katharine used the character to make fun of pretense. The sub-deb says that her mother had picked books from a bookshop to match the green color of the school library decor, with no regard to their contents. "I must say it certainly looks nice," remarks the sub-deb. "I always said attractive surroundings conduce a girl to think."

"Diary of a Sub-Deb" shows Katharine full of the confidence and bravado of a graduating senior. Making fun of intellectuals and of her school, the piece manages to be both funny and insightful. Surprised by recognition of her leadership when she was elected senior class president that year, she must have felt encouraged to be bold. Starting as business manager in December 1933, Katharine was also charged with keeping *The Tatler* afloat in the midst of the Depression, which meant finding new sources of revenue for advertising. Like any good leader, Katharine drew on her best contacts, in this case her father, who months earlier had bought a down-and-out newspaper at auction in Washington, D.C.

Eugene, disappointed with the policies of Franklin Roosevelt, the newly elected president, had resigned as head of the Federal Reserve. The sale of the *Washington Post* had come at a perfect time for Eugene, who saw the paper as a powerful way to continue to serve the public interest. But his leap into the new venture came as a total surprise to Katharine. She was living at school, and her parents had not bothered to mention it to her. While she had read about the sale of the *Post* to an anonymous bidder, she'd had no idea it was her father. Joining the family in Mt. Kisco at the end of school, she learned about the purchase when she overheard her parents in conversation. It was an exciting discovery for a girl already showing an interest in writing and publishing.

That winter, Katharine secured a full-page ad from her father's paper for *The Tatler*. In her end-of-the-school-year report, Katharine owned up to the tactic of "appealing to the softer side of . . . parents for funds." She also gave some journalistic advice to the younger girls who were taking over the paper, telling them to write up events "in an interesting fashion" and counseling them that the paper and the girls would "become more alive" as a result of "listening and watching more carefully." The graduating class made a prophesy that year that Katharine would become "a Big Shot in the newspaper racket."

Madeira had sparked Katharine's way of "thinking about thinking" about the wider world and about her leadership potential. Yet the school had also encouraged a narrow direction for her life. Katharine later said, "Subliminally, you absorbed the idea that women were put on earth to find a man, make him happy, keep house, have children." When she graduated in 1934, Katharine embodied the school's contradictions. Her writing had snapped with wit and youthful wisdom, her leadership was recognized by her peers, yet Katharine left feeling "fairly different and shy," with only a few friends. Foreshadowing the self-flagellation that often accompanied her later leadership decisions, Katharine credited Madeira with giving her a "curious hair shirt discipline." Her classmates saw her as a person with integrity. They wrote by her class picture, "Those about her from her shall read the perfect ways of honor." In her flattened estimation, Katharine saw this as the euphemism for a "Goody Two-shoes." Her years of enduring Agnes's criticism made it difficult for her to accept compliments without deflating their intent. She had acted as a leader at Madeira, yet felt inferior—a duality that would haunt her.

The compass pointed north for many Madeira girls after graduation. The single-sex Seven Sister Schools—Vassar, Smith, Wellesley, Bryn Mawr, Barnard, Mt. Holyoke, Radcliffe—were a well-traveled route. Katharine planned on attending Vassar in the fall of 1934. For the summer, rather than join her siblings at Mt. Kisco, the family estate in New York, she worked at her father's new business.

Filled with scandal mongering, the *Post* ranked at the bottom of the city's five newspapers. "Pa started with nothing but a fifty-thousand circulation, a beat-up building, and an Associated Press franchise," Katharine told an interviewer years later. The fifty-seven-year-old banker would spend millions of dollars to turn the *Post* around, but he didn't mind. Eugene had a $30 million fortune and a mission to "tell the truth . . . and not be an ally of the special interests."

Eugene's paper lived up to his creed. During World War II, when Japanese Americans were suffering discrimination, the *Post* stood out as one of the few papers in the country to question government actions. When a three-star general said, "A Jap is a Jap; it makes no difference whether he is an American citizen or not," the *Post* wrote of the American war dead who were "Nisei," or Americans of Japanese descent, and asked, "What was that you were saying, General?" The commentary showed Eugene's leadership touch. He gave his editors leeway, rejecting conformity and hiring people for their character and intellect. Working at the struggling company as a copygirl, or messenger, Katharine absorbed her father's brand of leadership. She also met women journalists who reacted differently from her mother's uncompromising and often exasperating tirades. Mary Haworth was adviser to the lovelorn who would earn a reputation as a "scourge of wrath for selfish simpletons," as well as a "scrupulous counselor." Katharine made friends with her and reporter Malvina Lindsey, and she left for Vassar firmly attached to her parents' new project.

Katharine carried on a brisk correspondence with Eugene and Agnes, commenting on her daily reading of the paper. Eugene kept Katharine up on the business, filling her with details and keeping her closely involved. Agnes had rediscovered her newswoman spirit, writing a blistering series on President Roosevelt's new Works Progress Administration. Consistent with a recurring theme of her life, Katharine's words and actions were out of sync with her low self-confidence. She thought of herself as "un-opinionated," yet she shared strong opinions with her parents. "The 'human interest' that was jammed down [the *Post*'s] throat at first and looked so awkward," she wrote them, "seems to be getting underneath the news now." After a few other minor comments, the seventeen-year-old advised her parents to be "encouraged as a whole."

At Vassar, Katharine again wrote for the school paper, the *Vassar*

Miscellany News. Her copy, according to another student writer, was "crisp, accurate, no-nonsense," and on time. Her peers found her diffident but with an inner self-confidence, "an observer rather than a joiner, a very private person." She listened carefully to all points of view and was known for making up her mind for herself, a style she never lost. In her second year, the December 1935 issue of the *Vassar Miscellany News* included Katharine in a list of members of the class of 1938 who were elected to the position of apprentice editors on the editorial board. She encountered new ideas—a strong strain of left-wing ideology that came through in classes and among her colleagues on the newspaper. The Depression had fostered a leftward tilt to the political views on Vassar's campus. Turning from her parents' Republican allegiance, Katharine became a New Dealer. Finishing her sophomore year, the publisher's daughter once again spent the summer at a newspaper, this time the *Mount Vernon Argus* in suburban New York. She worked as unpaid secretarial help, wrote a few announcements, and an article about female doctors. It earned her a byline—her first. She sent it to her father, who praised the writing with proud restraint. "It looks quite professional," he wrote his favored daughter. Katharine decided that she enjoyed being a working woman.

As junior year at Vassar approached, Katharine felt restless. She had been in London over the summer and told her father that she wanted to spend a year at the London School of Economics. He objected but offered agreement to any school stateside. His daughter responded quickly. Why not the University of Chicago? She had read that the new president, the young, handsome Robert Maynard Hutchins, was "revolutionizing" the school. The words "intellectual ferment" stuck in Katharine's mind. There were boys on campus too, and she'd never lived in the Midwest. Chicago it would be. The choice was informed and impulsive. True to the Madeira motto, Katharine was making haste slowly.

She had chosen wisely. Hutchins took to vigorously attacking the methods of higher education in America and demanding reform. Starting with a base in the great books, guided by the thinking of Aristotle and Aquinas, he challenged students in every discipline to understand concepts and practices within and across areas of study. At Chicago, Katharine had no choice but to challenge her intellect. She majored in American history, took classes in the great books, and toughened up intellectually with Socratic debating questions such as "What are good values?" She took seminars and honors courses that were described by a fellow student as "an intellectual boot camp that broke lesser mortals." According to a friend, Katharine studied, "like a dog," and thrived.

Politically, she became a "committed liberal" and rejected the Communist leanings of many of her friends, joining the anti-Communist wing of the American Student Union (ASU). She learned left-wing tactics in the ASU and argued politics with the campus Communist Party leader. Walking around campus with long confident strides, but striking her peers as "diffident and shy," Katharine's intensity fit a university that stressed intellectual pursuits over an active social life. Even drinking bouts at the local bar revolved around talk of "FDR, Hitler, truth, beauty, and Aristotle." Exasperated by Katharine's serious nature, one friend urged her to "live a little." She lived as she chose, however, on a campus that was a brilliant extension of the rich world of ideas she had known for as long as she could remember.

Katharine gravitated toward people and events that brought her close to journalists. She befriended a young man named Ralph Beck, who wrote freelance stories for the *Chicago Daily News*. He called one day to invite Katharine to accompany him to the nearby Republic Steel plant, as he'd heard there might be a violent clash between the company and the union picketers. She jumped at the chance and found herself in the middle of a historic and bloody day in labor history, May 30, 1937.

Katharine witnessed what came to be known as the "Memorial Day Massacre." A crowd of about fifteen hundred, including wives and children of strikers, marched across the prairie to demonstrate in front of the Republic Steel plant. The police were determined to protect the company. With little provocation, they began beating the demonstrators with clubs and throwing teargas. Soon after, shots were fired. Four protesters were killed and six more mortally wounded. Women and children were beaten. Dozens were left with gunshot wounds; most shot as they fled in panic. Katharine watched in fear and returned to join a vigil supporting the union cause. As the strike wore on, she used her connection to the *Post* to get a tour of the plant to help Beck with his reporting on the strike. When her father came to visit, a student friend of Katharine's asked Eugene if he worried about his daughter being around radicals. "Not at all," he replied. "She'll have a lifetime to hobnob with conservatives." He could hardly have imagined how prescient a comment he had made.

Eugene kept up an active correspondence with his daughter as if she were a member of his staff. He was gradually winning his battle to build a better paper, and he wanted Katharine in on the action. "It is much better sport fighting to get [to the top] than trying to stay there after you have gotten there," he wrote her. He had a vision of his favorite daughter working at his side.

Katharine graduated from the University of Chicago in June 1938. President Hutchins led the ceremonies in "the beautiful Rockefeller-built chapel." Eugene and Agnes didn't show up, but Katharine later insisted that she took little notice. Her friends organized a party at their favorite bar, Hanley's. She left for the farm in Mt. Kisco unsure of her future but not without ideas. The previous year, she had written her sister about her ambitions, saying, "Putting aside an unanswerable question at this time, my ability to be a good reporter, which is a gift given by God to a very few, I mean GOOD reporter . . . What I am most interested in doing is labor reporting, possibly working up to political reporting later." She knew that her father wanted someone willing to "go through the whole mill" and eventually be his assistant, but she said she thought that would be "a first-class dog's life."

On the Waterfront

After graduation, Katharine joined her father on a trip to San Francisco, and she fell in love with the city. Eugene set her up on a ten-week trial basis with the *San Francisco News* at the salary of $21 a week. In the grip of a widespread strike by workers throughout the city, San Francisco turned out to be the perfect proving ground for Katharine's journalistic instincts. Her first report on a meeting between employers and labor representatives earned her high marks. "She phoned in such an excellent account that she promptly was sent on more and more important stories," a *News* executive recounted. "Soon she was our chief outside reporter on the strike. Seldom have we seen anyone take hold of a tough assignment as she did." She became the "legman" for the labor reporter on the paper and embedded herself at the waterfront. The volatile activities of the longshoremen and warehousemen—negotiating with the employers and fighting over labor turf—were fertile ground for a young reporter.

Soon Katharine, blurring the lines between journalism and friendship, kept company with union leaders, including the legendary head of the longshoremen's union, Harry Bridges. Bridges, an Australian, had built a new, militant organization of dockworkers and had led them in a bloody strike that shut down the city of San Francisco in 1934, four years before Katharine's arrival. The strike brought Bridges to national attention. The local business community hated the tough, powerful labor leader with a vengeance. They had been trying for years to get him deported as a Communist, but Secretary of Labor Frances Perkins, who at the time controlled immigration decisions, refused.

There were four newspapers in San Francisco at the time, but only the Scripps-Howard *News,* the paper on which Katharine worked, had any labor sympathies. The other three, most notably Hearst's *Examiner,* wrote rabid editorials and featured screaming antiunion headlines. The labor men were "radicals" and "revolutionaries." They were "Communists," and if they succeeded, "California would be no more fit to live in than Russia."

Bridges, along with his labor friends, began sharing drinks with Katharine in the saloons along the waterfront. Listening to the stories, plans, and political arguments of these labor leaders, Katharine glimpsed a fascinating and previously unknown world. The sights, sounds, and smells of the waterfront seemed exotic to her. Bridges and Eugene Patton, head of the warehouse workers' union, cast large and charismatic shadows. They had battled police and employers and had dreams of creating a more equitable world.

Katharine must have heard echoes of Miss Madeira's call for a just distribution of wealth, as well as the political and economic arguments of her radical college friends and professors. Bridges, Patton, and their friends were the real thing, and Katharine was infatuated in more ways than one. They enjoyed her company as well. According to a friend, Bridges "thought she was smashing." She fell into a romantic relationship with Patton that ended when she learned that he had a wife and a drinking problem.

The *News* kept Katharine on after her two-month initiation. She dug into the work, sensing that the threat of war in Europe made it essential for her to "learn the game well." After nearly eight months, her father pressed her to return to Washington to work for the *Post.* She reluctantly agreed. As the boss's daughter, she decided she couldn't be a reporter as she had been at the *News.* To avoid an awkward situation, she put aside the reporting she loved in favor of becoming an editorial-page employee. *Time* magazine reported on her move. Featuring a picture of a smiling Katharine in a ball gown, the article noted that "comely, twenty-one-year-old Katharine Meyer" would move to Washington, D.C., to work for the *Post* for $25 a week. Her father was quoted as saying, "If it doesn't work, we'll get rid of her." Katharine knew he meant it.

Back in Washington, Katharine edited "Letters to the Editor," served as a proofreader, and wrote 103 light editorials in her first nine months at the *Post*. Of Lou Gehrig she wrote, "It took the persistent march of a cruel disease to slow his bat." She wrote about the dangers of spotted fever, a waiter who dropped a tray of drinks on British royalty, and the "Beauty and Brains" contest sponsored by her new employer. Despite her job writing lighter pieces, editor Felix Morley thought she was being groomed as the "eventual owner-publisher." Eugene had married a strong, independent woman. It didn't seem far-fetched that he would groom their daughter for leadership.

Katharine dove into her job with energy and perhaps a sense of future rewards, but she also found her social footing. Young and anxious to rediscover Washington as an adult, Katharine joined a group of young men and women looking to make their mark on the world. Among her many new acquaintances was the tall, angular, intense Supreme Court clerk named Phil Graham. They met in 1939, when they were in their early twenties, both New Dealers who shared friends and bright futures. Phil came to Washington straight from Harvard Law School. The craggy-faced editor of the *Law Review* seemed effortlessly brilliant to his peers. His former law professor, Supreme Court Justice Felix Frankfurter, treated him as a favorite son, and the young man arrived in the capital with the entry-level makings of a star. His wit and irreverence captivated people in both professional and social circles. It was no wonder that Katharine Meyer came under his spell.

They quickly fell in love. Katharine's working life in San Francisco, the experience she was getting on the newspaper staff, faded in the excitement of emotions that led up to their engagement and wedding. Of San Francisco, Katharine wrote later, "I loved those months . . . as I have loved few times in my life." Yet she traded the passion she felt as a reporter on the distant, turbulent waterfront for her love of Phil and the life they dreamed of building together.

Phil, with his shining self-confident ambition, was a buffer for Katharine from her mother's attacks. Agnes thought Phil was wonderful. By marrying him, Katharine won some measure of her mother's approval. She felt privileged to be around him, and privileged to take care of him, reveling in his quick wit, his wisecracks, and his ability to have fun. In her earlier experiences, Katharine gravitated to radicalism and action, but after coming home to Washington she let this instinct be eclipsed by love and her sense of duty to her marriage. She had traded in her reporter's hat for an apron, substituting one persona for another, much the way her mother had. She would spend the next twenty-three years, as David Halberstam wrote in *The Powers That Be*, "painfully shy, unsure of herself, feeling very much in Phil's shadow . . . awkward and dowdy." Katharine faded into the background as a wife, mother, and, though few people realized it, a leader-in-waiting.

CHAPTER TWO

PHIL GRAHAM'S WIFE

"Personal visions are always multifaceted—they always in-clude deeply felt desires for our personal, professional, organi-zational, and family lives."

—Peter Senge

When Katharine wrote her Pulitzer Prize–winning autobiography in 1997, she devoted nearly a third of the book to the years between 1940 and 1963: those that encompass her marriage to Phil. Readers learn far more about her husband and the business of the *Post*, how-ever, than they do about Katharine. In this way, through both struc-ture and substance, the book reveals its author as a woman in the context of her times—the classic "woman behind the man."

As her friend June Rossbach Bingham put it, "Victorian values were very dominant in the upper reaches of society. Men were heads of the household. Boys were more important than girls." For Kath-arine, and so many women of her time, these rules were accepted and unquestioned. Acceding to the customs of her generation, she gave up her professional ambitions, spending more than two decades as a wife and mother, for the most part, outside of the workplace.

Her upbringing had given Katharine the tools to be a superior leader, but her era demanded otherwise. Like her mother, she would face the inner tension of desiring a role in the larger world but accepting her place in the confines of home and family. June Bingham recalls that "Katharine was stoic. She didn't speak up, but you could feel her mind working. She was reticent, careful, obliging. We all felt it was our duty to be good wives, daughters, and mothers." And so, on June 5, 1940, Katharine started her married life, adopting Phil's ambitions as the substitute for her own.

Phil and Katharine exchanged vows on the magnificent grounds of her parents' estate in Mt. Kisco, but the more memorable backdrop, an argument about the role of patriotism in the classroom, was out of place for a wedding day. Two days earlier, Phil's mentor and new boss, liberal Supreme Court Justice Felix Frankfurter, had shocked his friends and court watchers. He had written the majority decision in a case that upheld the right of states to require public school students, irrespective of their religious beliefs, to salute the flag. Frankfurter's decision outraged the groom and his best man, Edward Prichard. As the guests gathered for the ceremony, Prich, as he was called, along with Phil, Katharine, her sister, and others challenged Frankfurter's assertion that national unity, created by such symbolic acts as saluting the flag, was more important than the students' religious interests. As the arguing intensified and voices were raised, Prich was brought to tears, and the minister was left waiting for an hour. Finally, Frankfurter grabbed the bride firmly by the arm and took her for a walk to calm down.

In retrospect, the discord on a day that was meant to be uniformly joyful must have struck Katharine as portentous. Tension, arguments, and overwrought emotions were to be a constant theme throughout her marriage. The new bride had had some foreshadowing of this even as she took her vows. At a dinner dance after the engagement was announced, Phil had hit the liquor with frightening abandon. Katharine stood by as his behavior became "out-of-hand" and "frenzied." Her brother, Bill, who also attended the party, was looking out for his sister. He cautioned her to think hard about marrying a man who could act as Phil had. Katharine decided to confront her fiancé and began considering an end to the engagement. She planned to talk to Phil the next night, but he showed up with a friend, the moment passed, and Katharine fell back into the intoxicated state of young, uncritical love.

Once married, Katharine learned that her prenuptial fears were justified. Phil's reckless drinking and unpredictable moods generated strife. Perhaps in reaction to this, or in opposition to her mother's independent style, the new Mrs. Philip Graham contrasted sharply with the free-spirited, industrious, and bright young woman of her single years. Despite a limited amount of work at the *Post*, her focus narrowed to home and family, her ambitions seemed to fade, and her intellectual efforts didn't rise above the "doormat" description she gave to herself. Her life revolved around Phil. According to a close friend, Katharine "had tremendous faith in him. She had a genuine fascination in the workings of his mind . . . he always amused her. He was a very jazzy influence in her life." Friends said he helped her worry less and "lightened her personality," but they could not see the private cost of living with his fragile genius.

A Wartime Mother

The newly married Grahams moved to an unassuming house in a modest neighborhood of Washington, D.C., near Georgetown, on Thirty-seventh Street. They were determined to live on their own resources, rather than on Katharine's family's wealth. Their intentions were only partly fulfilled. Katharine brought a lavish trousseau to the marriage and a generous cash gift from her aunt. Her father would sneak cases of good whiskey into the house when Phil wasn't around for his daughter to serve to guests.

Striving to be a dutiful wife, Katharine proposed quitting her job to take care of her husband. But Phil insisted that she continue working at the *Post*, her salary going to Mattie, a maid who cooked, cleaned, and took care of the laundry. For Katharine, who had never learned domestic skills, Mattie provided a needed relief—and with Phil spending long hours as a clerk at the Supreme Court, she felt free to work on the demanding "Brains" section of the paper. She wrote about Eleanor Roosevelt at the beginning of FDR's third term as president and about the trial of Harry Bridges, the labor leader in San Francisco she had socialized with as a reporter. She joined the Women's National Press Club with a recommendation from the *Post*'s managing editor, who said she was a "thoroughly competent reporter." Despite the challenge of her job at the *Post*, Katharine's focus began to shift to her new role, especially in the summer of 1941, as her first pregnancy progressed.

Unfortunately, the young couple's hopes for their first baby were short-lived. Katharine suffered a miscarriage early in the pregnancy. A few months later, she was pregnant again. Before the year was out, the United States would be bombed at Pearl Harbor and drawn into war on two fronts in World War II. Throughout the year, the sense of impending war spurred many young men to join the military, and Phil yearned to be among them. At the same time, he knew how Katharine had suffered from the earlier miscarriage. As this pregnancy progressed she felt "deliriously happy," and Phil decided to put off his plans to enlist until the baby's birth.

By the May due date, Katharine had happily taken on the life of "a vegetable," feeling tired and uncomfortable and more than ready to give birth. Why was this baby taking so long? Labor was induced, but four days passed before it took hold. Then crisis struck. As the baby's head emerged, the umbilical cord twisted around his neck. In the understaffed wartime hospital, the doctor, busy with other births, arrived too late. The child died. Katharine's sense of guilt and loss was still palpable in the autobiography she wrote half a century after the trauma. She had "suggested" that the doctor induce labor, "but it was too soon and the baby wasn't ready," she wrote, seeming to imply that she caused the stillbirth by her impatience. When Phil told her the sad news, she couldn't believe it, never having heard of anyone who had lost a baby. She took the loss as a personal failure, more so because the baby had been a boy and would have carried on the family name. Her friend June Bingham recalled that "Kay saw it as a bitter humiliation." She feared the worst catastrophes for the future—that Phil would join the army and never return; that they would never have children.

Phil did join the Army Air Corps in 1942, and the young couple set off on a series of postings. Katharine followed her husband, filling the role of dutiful army wife, "slightly resentful" of his domination but deeply in love. To her, Phil stood apart as a "marvelous, fantastic, magical, charismatic genius." She remembered their early married years as a time of fun together, a time of "constant growth and learning, and always a lot of laughter." Phil encouraged her to be independent of her parents. He enjoyed casting off convention and being spontaneous. Katharine came across as a slave to order and regimen. Phil showed little interest in restraint. His new wife, still in her mid-twenties, gained a new perspective at a formative time. The good feelings, however, weren't easy to sustain as the young couple shifted from Atlantic City, where Phil did basic training, to Sioux Falls, South Dakota, where Katharine got pregnant again.

This pregnancy had problems as well, and the doctor prescribed constant bed rest. Katharine was certain another miscarriage was on the way but was proven wrong. Her hopes were restored just as Phil got an appointment to Officer Candidate School back East. Katharine moved home with her parents in Washington for the last months of her pregnancy while Phil trained near Philadelphia. After his training, Phil was shipped off again, this time to Salt Lake City, and

Katharine knew she would face childbirth without him. She found some consolation in spending time with her father, who pressed her to help him with the *Post*. She took an unpaid job combing other newspapers for ideas, and reviewing their handling of the news.

Katharine's older brother, Bill, studying to be a doctor, steered her to Johns Hopkins Hospital in Baltimore for obstetric care. Before the birth, Katharine moved to the posh Belvedere Hotel in Baltimore with her sister-in-law along to help. She stayed there, "nervous, edgy and vulnerable," for four weeks, missing her sister Bis's wedding at Mt. Kisco. Finally, the baby, Elizabeth Morris Graham, arrived on July 3, 1943, the very day Phil returned. Katharine replaced her fears and disappointments with joy and relief. She had been pregnant, or recovering from her pregnancies, for most of the first three years of her marriage. Finally, she could focus on running her little household.

Shortly after Lally (as they nicknamed their daughter) was born, the fabric of their marriage began to deteriorate. While Phil could have fun, Katherine was expected to handle the drudgery of their life. Katharine recalled the move from the apartment they had in Harrisburg. Phil had gotten so drunk the night before that he didn't help pack a thing. As Katharine put it, she did all the "pulling and hauling." Besides the heavy drinking, Phil also seemed fragile, often complaining of fatigue or illness.

Hidden behind the comforts and conventional trappings of the Grahams' married life was a glowering shadow. Over the next dozen years, Phil's mental illness, what is known today as bipolar disorder, would become more severe. Because of her deep love for him, as well as her steadfast commitment to their marriage, Katharine was forced to develop in ways she had never considered. Her friend June says, "She had to learn to be a careful judge of people, to pick up on nuances because of Phil. People with his problem could be a danger to themselves or to others, including the children. As her family grew, she also had to help her children through the parental schism caused by Phil's illness." Katharine lived married life on a razor's edge, and few people, other than her closest friends, realized what she was going through. One of her best friends, Polly Fritchey, said, "Phil was very difficult, all hopped up. You could hardly stand it, the tension was so strong." But Katharine did stand it. She maintained her sanity as his slipped slowly, in fits and starts, from her grasp.

Katharine maintained the facade of a conventional, untrammeled life. Phil, for his part, was able to hold his volatile personality in check as he pursued his career. Katharine had intended to take care of her household on her own but soon decided, like others of her era and social class, to bring in some help. She hired Mary "Mamie" Bishop, who ended up staying with the Grahams until her retirement. The young couple also employed a housekeeper. Thanks to this help, Katharine found time to volunteer in the war effort, working at the Ration Board in Harrisburg.

Transferred back to Washington for Phil's new job with the Special Branch of Intelligence, Katharine found herself joining the ranks of home-front wives whose husbands had gone off to war. Phil was sent to the Philippines, and Katharine, again pregnant, went back to work in the circulation department of the *Post*. She found the department disorganized and poorly run, but she was in no position to make change. Instead, she observed and remembered. From her autobiography it's clear that it was difficult for Katharine, a person with a self-described "passion for order and routine," to watch the circulation department blunder along. Little did she realize that far in the future she would have her chance to set that department, and all the others, on the right course.

Katharine also socialized with friends. June Bingham recalls a favorite French restaurant on E Street, where the two would often have lunch. The maitre d' always gave the two white-gloved, attractive young women the best table at the front of the restaurant. But Bingham recalls the time they arrived for lunch both in the late stages of pregnancy. The maitre d' hid them and their protruding stomachs at a table in the back, next to the swinging kitchen door. The two mothers-to-be shared an uproarious laugh. They also had serious talks. "Kay cared a lot about world events and people. She didn't care much about clothes. We had unfrivolous talk, not about hair and nails, but about raising our children and the war." Bingham also recalls that "we all tried to do a little entertaining, although we were all so tired from helping with war work."

Katharine stored up her ration points to buy a nice piece of meat for her first dinner as a single hostess. Phil's close friend Ed Prichard was a guest, along with the Binghams, the liberal philosopher Isaiah Berlin, and Donald Maclean and his wife. Bingham recalls that during dinner, "voices rose, and Prich, who was vastly fat, and Donald Maclean started attacking Berlin. They accused Berlin of fraternizing with fascists like Alice Roosevelt Longworth. I was bewildered, having no idea that Maclean was a Communist." Only later would everyone learn that both Macleans were Soviet agents. Katharine's first dinner party ended on a bitter and angry note, with Berlin vowing never to speak to Maclean again.

Shortly after the disastrous dinner party, Katharine began house hunting. The baby she was carrying would strain the limits of the house they were living in. The Grahams' second child, Donald (Donny), was born just days after President Roosevelt died in April 1945. Mamie now had a second charge, but on her days off, Katharine took over as full-time mother. She was challenged not only by her inexperience but also by trying to live up to Mamie's difficult standards, such as hand-squeezing beef juice. Like every mother, Katharine had memorable disasters that included minor damage to the children in the way of bumps and bruises, but her confidence as a mother grew over time; less easily learned were the behaviors she needed to ease the relationship with her husband after he returned from the war in the fall of 1945. Phil could be engaging one moment and angry the next, overwhelmingly needy or in charge of everything. Adding to the complexity of their relationship was Phil's new job. At her father's insistent urging, Phil became associate publisher of the *Post* on January 1, 1946.

Leadership in the Shadows

Phil had a pet name for Katharine. He called her "Kate." If he meant a reference to *The Taming of the Shrew*, with himself in the role of Petruchio, few of the couple's close friends would have been surprised. Bingham, however, came up with a better reference. "Kay was a 'patient Griselda.'" Like the character immortalized by Chaucer, Katharine would endure years of escalating abuse while projecting a controlled, accommodating demeanor. She said she was married to a "myth," a man superior to herself. Her pleasure was to "meet his trains, pack his bags, pay his bills, serve as the butt of family jokes, and make sure [the children] don't get out of hand": a sad list of accomplishments she ably fulfilled.

People viewed her as the meek complement to Phil's outsized personality, but that simplistic perspective overlooks the silent strength it took to raise her children and sustain her marriage. She became "durable." She found the inner fortitude to help her depressed husband, sometimes by spending as long as eight hours just talking to him nonstop. She lived with his pain, and her own, the abiding ache of desperately wanting to stop the suffering of someone you love. Katharine developed a quiet and deep resilience that would not be fully recognized until after she emerged from Phil's growing shadow. Her husband's prominence increased as her father elevated Phil's stature in the company. Eugene convinced the young husband and father to take over as publisher just six months after Phil joined the company.

Katharine's days became overfilled. With a three-year-old and an infant, her prominent but difficult husband, and a drive to challenge herself, she seemed constantly on the move. She also had a new house to run. She and Phil had fallen in love with the Georgetown house that sat on top of a hill called the "Rock of Dumbarton." Viewed from the outside, the grand-looking brick house was, she felt, too formal for her modest taste. Phil was sure it would be too costly. Once inside, however, they envisioned their growing family in the spacious, light-filled rooms. Katharine negotiated for weeks with the owner, Major Bill Donovan, only to discover that her father had closed the deal at a dinner where he sat with Donovan. She asked why he had interfered. "When it's where you want to live, don't bargain," Eugene replied. Although he turned out to be right, and Katharine lived on her Georgetown hilltop for more than a half century, she once again found her authority over her own life usurped.

Dating from the early nineteenth century, the house had large green lawns running south in the back to a view of the city of Washington, and at the front separating the house from the street. She saw it as a house defined by her children. "It used to be the neighborhood playground," Katharine explained. "Baseball reigned in the spring and summer and football took over in the fall." She tried to plant grass on home base, but it never lasted through the fall sports. "Our boys and their friends would come in and out, and we never locked the front door. It was lovely for children." She let her son use the living room for practice with his band. This room, that years later would host the most formal dinners, had a linoleum floor with tricycles and bicycles scattered about. Katharine had breakfast there with the children every day before she drove them to school. "Phil used to call [it] the Shredded Wheat room," she explained to an interviewer. Years later her youngest son would say, "Everyone tells me that my mother is a world-famous figure, but to me she is still the lady sitting behind a box of Wheaties."

The children took an increasing amount of time, as did running and decorating the eight-bedroom house. She supervised the cook, an incompetent laundress she didn't have the heart to fire, and the steady stream of home decorating and repair people. Schools had to be chosen, activities arranged and supervised, and calendars planned and adjusted. She was almost always home when the children finished school. There were also social and professional events to organize and attend, and Katharine increased her work for social causes. The Community Chest, the National Symphony Orchestra, and the Children's Convalescent Home found her an active volunteer, and she accepted an appointment on the National Capital Sesquicentennial Commission.

In her autobiography, Katharine also describes her behind-the-scenes role as her husband made critical business decisions such as acquiring the *Washington Star*, shaking up the staff roster, influencing politics, and expanding to new media areas. She signaled her involvement in these activities through the editorial "we." After the *Post* acquired the *Times-Herald*, Katharine wrote proudly that "we" had newspapers that covered the market. She described the resignation of a key editor because of heart disease as a great loss for "us." These business changes were important for her as a major stockholder, and as part of the family that had turned the paper around, but her comments have a longing quality. Her primary role, caring for house, husband, and children, didn't allow for leadership in any of the major decisions confronting the business. Instead, for two decades, Katharine wafted in and out of the family business, sometimes holding minor jobs, but never in a leadership role. Phil remained the man in charge. She held back, concerned and emotionally involved, yet conscious of the decorum required of her subservient role.

In 1947, about the time Donny turned two years old, Katharine returned to work to write a column called "The Magazine Rack," a review of interesting stories in magazines. Even if the column did take only a day to write, Katharine felt the pressures of being a working mother. By that autumn, handling another pregnancy was also part of her hectic life.

A Courageous Choice

Katharine had little trouble with this pregnancy and asked her doctor about a new birth technique just coming into vogue—natural childbirth. With her history of a miscarriage and the tragic end of her second pregnancy, her doctor advised against it in strong terms. Physicians at the time were not trained to treat childbirth as a routine event, nor did they consider that it could be painless. They believed that conventional interventions were safer for the mother and child. Leaving childbirth to nature and becoming observers in the process ran counter to doctors' ingrained practice and belief. Katharine took her doctor's advice, however, as a challenge, despite the trauma of her previous birthing experiences.

She had clearly educated herself about the revolutionary ideas of Grantly Dick-Read, who advocated methods of relaxation, exercise, and diet that would lead to a "conscious, joyful" childbirth. She probably read Dick-Read's book *Childbirth Without Fear*, which is both medical text and inspirational tract. He wrote that his method would lead to "a sense of exaltation and incomparable happiness." Bingham explains that many women at the time felt that they "didn't want to be robbed by these men [doctors] who wanted to make it convenient for themselves. It was *our* experience, *our* uterus, *our* baby." Katharine set out to birth her third baby as she chose.

She began the labor without the normal anesthesia. She didn't, however, have the painless experience that Dick-Read promoted and began to think she would have to get drugs, when finally her second son was born. Despite the intense pain, and its aftermath, Katharine wrote about how pleased she was to have chosen the natural way. At a time when she had faded into the background of Phil's prominent life, when she had sidelined her ambitions to devote herself to family, Katharine's birthing experience shed light on her deeper feelings. She chose to challenge herself in one of the few areas where she still had control—having a baby. She chose to fully experience the moment, despite the chance of complication and pain, rather than be in a state of anesthetized semiconsciousness. The birth of William Welsh Graham, in May 1948, provided a glimpse of Katharine as she had been before her marriage, curious, challenge seeking, independent, and quietly—but with determination—charting her own course.

Burying this part of herself had its costs. Evangeline Bruce, a close friend, said that Katharine was in "despair" over "living intellectually off Phil . . . she found it utterly demeaning to be an appendage, to subsist in her husband's shadow." Chafing at the contours of her life didn't prevent Katharine from learning skills and styles of behavior that influenced her later leadership in the professional world.

Like so many women in the primary parenting role, her responsibilities were rife with lessons of leadership. Katharine's family became her ambition. She took her role as mother as seriously as any she had had, and her home proved to be fertile ground for her development as a leader. She made it her primary job for twenty-three years. As the conscientious parent of four very bright, sensitive, and often difficult children, Katharine had every chance to learn about mediation and arbitration, listening well, teaching values, recognizing and building on positive traits, and modifying negative ones, all lessons for leaders.

Home was an ever-changing proving ground where interpersonal skills were tested, values were honed, and multitasking was the rule. She found genuine satisfaction from getting up in the morning and having breakfast with her children, arranging their days, being there for them after school. To her, life "seemed so unglamorous—houses, children, boards and good works," yet she writes that she loved it, and her devotion to Phil was unmistakable. Her life revolved around him and the children, "endless carpools, mothers'-group meetings, birthday parties, riding and tennis lessons, field days, dogs, doctors' and dentists' appointments." Years later she said of this period in her life, "It was wonderful, and I learned a lot from [Phil], and I had a wonderful time, and we had four children and we loved them, and we traveled." Like millions of women today who disproportionately leave or stop out of the workplace to stay home with children, the social role of mothering had exaggerated importance for Katharine's professional life. She would be ahead of her time in transferring many skills and attitudes from home to work when she reentered the workforce full-time almost two decades later.

Despite the numerous areas in which parenting and leadership overlap, in Katharine's day there was no recognition that parenting was a form of leadership. Today, that has started to change. After interviewing more than one hundred primary caregivers (mostly women) in a number of fields, Ann Crittenden finds, in *If You've Raised Kids, You Can Manage Anything*, that all the skills companies value are gained and improved through parenting. Similarly, the car manufacturer Volvo has found that male executives who take paternity leave return to work as better managers. Only recently has research begun to prove that executives are influenced by the multiplicity of their roles in the larger world, including parenting. Teaching children the challenges of responsible independence creates leaders who know how to empower others to lead. For Katharine, this would become apparent during her professional years as she effectively delegated authority. Katharine also gained the perspective of a person who is required to prioritize a variety of demands. She cared for Phil with his extreme illness, she mothered a brood, and she remained a dutiful daughter to a demanding and difficult mother. The juggling of these roles meant multitasking in a literal and emotional way. If Katharine seemed removed and moody at times, if this balancing act resulted in, as a friend put it, "Billy Goat Gruff days," it was no wonder. But the experience of responding effectively to these varied responsibilities gave Katharine a rare sense of empathy on the job.

Mary Beckner, a longtime employee in the *Post* classified department, remembers one such instance after Katharine became head of the company. Beckner mentioned that her youngest son, a boy with a form of dwarfism, loved football. He wanted a helmet, but Mary couldn't find one for him. Somehow Katharine heard the story and showed up in Mary's department with a helmet for her son from Washington's professional team, the Redskins.

Katharine developed a caring interpersonal manner based on her years spent navigating within and between her roles. "She tried to get into the person and understand them before telling them things," Beckner observed. When she took over the company, the male executives would misunderstand Katharine's approach. Their experiences and development as leaders had been too dissimilar. They couldn't appreciate that she had grown as a leader during her two decades as the woman behind Phil Graham.

One Life Ends

In July 1948, Eugene Meyer sold 100 percent of his Class A stock in the Washington Post Company to Katharine and her husband, making them the sole owners. Phil had received a gift of $75,000 from his mother-in-law for his birthday. That money, together with some money he borrowed, allowed him to buy his 3,325 shares. Katharine only received 1,325 of the voting shares, her father explaining, "You never want a man working for his wife." Years later, Katharine's friend Gloria Steinem would label Eugene's action "patriarchy pure," an example of the powerful system that keeps women in families of inherited wealth from ascending to leadership. In her memoir Katharine writes that she felt completely in "accord" with her father's explanation, although the decision had ironic consequences. In order to allow Phil to pay back the debt from buying the stock, Katharine began paying all the couple's expenses, except those that were personal to Phil. She used the money from the trust fund set up for her by her father. Phil wasn't working for his wife, but she was supporting him. His latent, unspoken, and perhaps largely unconscious resentments over the arrangement would bubble to the surface in coming years.

The young couple's prominence, power, and prestige grew with the transfer of ownership of the company. *Time* magazine put Phil on the cover in April 1956. He had become, in the words of author David Halberstam, the "incandescent man." He dazzled Georgetown socialites and future presidents Kennedy and Johnson. He loved playing the political power broker. If he occasionally got so drunk that he passed out on the floor, or so vulgar in his language that people walked away in disgust, his transgressions were mostly overlooked.

These episodes, however, were the rare public display of his darker, secret side. Signs of what would be diagnosed in the 1950s as manic depression became apparent as early as grade school, when his blistering anger at a Sunday school teacher got him expelled from class. Later, out-of-control drinking in college led his father to pull him out for a term. Once married, he spent tearful, depression-filled nights with Katharine at home, where he despaired of his talent. The brighter his star shone as head of a rising newspaper, the more Phil's inner demons led him to question his role as media mogul. Had he simply married the boss's daughter? Would he ever be recognized for his own talent? The idea that his position had been handed to him rather than earned ate at his psyche.

Little was understood about manic depression at the time. Katharine, baffled and often hurt by Phil's behavior, tried in every way to ease his obvious emotional pain. She became his social secretary and companion, traveling to business events with him and organizing the social whirl around his erratic requests and behavior. In many ways he was like another child. He needed her to sit with him when he bathed, for example, and was once infuriated when Katharine left him alone for the weekend, though he had encouraged her to do so. Looking back, Katharine realized that their worst moments came during his mood swings, but at the time she simply worked harder to smooth their life together.

In 1951, the Grahams bought the 350-acre farm in Virginia that they called Glen Welby. Though it added another job of decorating, maintenance, and scheduling to Katharine's duties, the property also offered a sanctuary for family time. The next year their fourth and last child, Stephen, was born. Katharine seemed to be succeeding where her mother had failed—providing her children and husband with unstinting, selfless support and love. She would soon learn that, in the case of her husband, no amount of self-sacrifice would be enough to fend off disaster.

Phil was a supercharged manager. "He cannot keep still. He cannot keep silent. With this wild and restless brilliance he must play Pied Piper to every man and woman that comes into his ken," a British journalist wrote in 1961. He "flooded" the *Post* with notes praising and criticizing stories, taking issue with headlines, targeting misspellings and "even the content of the crossword puzzle." He worried over the bottom line, trying to trim overtime, find new advertising, and attract more readers. He oversaw the move to a new building in 1949 to replace the nostalgically loved but crumbling and cramped E Street location. He took the company in new directions, buying into WTOP Radio in Washington, D.C., as well as a TV station renamed WTOP-TV. Then he bought WMBR-TV in Jacksonville, Florida, later renamed WJXT and destined to be a profit center for the company. His pace and responsibilities were a toxic combination with his excessive drinking and mental illness. Behind the bravado, charm, and exuberant energy was a brittle man who often saw the world as threatening and overwhelming.

As the years passed, Phil's various illnesses intensified, as did his drinking and arguing with Katharine. She wrote that the quarrels were often "violent." One dinner party at the Grahams' home in the spring of 1951 ended with a vitriolic argument among the men about politics during World War II. Katharine's friend Evangeline Bruce had been at the party and noticed a few days later that "Kay's arms and legs looked swollen and bruised." Sometime during the first half of that year, Katharine suffered another miscarriage.

Like Agnes, Phil was also a master of the cutting remark, and he felt free to direct them at Katharine with cruel frequency. No wonder that she froze and grew "over worried" when he began drinking at home or on social occasions. He once asked dinner guests if they knew what Kay did every morning. After a pause he said that she "looks in the mirror and says how lucky she is to be married to me." One night, in the spring of 1954, driving home from a party, he got drunk and threw an angry fit. He insisted on getting out and walking while Katharine drove slowly alongside, watching him burn with rage. A day or two later, a neighbor saw her outside looking unsteady, and showing "a very painful-looking black eye." Like many victims of domestic abuse, she blamed herself, even in her autobiography written so many years later, for not handling Phil better. She recognized that he made up reasons to rage at her, yet excused him, blaming his pressures instead. She never guessed that he had any underlying mental illness, and she didn't share her distress. "What was not said in those days was as important as what was said," her friend June Bingham explained. "I marvel at how lonely it was for us because we didn't share our troubles with each other. It wasn't done."

Phil's self-doubt, magnified by his illness, grew like a relentless cancer. By the second half of the 1950s, his work habits had become erratic. Katharine became the focus of his angry, humiliating attacks. He made fun of her failure to dress or wear her hair with style. He called her "Porky" for the weight she gained after four children and two unsuccessful pregnancies. Katharine came from Jewish roots, but despite her family's thorough assimilation Phil peppered his diatribes with anti-Semitic remarks. He called her a "Jewish cow." He targeted his jokes at her when they went to parties, and he frequently humiliated her in front of their children.

Friends watched in horror as Katharine laughed at jokes made at her expense. She didn't strike back. Phil's attacks rekindled and reinforced childhood feelings of paralyzing inadequacy. She had never felt more inferior, insecure, or confused. At a women's lunch given by Lady Bird Johnson in the mid-1950s, congressional and newspaper wives were asked by the future first lady to say a few words about their summer activities. Katharine sat in terror when it was her turn to speak, unable to say a word. At the annual party the Grahams gave for *Post* employees at Glen Welby, Katharine stood around numb with anxiety, barely greeting people. Much of her conversation revolved around apologizing for Phil's vulgar comments. Meanwhile, Phil played the part of powerful host, reserving most of his charm for other men's wives.

In 1961, with the *Post* dominant among Washington's three news dailies, Phil conceived of sharing the costs of foreign coverage by creating a news service with the *Los Angeles Times*. His concept dramatically improved the paper's foreign coverage and eventually became profitable as a subscription service for other news outlets. He took part ownership in the Paris *Herald Tribune,* and bought *Art News.* He also began negotiations that same year to buy the newsweekly *Newsweek,* based in New York. In one of his most brilliant acquisitions, Phil gained controlling interest in *Newsweek,* valued at $15 million, and paid out only $750,000 in cash. In the midst of the deal making, Katharine came down with an active case of tuberculosis. She kept her condition secret from Phil until *Newsweek* had been bought, not wanting to distract him. She speculated later that stress contributed to the unusual occurrence of contracting the disease. Her body, if not her will, seemed to be breaking down under the pressure of Phil's torturous emotional descent.

As the pressures of business and family grew, Phil's behavior became more bizarre and extreme. Katharine tried to hide the embattled side of their life from public view and from the children, even as she lived in dread of his actions. His depression had begun to escalate after 1957. Eugene's health was declining at the same time, and while Katharine's family was on a trip to Europe in 1959, Phil and Katharine had to return suddenly to her father's deathbed. She had been his adored daughter, and his loss compounded her despair with Phil's illness. Finally, Phil turned his increasing disgust with his wife into the harshest indignity.

On the afternoon of Christmas Eve, 1962, Katharine answered the phone just as Phil lifted the receiver in another room. She overheard the unmistakable conversation of two lovers as Phil spoke to Robin Webb, a journalist at *Newsweek* who had become his paramour just weeks earlier. As Katharine wrote in her autobiography, the world that she had known and loved ended for her. When she confronted Phil, he told her of other affairs. Soon afterward he left to live with Robin and demanded a divorce. During the horrible months of his open infidelity Katharine would hear of his exploits: trips to Puerto Rico, dinners with old friends, lavish stays at grand hotels.

The journalist Mary McGrory was part of a group of women friends that Katharine leaned on for support during this period. McGrory recalled a dinner where Katharine worked hard to put on a calm public face. John Walker, head of the National Gallery of Art, was also a dinner guest. McGrory told a humorous story about driving a nun from Baltimore to see a special exhibit of the Mona Lisa at the Gallery. McGrory had Walker and Katharine laughing as she told of getting hopelessly lost with the poor nun in tow. McGrory noticed, however, that her hostess had to keep tipping her head back as her eyes threatened to overflow with tears.

The final evidence of Phil's descent into insanity took place in front of his peers in January 1963. At the annual meeting of newspaper owners and publishers in Phoenix, Arizona, the famous publisher of the *Washington Post* rose from his seat and took over the podium without warning or invitation. He called the audience names, singled certain people out for particular scorn, identified a woman he claimed was having an affair with his friend President Kennedy, and then started to strip off his clothes. He was whisked away to Chestnut Lodge, an institution for mental illness where he had stayed before. He soon begged Katharine to take him back, and she agreed with a mixture of joy and trepidation.

The humiliating incident in Phoenix, however, and his stay at the institution did little to change him. He returned abruptly to his lover Robin and tried to draw up legal documents to give her Katharine's share of company stock. Katharine was terrified and infuriated by the move, hiring a lawyer to protect her interests even as she hoped that Phil would come back to her. By June 1963 he had become nearly paralyzed, both emotionally and physically, by his overwhelming depression. He told his doctor that he wanted to end the affair with Robin once and for all and return to his wife.

Katharine was ecstatic to have him back, at the same time agreeing with his doctors that he would return to Chestnut Lodge to help his recovery. After six short weeks he convinced his doctors and his wife that he was well enough for a trip to Glen Welby. Despite his previous episodes of violence and suicidal despair, the doctors gave permission for a weekend away in Katharine's care. She felt hopeful and told friends that Phil seemed much better; but he was not. That weekend he took his life. He was buried in Oak Hill Cemetery, across the street from the couple's grand house on R Street, his grave always in view from Katharine's window.

With Phil's death, Katharine's role as wife ended forever, as did her place in the constellation of Phil's universe. Yet her married life had forever shaped her as a leader. Not only would she carry her experiences as a full-time mother into the workplace, she would also bring the sensibilities of a person who had witnessed and felt the deepest possible despair. "Whatever strength I had," Katharine said in 1997, "was enhanced by dealing with Phil's illness." Perhaps her life with Phil also explains her later impatience with those who treated work frivolously. In her married life, where disaster loomed with regularity, there was little time to be frivolous. Her staff would learn that no matter where in the world she traveled, no matter the duress of time or place, she expected to work, not sightsee. She was also filled with compassion for her friends and individual employees, showing concern and take-charge strength in personal crises. More than most, she had been battle hardened, if not by the business world, then by a world where human tragedy was inevitable.

Nine years after Phil's death, in a rare candid conversation about her marriage, Katharine opened up to three of her friends. She was having drinks with Joe Alsop, Meg Greenfield, and Haynes Johnson at her house before going to a play. Johnson had been covering the 1972 presidential campaign for the *Post*. He had written an extensive piece on Democratic vice-presidential nominee Tom Eagleton's mental illness, which, when disclosed, caused Eagleton to withdraw from the race. Katharine seemed eager to let Johnson know that she understood the problem. "You have no idea how bad it is; if you haven't gone through it you can't know," she told her friends. She spoke with candor and from the heart about the ups and downs and unpredictability of the disease, Johnson remembered. She didn't seem embarrassed or maudlin as she described the pain and confusion that had marked so much of her life with Phil. Instead, she seemed to have come to terms with that phase of her life, and having sought wisdom from its trials wanted to share with others what she had learned. In this way, she turned personal tragedy into opportunity, choosing understanding over continuing despair, as every leader must do.

As Phil's wife, Katharine had survived and grown in unexpected ways. As the new CEO of the Post Company, she would step onto a bigger stage. Once again, but in a different context, she would face attacks on her character and competence. Once again, she would struggle with her insecurities. Once again, she would confront new challenges and cope with her despair at finding solutions. But making the conventional choice of marriage to Phil had brought her great and unexpected pain. After his death, she was ready to defy convention and accept the consequences.

CHAPTER THREE

THE VAGABOND QUEEN

"Re-adjustment is a kind of private revolution."

—Eleanor Roosevelt

Phil's death put Katharine through her private revolution. His violent end led to a radical shift in Katharine's view of the world and it of her. But along with the sudden imperative to reinvent herself came the longer, more difficult problem of her evolution as a leader. She had to hone her skills for the job as head of the company, devise her role, and develop her day-to-day style as an executive. She faced her own tests of inner resolve and confidence as well as those imposed by others gauging her leadership.

Katharine could have chosen a much easier course. Money was not an issue for her or her children. A quiet life, or that of society matron, would have been a conventional and unremarkable choice. She had spent years as a volunteer working on the problems of poverty in the District of Columbia. She could have continued her uncontroversial good works. Instead, Katharine chose to turn fate into purpose. She refused to wallow in her personal needs. She elevated values over personal feelings, an approach that would mark her leadership. In the very earliest days of Katharine's greatest life trauma, there were unmistakable glimpses of leadership character.

Character. It ran like an unbroken lifeline through the maze of first experiences making up Katharine's early months as head of the company. If some decisions were shaky, if she seemed blundering or ineffectual, a moral and ethical grounding kept her exploring her role as a leader. That grounding started with her father's vision of public service. By carrying that vision forward Katharine honored generations of Meyers who had worked for the public good. She also hoped to insure the continuation of their vision for future generations. Her mother had also called for a commitment from her children to build a better world. For all her self-perceived failures as a wife and mother, Katharine could not turn away from these core values, despite the difficulty and risk.

Values-based leadership creates a certain type of leader. While Katharine would grow into a CEO who insisted on good business practices and aggressive profit margins, she had an aspiration for herself and her employees that drew on a cause bigger than any one person. As Bill George, the former CEO of Medtronic, writes, the best leaders "have a deep sense of purpose and are true to their core values." Margaret Heffernan, who has studied and written about women executives in U.S. and UK businesses, writes that all the female business leaders she has met "are passionate about . . . building companies that match their values, where they can be themselves, have whole lives, be honest and open and have their innate skills recognized." Katharine took on the job of building a values-based company from the start.

Katharine's first hundred days, bookended by two violent deaths— Phil's and President Kennedy's—were a tense, lonely, and trouble-filled time. Most people would have reversed course, but Katharine stuck by her decision, even as she began to realize that it was far more difficult than she had imagined. She had toughness under her prim blouses and sensible skirts. Her father "brought her up firm and able to make up her mind," June Bingham explains. She was, however, naive in her view of the future. Like anyone who dramatically alters their life, she overlooked the unintended consequences of her decision to take over. In many ways, leadership sneaked up on her. As Michael Watkins points out in *The First 90 Days,* new leaders' behavior sometimes acts like a virus. A new leader's early actions can "alienate potential supporters, undermine her credibility, and stimulate defensive reactions." With her lack of experience and preparation, Katharine contributed to a rocky transition where the virus of mismanagement combined with mistrust of an unusual and unknown leader.

Finding Her Way

No one had elected or appointed Katharine. She had no constituency within or outside the company, other than friends, some of whom doubted her course. According to Ben Bradlee, most of her friends and colleagues in the newspaper business "secretly wanted her to sell them the *Post.*" They seemed to forget that unlike her father and husband who had started at the top, Katharine had experience as a journalist and on the *Post*'s staff. Even her longtime friend Chip Bohlen asked, with the best of intentions, "You're not going to work, are you?" He expected her to stick with convention, remarry, and remain on the business's sidelines.

She told friends that she was "rusted up inside." They called her early days the "'groaning and sighing, it's impossible, poor little me' phase." This period, she avowed, was just an interregnum until Donny got out of college and was ready to take over. "I didn't go in intending to take over," she said. "I thought I'd just be a family coordinating hand for a while." She gave herself little credibility, instead taking the role of a meek lame duck. Later she could admit that in the early days it took her "some while to cease thinking constantly of a certain scene from the old musical comedy *The Vagabond King* . . . when the suddenly enthroned vagabond—for the first time dressed in royal robes—descends the great stairs, slowly and anxiously, tensely eyeing on either side the rows of archers with their drawn bows and inscrutable faces." She felt like an imposter who feared discovery at every turn.

Katharine had good cause to be struggling with *imposter syndrome*. The imposter phenomenon is hard to break because it develops early in childhood. It is seen most often in families where achievement-oriented messages are strong, and children do not receive recognition or praise for their accomplishments and talents.

In her household, Katharine recalled that "many people were put down as dreary or routine, and I thought I was among them." She said of her mother, "She condescended a lot to other people, and especially her children. And so, while she was demanding great things of us, she was also, in a way, undermining our ability to fulfill them." In a classic example of imposter syndrome thinking, Katharine thought that everyone else in her household was living up to her mother's impossible standards. "I thought I was this peasant walking around among brilliant people," she told an interviewer years later. Imposter syndrome research also found that little girls particularly are socialized to think that their achievements are based on luck or sympathy rather than talent. Katharine would struggle with her imposter fears through most of her life.

She decided, despite these deep-seated insecurities, that whatever she did, she would act as herself. Early on, Katharine realized that she "couldn't try to be someone else, least of all Phil." It is a decision that may sound simple in retrospect, but in the context of Katharine's era and the immediate aftermath of Phil's suicide, it was another example of character and courage.

In the fall of 1963, Katharine struggled in the throes of the first stage of her grief. While loss is difficult for everyone, those who lose loved ones to suicide often experience particularly volatile emotions. Phil's sudden and public death initially left Katharine shocked and confused. Denial and the desire to escape from emotional pain are often pervasive during early stages in grief, and she alludes to this in her autobiography. She found Phil's illness and death "difficult to talk about . . . I just shut the door." As his wife and committed caretaker, his death must have felt like her failure as well, further damaging her sense of self-worth. Compounding her grief were doubts about her actions as a mother immediately after Phil's death.

Lally and Donny were nearly adults, close to each other at Radcliffe and Harvard, and so able to comfort each other. "It was tremendously important to have [Lally] there," Don Graham remembered. "That was a horrible time." The other two boys were still at home. Bill was fifteen, and Steve only eleven years old. Phil's death created a family crisis that called for a different kind of leadership than what was called for at the *Post*. In this regard, Katharine felt she had failed. Looking back, she realized her younger boys needed support, guidance, and a compass to navigate the uncertainty of change. Instead, she sent them back to their summer camps after the funeral. Pressured by her daughter and a friend, Katharine joined her mother who, too convulsed by the tragedy to travel, remained on a cruise near Istanbul after learning of the suicide.

In a poignant passage of her autobiography Katharine writes that her decision was "so wrong" for her boys, and she recalls it with obvious emotional pain. Unlike her mother, who showed little capacity for self-reflection, Katharine carried on an unforgiving inner life. She felt she had failed the sons she loved by going "blindly and mindlessly" forward.

Few people, of course, would blame her for any decisions made so soon after the trauma she experienced. Steve, her youngest, said "the dramatic change was my father's death. Her working on the paper, I barely noticed at the time . . . I didn't even question it . . . I was too wrapped up in being unhappy." But Katharine blamed herself. She simply went along, unable to decide what was best, and the consequences would haunt her as she pushed ahead in her new job.

Katharine had held her emotions close for so many years that few people, other than close friends, could have realized the searing pain she endured. She walked through her new world lonely and "painfully shy." She saw no future except that which existed within work. Looking back, she described herself as "taking a veil." To friends she said she was becoming a kind of monk. Every reminder of Phil cut like a fresh wound; looking at his handwriting brought on a rush of memories. In the midst of this intense pain, numbed by it, she stepped up and into the top reaches of the media world. Was it a place to hide or heal? Would the ghost of Phil's leadership paralyze her? Would she sink under the weight of her grief? She could not know the answers to these questions as she struggled to lead in her own way.

It helped that the *Post* felt like home. It had been the family business since she was a teenager. She had worked there as an aspiring writer, and she knew many of the key people well. She felt she had absorbed a great deal about the business from her father and Phil and that she brought "some knowledge and appreciation of news and journalism." But her proximity to power and information, though helpful, was inadequate. "I'd been very close to my father and to my husband—but when I was thrown in there, it was an entirely different thing," she told an interviewer. "I literally did not know how to use a secretary, much less how to manage a business." She also had the sense of stepping into the shadow of a legend. She "mythologized" Phil, lacking the perspective to see his accomplishments and failures with a clear eye, struggling to separate her vision from his.

It was 1963, and until that year women had been discouraged by the social order from acting on or even acknowledging their authentic selves. What we now call "Stepford Wives," those beautiful and obedient women described in Ira Levin's 1960s best seller, were the ideal. But then Betty Friedan published *The Feminine Mystique*, opening the first fissure in the cultural walls that circumscribed women's lives. Katharine surely would have read this explosive book or at least have been aware of its implications. Her realization that she had to lead in her own style showed an intuitive feminism, explained perhaps, as her friend June Bingham said, as a "rebound from being dismissed by Phil for all those years."

Katharine could have chosen to be a pale imitation of either of the two men she both loved and admired who had run the paper—Phil or her father. On the cusp of the second wave of the women's movement, she might have chosen to be an early entrant into the ranks of professional women who were trying to lead by mimicking a male style. Adopting men's command and control leadership style, spouting sports metaphors and wearing bulky shoulder pads, this leadership vanguard tried unsuccessfully to trade authenticity for power. Katharine seemed to instinctively know better, and while she might never think to do so, she probably had Agnes to thank.

Despite her anger and disappointment in her mother's behavior, which carried on from childhood through her marriage, Katharine couldn't help but be influenced by her powerful presence. Agnes was nothing if not her own person, forever chafing at the constraints of her marriage and following her own instincts and desires. The author and journalist David Halberstam called her "a tough, driving, audacious, independent woman who seemed to have sprung from a Wagnerian opera." Katharine rebelled against Agnes's model as a wife and mother, enduring even Phil's abuse rather than being the distant partner as Agnes had been. But once Katharine found herself in the uncharted territory of corporate leadership, her mother's style became more appealing.

Agnes, still very much on the scene, encouraged her daughter to take charge. She served as a reminder that Katharine's deepest understanding of womanhood grew from her mother's fierce individualism. Katharine had seen Agnes provide a compassionate side to the *Post*, persistently reminding her husband that government clerks were as important as presidents to the paper's success. Katharine watched her mother, the undaunted reformer, fighting the Catholic Church over opposition to federal aid to public education and being an early antagonist of Senator Joseph McCarthy and his witch-hunting anticommunism. Katharine's lifelong paradox as an insecure yet successful executive, a conventional woman who embraced an unconventional role, a gossip and tight-lipped CEO, could be traced to the paradox of Agnes. While Katharine would never adopt Agnes's flamboyance, she would far outpace her mother's attempts to make a singular mark on the world.

After announcing her intentions to assume control to the *Post* board, Katharine took another extraordinary step toward establishing her leadership. Only days after Phil's death, she had a negotiation with Fritz Beebe that established her future role. Beebe was the tall, cigar-smoking New York lawyer who had helped broker the acquisition of the *Times-Herald* by Phil Graham and then been appointed chairman of the company. Beebe had only been at the *Post* two and a half years. They were volatile years in which Beebe had to steer the business around the shoals of Phil's increasingly destructive behavior. Katharine appreciated what he had done. "He was so decent, so wise," she said. "He had a brilliant corporate mind . . . he saved us." Yet, despite her faith in Beebe, Katharine moved quickly to secure her position and power.

In the four days between Phil's death and her departure for Europe to join her mother's cruise, she discussed roles and titles with Beebe. He wanted to stay on as chairman and have Katharine take over Phil's role as president of the company. Katharine pushed back, fearing that the plan "might entail his being boss and my being number two." Her instincts were sound. Later research would show that even when women have "the traditional emblems of leadership," as psychology professor Virginia Valian explains, they are less likely to get the deference that men in the same title and position receive. Beebe agreed that they would work on a coequal basis, after which

Katharine agreed to accept the existing titles. Katharine called it a "business marriage." The relationship would evolve over time, as marriages do, but she insisted on a full partnership role from the beginning.

Katharine's discussion with Beebe was influenced by the fear she had experienced when Phil had tried to take over her share of the company and give it to his lover Robin Webb. In her new role, Katharine wanted her position secure and understood. But the talk with Beebe also revealed the complex internal instincts driving Katharine's actions. Much has been made of her insecurity, fear, and inexperience. She described herself initially as simply being a "placeholder" for her son, an image of passivity that fit with her former life. A placeholder, a sort of bookmark in the pages of the company's history, was no threat to anyone. She said she was "congealed" with fear about running the company and that she made the decision without realizing the enormity of the task. These characterizations, however, reveal only part of the truth.

Katharine also instinctively took charge and had a core of emotional steel. Her terror, her bewilderment, her almost obsessive self-doubt and flagellation were real, but they coexisted with a desire to live up to deeply held values and with extraordinary personal determination. Her father's values were paramount in her mind: Tell the truth; make the newspaper "a commercial success;" remember that a newspaper's duty is aligned with the public good, not the private interests of its owner; don't be beholden to special interests. "If you give [people] the truth," her father had said, "and back it up with clear explanations and sound arguments, you are exercising very great power in a very useful way." His daughter understood that she had inherited an uncompromising and challenging philosophy for her paper. She intended to live up to that philosophy by leading in her way. Less than a year after taking over she told an interviewer, "I believe an individual grows because he acts as an individual. . . . People perform best when they have the freedom to be themselves." Because Katharine gave herself that freedom, she developed a leadership style that worked for her and her company.

So Much to Learn

With her meager newspaper background, Katharine had an urgent task: to learn the business. She faced a steep curve in that regard, and the challenge of winning the trust and loyalty of the staff and her industry counterparts. Expectations were low; Katharine's included. Formerly content to take care of Phil and "clean up after him," she now had a newspaper that ranked sixth in advertising among all others across the country and had just passed its local rival, the *Washington Star,* for the first time. Daily circulation topped four hundred thousand, and while the newspaper was the flagship, there were the other media properties to oversee. The company included the magazine *Newsweek,* two art magazines, several television stations, and a news service. The newly minted businesswoman also inherited a cash-flow problem.

There were many "firsts" for the raw CEO. Some were emotional. Phil's very public death had exposed what Katharine had hid for so long: her torment in living with his illness. Whether she chose to share it or not, other people were now part of her personal struggle. They could only guess what she had been going through, but they could see clearly what she was facing, and they stepped forward to help. Agnes, for all her years of criticism and negativity, became a staunch ally. Katharine's daughter, Lally, continued to tell her mother, in person and in letters, that she believed in her, that she saw her as a woman of talent and promise. Friends—like Scotty and Sally Reston, who flew back from a European vacation when they heard about Phil—came together to help her at every turn. Katharine's loneliness was eased by this extended support system.

She also began to see that the task ahead could be accomplished with many levels of collaboration, both formal and informal. Her willingness to turn to others was an aspect of her interpersonal style. She pursued the insights and knowledge of others, and some of the male leadership of the company viewed this as a sign of weakness. They resented her going outside the company for advice. They didn't understand her relentless questions, taking them not in the spirit of learning but as challenges to their authority. Her friend Gene Patterson saw her behavior differently. "She read people very well. She laid way back and gathered information, asking questions, concealing where she was going, and then making a decision about what was best for the paper." If Katharine knew nothing else, at least she knew how to ask a question. What could be less threatening? She wasn't being presumptuous. She was anything but arrogant. She had always been the good listener, whether at her parents' table or in Phil's charmed circle. She certainly felt more comfortable seeking advice than giving orders in the foreign world of business. Thirty years later, Katharine's first steps could be seen in the relational leadership style that is still a common and effective strategy for women leaders.

In her groundbreaking paper in the *Harvard Business Review* in 1990, Judy Rosener, on faculty at the Graduate School of Management at the University of California, Irvine, described the style of a "second-generation" of managerial women as "unique to their socialization as women and creating a different path to the top." Rosener defined an "interactive" leadership style that stressed inclusion and participatory communication. One female CEO interviewed by Rosener said, "When I face a tough decision, I always ask my employees, 'What would you do if you were me?'" Katharine pioneered this style in an era before such differences were recognized or valued, showing herself to be a leader ahead of her time.

Although she found wisdom and comfort in the advice of others, she also realized the limitations of this approach. She wrote, "When I had to decide something, I asked the advice of everyone I could, often irritating those closest to me, who felt, understandably, that I should trust their judgment." Katharine knew, however, that the object was not the decision itself but the development of a very new and earnest executive.

Following her friend Walter Lippmann's advice, Katharine read her paper in the morning and later in the day asked to speak to reporters who had written stories that interested her. She sat in the conference room as the editors went over the "daily news budget," the stories that reporters were working on for the next day, and decided what would go on page A-1. "I was paralyzed with fear at first," she told an interviewer. "It was like being the new girl in school. You're disoriented. You don't know what your role is. The first time I ever asked a question at one of our private editorial lunches, I thought I'd die." Instead, she hid her fears and continued learning. She found her way to the circulation department, where she had worked briefly years before, to understand the network of dealers and carriers, and their unique incentive system. She studied the complex operation that turns copy into a printed newspaper. She met the compositors, printers, and makeup people racing to get the "dummies," sheets with only the advertising laid out, up to the editors. Then she watched the printers clatter at keyboards, the setup of Linotype slugs and photoengraving plates, and the proofreaders as they examined the final copy. She followed the hundreds of plates that were sent to the pressmen for printing on the huge rolls of paper fed into enormous, gulping machines. She would need to understand it all in order to track production costs and make financial decisions to underwrite new technology and machinery.

Katharine also explored the larger professional world, joining her first business board. She lunched with other executives, organized a business dinner, visited the Chrysler Corporation, and attended an event at the White House honoring President Tito of Yugoslavia. President Kennedy had been close to Phil, but he had intimidated Katharine. At her first presidential lunch in her new role, however, she felt emboldened to hand him a preelection poll, never imagining that he would die before the election year began. She got caught up for the first of many times in pressure from the White House to kill an editorial. Franklin Roosevelt Jr., an undersecretary of commerce, had accompanied Jackie Kennedy on a trip on Aristotle Onassis's yacht. Since Onassis did business with Roosevelt, the *Post* was about to criticize the apparent conflict of interest. After a call from the White House, Katharine agreed to talk to the editor, but the editorial ran anyway.

Katharine began to learn the literal and figurative limits and power of a CEO's voice. Making speeches came with the territory of being president of the company, but Katharine froze with terror at the thought. Her first test came at an advertising-sales meeting in Puerto Rico. With some help from a former speechwriter for President Eisenhower, who was on *Newsweek*'s staff, she made a seamless debut on "wobbly knees." Her speech-giving agonies, however, would last for a long time. She decided to hire a speech coach, overcoming her fears through knowledge, practice, and determination.

Other challenges were not so successfully met. During a strike at the *Post*'s rival newspaper, the *Washington Star*, Katharine passed a comment on to *Post* publisher John Sweeterman. She told him that Jim Reynolds, a member of Kennedy's labor department, thought that the *Post* should not support the *Star* against the strikers, as Sweeterman had been planning to do. The decision had long-term implications. The two papers had always stuck together in labor conflicts. Without a united front they were far more vulnerable to pressure from the workers. Sweeterman was well aware of the history of mutual support, yet he took Katharine's comments as a command. *Star* management capitulated to the strikers and bore a grudge toward the *Post* that would haunt Katharine during her own labor crisis years later.

Katharine took on the blame herself for "the mistake" of passing the message on to Sweeterman, accepting responsibility for the final decision. But the incident may have had more subtle and political undertones. Sweeterman had resented her leadership from the start. She irritated him, and tension bubbled up regularly between them. By treating her comment as if it had been an order, even though Katharine said otherwise, Sweeterman appeared to be setting her up. If Sweeterman had hoped to leave the *Star* without support in their labor negotiations, Katharine's call offered convenient cover. It had the added benefit of making her the villain should things go bad. It's evidence of Katharine's political naïveté that she failed to see Sweeterman's possible hidden motives, even years later as she recounted the event in her autobiography. Despite the unpleasant turn of events, the incident showed Katharine that her "voice" as leader had power, including the power to backfire with a bang. The wisdom of experience would teach her to use it well.

Perhaps the most visible first for Katharine as a woman leader came from the attention she received in the media. Katharine's rise coincided with a growing and vocal feminist movement. President Kennedy had appointed former first lady Eleanor Roosevelt to head the first Women's Commission in 1961. Title VII of the 1964 federal Civil Rights Act unexpectedly included sex discrimination in the workplace as a violation of rights. Books and articles were flooding readers with discussions of women's role in society, and by 1966 the National Organization for Women issued a rallying cry for women to become more politically active on their own behalf.

Katharine, the head of a rising paper in the nation's capital, stood out as the women's movement sought to highlight women with power. There were other women who had preceded Katharine in running large papers. Dorothy Chandler and her son ran the *Los Angeles Times* in 1960. Alicia Patterson had been editor and publisher of Long Island's *Newsday* for twenty-three years before Katharine came on the scene. In Washington, Alicia's cousin Eleanor "Cissy" Medill Patterson had been the editor and publisher of the *Washington Herald,* and Eugene Meyer's nemesis, until her death in 1948. For thirty-seven years, Dorothy Schiff owned and edited the *New York Post*. But Katharine's story had pathos and drama, and the wealth and political influence of her business was larger than any of the others.

The early stories played on her lack of ability and experience. Portraying her as the inept widow who inherited her throne made for an easy storyline, and it also fit the way Katharine projected herself. Asked in an early interview by *Newsweek* about her experience at the *News* in San Francisco she said, "I was the youngest and silliest girl on the paper." She seemed to be encouraging everyone's worst perceptions of her initial foray into managing her own press. Over time she would grow more sophisticated, as would the public's understanding of her leadership.

In the first months after Phil's death, Katharine pitched from success to misstep, from glimmers of confidence to abject loss of faith in herself. She got along by reacting rather than planning, vaguely determined to learn more, but unsure of her priorities. In this difficult emotional state, and still reeling from Phil's death, Katharine was swept into a sudden national trauma.

On November 22, 1963, Katharine was in New York for a meeting at *Newsweek*. She had brought her old friends, historian and author Arthur Schlesinger Jr. and economist John Kenneth Galbraith, both presidential advisers. As they were having drinks, a breathless aide told them that President Kennedy had been shot. Katharine immediately flew back to Washington and joined her friends as they rushed to the White House and witnessed the organized chaos as Vice President Lyndon Johnson became the new commander in chief.

The next day, Katharine returned to the White House and called on Lady Bird Johnson. The new first lady spoke candidly. She and her husband were horrified at losing Kennedy, more so because it happened in their state of Texas. Suddenly thrust into a role she didn't expect, Lady Bird said, "I feel like I've walked on stage for a part I've never rehearsed." Katharine understood exactly what she meant.

CHAPTER FOUR

"POWER HAS NO SEX"

"The first problem for all of us, men and women, is not to learn, but to unlearn."

—Gloria Steinem

There was no escaping it. Katharine wasn't just a company president, a corporate executive, a journalist, and a business owner. Most of the world appended "woman" before any description of her role. "There were men everywhere," David Halberstam wrote about the world Katharine entered. No matter what she did, Katharine faced the inescapable mirror of her gender at every turn.

Nearly twenty years later, Katharine's son, Don Graham, then publisher of the *Post*, echoed Halberstam's observation. Commenting on his mother's autobiography, her son had one suggestion: "I think that I would go back and try to expand on—because nobody in 1997 is going to understand—what it was like to be a woman CEO of a corporation in 1963, because it colored everything." No doubt Katharine was proud to have raised a son with more awareness of sexism than her male colleagues when she took over the paper. On the cusp of the presidential election year of 1964, Katharine was a sensible forty-six years old, and no one would have accused her of trying to draw attention to her sex. She wore her hair brushed straight back off her high, broad forehead, as she had done since she was young. Her clothes were conservative, buttoned up and simply adorned with a necklace and earrings. She was tall and had slimmed down, her large bones making her imposing if she chose to be, which was rare. Katharine came across as unfussy about her appearance. Fashion had never been her forte. She showed little concern about hairstyles and manicures; other priorities were on her mind.

First in order came the wrenching duality of her role as a working mother. She was, in today's parlance, a 24-7 executive, working long days, entertaining and socializing in the evening. Looking back, she wrote with touching self-criticism that her youngest children, Bill and Steve, had "lost both parents at once."

Katharine's mothering agonies preceded an era when a national chorus of working mothers would wrestle with the demands of balancing work and family. Katharine tried. She went to all of the boys' football games, took them along to events when she could, worrying that she was not as "present" a mother as she had been. Two decades after bearing her first child and making the commitment to home and family over all else, she upended this personal contract, one that she had paid dearly for. Why, when her children needed her most, did she reorder her priorities?

In explanation, Katharine wrote that her parents had gone out a lot, that she and Phil continued that pattern, and after he was gone she automatically continued the same course. But perhaps, in circumventing the pain and guilt of Phil's suicide, it was easier to sidestep the children as well. What could be a more searing reminder of her husband than his sons? Whatever her motivation, the boys occupied a guilty corner of Katharine's already wearied mind as she established herself as leader at the *Post*. Behind her distraction and insecurity on the job lay the interwoven strands of her recent trauma and her family duties. Minor incidents revealed the depth of her timidity, like the interchange recorded between Katharine and President Lyndon Johnson.

In December 1963, Katharine nervously held the phone to her ear as she waited for President Johnson to answer. Phil had been Johnson's political adviser and friend, but Katharine had been on the periphery of their relationship. She was calling to ask the new president to speak at the publishers association meeting the following year. Johnson started the call with a frankly salacious remark, suggesting he'd like to turn into one of the "young animals" on his ranch and jump a fence to see her. It was Katharine's first taste of the kind of sexualized teasing that she came to expect from him. Four months into her new role, her lack of confidence seemed to break down her good sense, as the president then took full advantage of her nervousness and lack of sophistication. When she asked if Johnson "might" consider speaking, Johnson said, "All right, okay. Yes, I will," to which Katharine replied, "Do you want to think about it, because—" Johnson cut her off saying, "I'll think it over, but I think I will." Katharine, still unable to see her victory, said, "[T]hey just wanted me to sound you out." But Johnson barreled along, taking the opportunity of having the new president of the *Post* on the line to pressure Katharine on an editorial position for the Civil Rights Act, then stuck in the House Rules Committee. When he instructed her to let her editorial board know of the House's recalcitrance, she dutifully replied, "I sure will." Katharine, who had sat nearly dumbstruck next to President Kennedy two years before, had not yet found her voice. She didn't believe that she could so easily command the attention of the president. Powerful men, whether in the White House or at her offices just blocks away, were intimidating.

Just eight months after the Johnson call, however, Katharine signaled a change. Senator Barry Goldwater, the archconservative from Arizona, had just won the Republican presidential nomination. Goldwater had called for severe cuts in social programs and the deployment of tactical nuclear weapons in the Vietnam War. His politics horrified Katharine. At the Republican convention she had witnessed the vitriol aimed at the press for its supposed liberal bias. She bristled at the condemnation, taking it as a strike at her values. She personally supported President Johnson's reelection even though she agreed with the *Post*'s long-held policy of nonendorsement. Katharine decided to reach out to Goldwater to uphold the *Post*'s tradition of nonpartisanship. She sent him a letter inviting him to the paper or to *Newsweek* to get better acquainted. As the leader of a major media company she wanted "complete and accurate reporting," writing that the news industry had "a solemn obligation to this kind of news reporting and that much depends on our ability to fulfill it." Katharine was beginning to act like Eugene's daughter.

Even President Johnson got a taste of the newly minted Katharine when he swept her away to his ranch after the Democratic Convention in August 1964. The surprise invitation landed her on a plane to Texas with the Johnsons, vice presidential nominee Hubert Humphrey, presidential staff, and the press pool. The visit proved a rare opportunity to hear campaign strategy. She joined conversations as an equal player, debating about issues of the day, politics and politicians, and the role Phil had played in Johnson's career. David Halberstam wrote that it gave her "new confidence" and "proved to her that she was in fact the publisher of the *Washington Post*." She may have arrived at the ranch with continued insecurities about her role, as Halberstam implies, but those feelings did not stop her from showing a newfound courage with men—even the president.

On the second day of the visit, LBJ and his guests headed to a country barbecue for the president's birthday. Johnson felt rushed, and once in the car he angrily told his wife that she had done a poor job of planning his time. To Katharine it sounded like an attack, and she couldn't contain herself. She reminded the president that his wife had "got you where you are today." The comment only stoked Johnson's anger. He lashed into Lady Bird, and Katharine erupted. "Oh, shut up, er . . . Mr. President," she told a chastened Johnson.

Was Katharine's response habituated by years of Phil's harangues? Was she trained to recognize verbal fisticuffs as a warning of abuse that, in her case, had escalated to violence? Or had Katharine found new courage with men? Did she have a new sense of entitlement to stand up for herself and, by extension, other women whose plight she understood? The latter seems likely. She was under attack, subtle but pernicious, from men on many fronts. Her consciousness of the gender stereotyping underlying her treatment had barely emerged, but after years of Phil's abuse, she could identify the oafish, ungrateful, and sexist behavior of husbands toward wives. It was a beginning.

Katharine had started to claim her "estate," that part of her that had been hidden or unknown even to herself.

Men Only

When Katharine took over, the *Post* was a male bastion in every department from news to editorial to business. While women had done outstanding work during World War II, when the majority of men were in the armed forces, they were quickly sidelined after the war was over. The women that remained had "women's" beats: fashion, education, welfare, and the "for and about Women" section, whose editor, Marie Sauer, tried unsuccessfully to rename it "for and about People." Male executives held little belief in women as leaders, much less that they may have had a style different but effective as compared to men. The company had only male managers, few women professionals, and, as Katharine wrote, "probably no women within four levels of me."

The business world was a man's world, and it had been a long time in the making. Centuries of thinking that gave men the presumptive leadership edge made it difficult for men or women to embrace the idea of women as leaders. Katharine wrote that her generation viewed women as inferior and "not capable of governing, leading, managing anything but our homes and our children." Male dominance seemed to be a birthright and an historical imperative.

Leadership scholar Bernard Bass wrote, "The study of history has been the study of leaders," but he might have added "male" leaders. As Bass describes, from Egyptian pharaohs in 2300 BC to the Old Testament, from Odysseus to the writings of Plato and Aristotle, and from Machiavelli to the "Great Man" theory of leadership of the eighteenth century to the present-day popular genre of great-leader-lesson-books, recognized leaders have been male leaders. "Women," said Katharine's friend Arthur Schlesinger Jr., "have constituted the most spectacular casualty of traditional history. They have made up at least half the human race, but you could never tell that by looking at the books historians write." The invisibility of her gender in history only added to Katharine's feelings of isolation.

Throughout her life, male leaders had dominated every sector, from government to politics to the military and corporations. In 1963, only one woman was head of a Fortune 500 company, Olive Ann Beech of Beech Aircraft Corporation. The stereotypes ascribed to women—nurturing, gentle, submissive, and emotional—were never correlated with leadership by those in power, as research three decades later would prove. Women who tried to lead in stereotypically male ways—directive, autocratic, hierarchical—cut against expectations in ways that made others uncomfortable. Either way, women who wanted to lead faced the bias that said they could not.

Instead, women were expected to be "feminine" in a way that left leadership to the opposite sex. A *Time* magazine article in 1963 described the mass media's idea of femininity. "Be thin, be smart, be gay, be sexy, be soft-spoken. Get new slipcovers, learn new recipes, have bright children, further your man's career, help the community, drive the car, smile." The atmosphere and attitudes of her time presented Katharine with few historical or contemporary role models and prejudiced others against her success.

At first, Katharine didn't see the problem. Her personal insecurities led her to overlook cultural sexism and fostered self-blame. She told an interviewer from *Women's Wear Daily* that any man would do a better job than she was doing. She told *Editor & Publisher* that, even in a field dominated by men, people "forget you're a woman." In explaining her failure to support the Equal Rights Amendment for women she explained that she didn't see the need, since "people just emerged or they didn't." Where other women had begun to see a mountain of discrimination, Katharine was so inculcated with the perceptions of her time that she gave tacit approval to the idea that sexism was just the way the world worked. "I was brought up in an era in which we were taught that men were superior," she told an interviewer in 1997, "and that we were to get married and have children and make them happy." Even as the women's movement became more prominent, Katharine drew away, slow to react. Her mother's comment, "Penis envy, that's all it is," didn't help. Katharine could not, however, escape the harsh reality of being a woman in a man's world.

As soon as she took over, men responded by using Katharine's gender to undermine her power. A *Time* magazine article published just after Phil's death speculated that an inexperienced woman like Katharine could never run the paper. Control would probably be given to someone like *Post* managing editor Al Friendly. On the business side, Katharine was routinely told not to worry her head and given a figurative pat. Behind her back she was called "Mama." The men who didn't like her style, her increasing assertion of authority, or who simply didn't like the idea of working for a woman, were more crass. "What she needs is a good f——k," became one of the sniggering comments in the whisper campaign. John Sweeterman, the brilliant business head of the newspaper, had little patience for his new boss or for women in power in general. Frank Waldrop, former editor of the *Washington Star*, explained that men like Sweeterman "didn't know much about women at all—okay you marry one, you hop into bed with her, have some kids, then you get on with your work." The comment explained a generation's worth of male attitudes.

At *Newsweek*, management continued a "long and strong history" of discriminating against women. Women were stuck in the role of researchers, and promotions were out of the question. Katharine had encountered this sexism shortly after taking over, on a visit to the *Newsweek* offices. Meeting with editors about a senior editor vacancy, she suggested that a woman be hired. Her idea met with patronizing smiles and the comment, "That would be quite impossible, Mrs. Graham. All those late Friday nights, everyone working together . . . it just wouldn't do." Katharine backed down, too intimidated to say any more.

Discrimination against women grew out of unthinking patterns of behavior based on stereotypes. Katharine's sudden ascendancy threatened this newsroom caste culture. If she could succeed, if she were allowed to succeed, long-held presumptions about the capabilities of women would be turned on their heads.

Surrounded by men, hardly speaking to women other than secretaries, Katharine internalized her male colleagues' negative expectations of her performance. "These men seemed to know what they were doing at all times and they always had the answers and they talked in a kind of insider's shorthand. It was very easy to feel slow among them," David Halberstam wrote. They were top in their industry and competed vigorously, often fiercely, for more prestige and power. They expected Katharine to stay out of their way. Top-level men at *Newsweek* had the attitude, "Sure, I'll cooperate with the poor widow lady, but if she tries to get in my way, I'll ignore her."

Though not proven at the time, research now demonstrates that competent individuals increase their chances of failure by doubting their ability. In a pattern that will be familiar to many women today,

Katharine failed to recognize the impact of the men's perceptions on how she did her job. Instead, she felt inferior, and she blamed the victim—herself. Katharine's abilities were further undermined by the stereotyped caricatures others had of her. She carried the "psychological burden" of worrying that she would confirm the worst stereotypes. This weakened her sense of "self-efficacy" or confidence in her success. She had fallen into a vicious and self-defeating cycle.

She could see that women were often invisible to men, or too visible. "I would go to a meeting. It would be addressed by a man saying very self-consciously, 'Lady and Gentlemen,' or 'Gentlemen and Mrs. Graham.' I mean, you'd always stick out as something unusual." At a meeting of the Bureau of Advertising, one of the many all-male groups she had joined, a friend of hers was leading a discussion on an issue that was unfamiliar to Katharine. He went around the table asking for input. Katharine, about to make the last comment, never got the chance. "I was thinking all the way around the table what I was going to say," she told an interviewer, "and then he skipped me! He ended at my right. He didn't ask me!" After an awkward silence where the group realized the gaffe, she managed to say a few words on the subject.

Repeatedly being the only woman in the room, as well as the outsider and nontraditional leader, both raised and lowered Katharine's consciousness. On one level, she found it "spoiling—and fun," on another it reinforced her insecurities. Gradually, however, her traditional views began to shift. She drove along on a two-track pilgrimage to understand herself as well as her new role, and she could no longer pretend that being a woman was irrelevant to her journey.

A Reluctant Feminist

Great leaders are marked by their capacity for learning, growth, and change. Katharine had read her Emerson, and the "foolish consistency" of her ideas about women's roles and abilities began to unravel. Her friends and associates, as well as the growing voice of women who were demanding equality, all affected her thinking. In 1969, her friend Elsie Carper, a *Post* reporter and editor, threatened to quit after reading Katharine's *Women's Wear Daily* comment that a man could do a better job running the paper. "If you feel that way," she told Katharine, "then I ought to quit and every woman on this newspaper ought to quit." Carper's outburst had a deep effect. That same year in August the *Post* wrote its first editorial on the new wave of the women's movement. Called "Not Such a Long Way, Baby," a reference to the Virginia Slims cigarette commercials of the time that celebrated women's progress, it criticized the exploitation of women throughout society. Katharine and her paper were slowly catching on.

Katharine's close friend Meg Greenfield, an editorial page editor, traveled the road toward feminism with her. As one of the few women who had made it in a man's world, Greenfield had little sympathy for the movement's demands. Instead, like other women in her position, her unique status gave her a sense of superiority. She kept a sign on her office door that said, "If liberated, I will not serve." But together, she and Katharine discussed the women's liberation movement, struggling to find a position of comfort. They took an intellectual approach, turning to books with feminist ideas. In *The Second Sex* by Simone de Beauvoir, Katharine no doubt recognized her earlier life in the author's description of men and women: "humanity is male and man defines woman not in herself, but as relative to him." Women, de Beauvoir argued, needed to become central to their own life stories. Katharine and Greenfield wrestled with these new ideas, confronted their discomfort with radical action, and tried to see beyond what appeared to them to be a movement based on man hating.

Besides her friends, Katharine also found a mentor in her journey toward feminism. Younger by a generation, Gloria Steinem marched at the front, literally and figuratively, of women who had united against sex discrimination. Steinem had trained and worked as a journalist. She had lived in India in the 1950s and been moved by the terrible oppression of women there. She returned to the United States to be a freelance journalist in the 1960s, finding her passion as a leader and feminist activist in New York City. A powerful speaker who rapidly became a feminist icon, Steinem believed in the possibilities of the women's movement. "Any woman who chooses to behave like a full human being," she said, "should be warned that the armies of the status quo will treat her as something of a dirty joke. That's their natural and first weapon. She will need her sisterhood." In this spirit, Steinem developed a friendship with Katharine that challenged the older woman's beliefs.

Steinem encouraged Katharine to "throw off some of the myths" of her old-style thinking. She challenged Katharine to remake her vision of who she was and what she could become, to shake off a lifetime of habits and ingrained beliefs. Steinem had a passion and brilliance that her older friend admired, despite the differences in their backgrounds and views. She guided Katharine to pull apart and come to terms with new concepts like questioning patriarchy and understanding her authentic self. In turn the older woman helped as she was able.

Steinem had dreams of a feminist magazine, but funding was scarce. "We had no funding. We were making dummies of the magazine out of our own money," Steinem recalled. Steinem turned to Katharine for help in getting *Ms.* magazine into publication. When Katharine sent $20,000, Steinem's former boss, *New York* magazine founder Clay Felker, called it "walking around money." But for Steinem it was "our first money when we had no money," and it launched a publishing phenomenon for the women's movement. Years later, Katharine told an interviewer that the women's movement had been an enormous help "to understand where sexism came from." Despite her misgivings about feminism, she had played a central role in building its outreach.

As Katharine came to discover the women's movement, it discovered her. Stories about the *Post* publisher burst onto magazine pages around the country. She was featured in eleven articles in ten national magazines, including *Vogue, Forbes, The New Yorker,* and *Business Week* between 1964 and 1975. In October 1974, she was on the cover of Steinem's *Ms.* magazine, with a story headlined "Meet the Most Powerful Woman in America." She became the poster woman for professional women who were "soft without mental flab, knowledgeable without aggressiveness," as a photo cutline described her in *Vogue.* Katharine struggled with personal contradictions that the news media often articulated. Could she be in charge, a leader and CEO, yet fit the feminine ideal?

In the *Vogue* article, written by Katharine's friend Arthur Schlesinger, she was praised as a "lady publisher," graceful, thoughtful, and sensitive. Acceptability as a leader, the article implied, required a certain type of prescribed femininity. In December 1968, *Harper's* profiled Katharine, saying she "commands the loyalty of her [all-male] court by being feminine, direct and invincibly knowledgeable." According to the author, Katharine "enjoys [the editors'] militant male democracy too much to wish to disrupt them." Despite its sexist slant, the article captured the continuing paradox of Katharine's leadership. "Behind her natural shyness and deliberate self-effacement ('I pick the wool off blankets') lies a bright core of pride; and the combination permits a wee penumbra of healthy vanity. By being tough, Mrs. Graham will make a proprietor's contribution. But there is a further, unique contribution that she makes by being a lady and a rather lonely widow and by temperament dependent on men." At that point in her life, Katharine probably agreed with the author's assessment. But gradually, she pushed aside old ideas and moved toward a popular phrase coined by the women's movement: "consciousness raising."

Her new consciousness, however, did not translate into strong demands on the men in the business, advertising, and production sides of both the *Post* and *Newsweek.* She only seemed willing to make changes around the margins. She sent her executives an article titled

"The Female Job Ghetto," evidently hoping they would be as willing to learn and try to change as their boss. She cautioned the personnel director against subconscious sexism for putting out a memo on new employees that referred to the men by last names and the women by first names. She suggested the elimination of such words as "'divorcee,' 'grandmother,' 'vivacious' or 'cute,'" where comparable words wouldn't be applied to a man, or to avoid clichés. Her approach avoided confrontation, even as women at the paper complained to her about what today would be called "micro-inequities," or the subtle differences in treatment that often deny women their due. They told Katharine about being assigned to the least interesting stories or being limited to interviewing other women, but Katharine showed no sense of urgency on their behalf.

Other women, however, were growing more than restless with second-class status and were looking for greater and faster change. Syndicated columnist Ellen Goodman recalled being hired at a newsmagazine in 1963, as a new college grad: "In those days, women were hired as researchers and men were hired as writers . . . and that was that." But the 1964 Civil Rights Act, which gave women the right to sue to stop sex discrimination, shook up the status quo.

The first salvo on behalf of equal rights for women in Katharine's company came at *Newsweek*. It had taken the magazine until March 1970 to publish its first cover story on the women's movement, titled "Women in Revolt." A woman reporter was commissioned as a freelancer to write the story because the editors believed they had no woman on staff qualified for the job. Conveniently, the writer was married to a star reporter. Explaining the women's movement, the piece said that women "with lovers, husbands, and children—or expectations of having a few of each—[were] talking about changes in social attitudes and customs that will allow every female to function as a separate and equal person." But the women at *Newsweek* were doing more than talking. On the day the magazine hit the stands, forty-six women at the magazine filed the first complaint of discrim-

ination by women in the media under the six-year-old Title VII of
the federal Civil Rights Act. When Katharine heard about the suit,
her reaction came across as tongue-in-cheek, but her ambivalence
was real. "Which side am I supposed to be on?" she asked.

The women sent Katharine a letter outlining their grievances.
Nearly forty years earlier, Eleanor Roosevelt had held the first-ever
press conferences by a first lady. She only allowed women reporters as
a way of encouraging newspapers to hire them and give them good
assignments. The war years increased women's opportunities, as male
reporters left to fight. But by 1970, the clock had been turned a long
way back. In their letter, the women told Katharine that they had
"rarely been hired as, or promoted to, the positions of reporter, writer,
or editor" and were bypassed for bureau correspondent positions.
They were given lesser titles and lower pay. They were excluded from
public functions, and, of course, the magazine did not even give the
cover story on feminism to one of its own female staffers. Determined
and organized, they had hired an up-and-coming young lawyer,
"highly articulate, tough, militant, black—and pregnant"—Eleanor
Holmes Norton. Private anger had flared into a very public battle.

Katharine reacted as an executive, a member of management, and
an "Aunt Tom," as she would later call herself. To one reader who
questioned the situation she wrote that the newsweeklies had "tended
to appear to discriminate against women, but they were making plans
to change, and the women should have discussed this with us before
they filed their legal complaint." In her autobiography, Katharine ac-
knowledges that her response was naive and unrealistic. The women
had had their fill of discussions, which the company president had
evidently never heard about or cared to address. Her fierce loyalty to
the paper colored her reactions. Steinem said that Katharine saw
"criticism of the *Post* as the greatest sin" and remained unadmiring of
Eleanor Holmes Norton, who went on to become the congresswoman
representing Washington, D.C.

In five months, the women had a settlement, but they sued again two years later, claiming management hadn't lived up to the agreement. Katharine hadn't paid enough attention to the problem, and that same year, in 1972, the *Post* was sued as well. At the time the *Post* suit was filed, the only women in upper management were Katharine and Meg Greenfield. In 1974, the Equal Employment Opportunity Commission found that the *Post* had discriminated against women, particularly in promotions. The *Newsweek* suit was settled at Katharine's urging, and the women got most of what they wanted. A third of all the writers and reporters would be women, and a third of researchers would be men. The women felt it was important to integrate what had been solely a woman's job. Training programs were put in place, and plans were made to move women into leadership roles as bureau chiefs and to have a woman senior editor within two and a half years. Hiring and promotion practices changed at the *Post* as well as a result of the legal action. Women, as well as minorities who faced similar discrimination, began to change the face, writing, and thinking of Katharine's growing media empire.

Katharine had undergone a transformation along with her business. She felt pushed to make changes but admitted that the pressure turned out to be for the good. "Gradually I came to realize," she wrote in her autobiography, "that what mattered was performance, that sometimes people might have to be helped to develop, and that it takes all kinds to make an organization run properly." She took pride in that, however bad things were at the *Post* and *Newsweek,* her enterprises were far ahead of her competitors.

The sexist attitudes that Katharine encountered on the job extended to the larger business world as well. Organizations that brought industry leaders together actively discriminated, and in some cases had been doing so since they were formed. The National Press Club didn't allow women members until 1972. The Gridiron Club, which had started in the 1880s exclusively to have an annual roast of politicians by white male members of the press, was even more recalcitrant. Washington bureau chiefs used the Gridiron roast to make their out-of-town editors feel important. Virtually every U.S. president had attended the Gridiron dinner, as well as every cabinet member and Supreme Court justice. The big-name guests were scattered throughout the audience, giving the out-of-towners a chance to rub elbows with the Washington elite. The Gridiron Club boasted that its members were the most distinguished journalists in the country.

Women had resented the club's all-male exclusivity for years. When Franklin Roosevelt attended his first Gridiron dinner, his wife, Eleanor, started a new tradition—the Gridiron Widows dinner. The First Lady invited all the women in the press to come, as well as the wives of the cabinet members and diplomats who were at the men's dinner. She also invited the only woman cabinet member, Labor Secretary Frances Perkins, whose gender trumped her position when it came to the men's dinner.

Eleanor Roosevelt's dinner cut through the pomp and gained a reputation as a more lively and entertaining event than that of the men. Still, no changes in membership were made until the organized agitation of the women's movement became focused on the club decades later. In 1970 women in the media began demanding Gridiron membership and picketing the dinners. As the pressure mounted, the club decided to invite fifteen prominent women to attend the dinner as guests in 1972. Katharine was among the group that included congresswoman and presidential candidate Shirley Chisholm, other women members of Congress, the anthropologist Margaret Mead, Mrs. Martin Luther King Jr., and the wives of President Nixon and Vice President Agnew.

Katharine had every intention of going to the dinner. Her instincts as a journalist and media CEO overwhelmed any developing feminist consciousness she may have had at the time. Then she received a letter from women on her own and other papers urging her to refuse the invitation unless the club gave women membership. Katharine's first reaction came across as typically moderate and self-defeating. She reasoned to herself that the club had no openings at the time and that the invitation was a "beginning." As *Post* reporter Sally Quinn put it, "She wasn't a raging feminist, but was offended that the Gridiron didn't take women. She didn't want to start a feminist charge. The question in her mind was how to encourage them to include women but not to rile up the men." Nearly ten years into her job as publisher, Katharine still failed to see that it wasn't her actions that riled the men—it was her position as a powerful woman.

Katharine's experiences with the fight against women's discrimination and her own lack of awareness led her to get more educated before finalizing her decision about the dinner. A group of women from the paper were invited to have a discussion about the Gridiron Club. It fell to Sally Quinn to make the argument that won over her boss. "If a country club excluded you for being a Jew," Quinn asked, "but said they'd like to have you come for dinner, would you go?" Faced with that logic, Katharine agreed to decline the invitation. She wouldn't defy her women friends and colleagues, but she wouldn't join them on the feminist barricades either.

Quinn did join the protesters, holding signs "like the suffragists" and standing in the freezing cold. "The men were slinking in in white tie," she recalled, "because they were totally embarrassed." Katharine was both curious and embarrassed. On her way to a restaurant with Meg Greenfield, they cruised by the dinner, but Katharine ducked low while Greenfield did the driving. They were worried about a "dreadful photo," if a photographer spotted them. The story is vintage Katharine: curious about the drama of activists and social change but a reluctant and cautious feminist.

In another blow to tradition, Katharine ended an antiquated social practice in Washington that required women to leave the men to their cigars, brandy, and serious conversation after dinner. One evening she and Meg Greenfield were at Joe Alsop's for a dinner party. Katharine had been working all day, taking part in an editorial-issue lunch, and "something snapped" as she thought about being dismissed from the table after dinner to join a discussion of "women's" interests. She told her host that she planned to quietly leave after dinner rather than be exiled for an hour. She hadn't counted on Alsop being upset enough to break with custom and keep everyone around the table. Word spread of Katharine's revolt, and although she had not meant to spark a rebellion, her action brought an end to the offensive custom.

Just as sexist practices were slow to change, it took Katharine time to understand how sexism affected her and other women and to figure out how to make change. In 1977, she invited Steinem to address the *Post* editorial board on the issue of extending the deadline for state ratification of the Equal Rights Amendment. Supporters of the ERA argued that there was no constitutional time limit for state ratification, and the amendment, already close to passage, just needed a little more time. Steinem was nervous about addressing the board. "I told her, 'You're a woman publisher and a Democrat, can't you do it?' But she wanted me on short notice," Steinem recalled. "I felt like a surrogate Kay, and I did poorly in that atmosphere of men in Brooks Brothers clothing and tweed jackets with elbow patches. A great deal depended on it and I was very intimidated on a class level." After Steinem's visit, the editorial board voted against supporting the extension. It was another example of Katharine going only so far and no farther. She brought in her feminist friend to argue the case, but she wouldn't try to influence the board herself as Phil or Eugene likely would have done on an issue of importance to them. She had created her own standards and she stood by them.

She began to practice a kind of personal feminism, showing open support for women at the company. In the mid-to-late 1980s, she let pregnant reporters know that they could use the sofa in her personal ladies' lounge to lie down whenever they wanted. After reporter Dale Russakoff came back from maternity leave, Katharine told her that she was amazed by the ability of the young women at the paper to work and raise children. Because the *Post* was a morning paper, flexibility and hours were big issues for women reporters who also had the role of primary caregiver for their children. With Katharine's support, limited flextime and job-sharing became an option. "[She] went out of her way to talk with women who worked at the *Post*," said executive editor Leonard Downie. "She encouraged them to move up and take leadership roles at the paper." Although her selection of executives remained predominantly male, she reached out to her friend Jack Valenti in the mid-1980s to help change her board. "I want a woman to go on the board, a very bright woman, can you help me?" she asked him. Valenti, then head of the Motion Picture Association of America, suggested his general counsel, Barbara Scott Preiskel. "I introduced Barbara to Kay and they hit it off," Valenti remembers. Preiskel went on the board.

Katharine also stood up for her own leadership. An interviewer in 1978 brought up criticism leveled at her by some of the executives she had hired and fired. Told that an unnamed source had said that "her mistake is not in picking bad people. It's in emasculating them," Katharine had a quick response. She had gone through enough battles to realize that the remark reflected gender bias. Her answer flashed with impatience over the pace of change. "That's the woman thing," she replied, "Christ . . . nobody says a thing [about *Washington Star* management changes]. And then I do it, and they can't stop talking about it." She had moved from being the victim to fighting back, from meek acceptance of the status quo to redefining conventional ideas. "The thing women must do to rise to power is to redefine their femininity," she wrote. "Once, power was considered a masculine attribute. In fact, power has no sex." Katharine had proved the truth in her remark, not by being an outspoken activist but rather by being a businesswoman unique to American corporate culture. "Women exercise power to," Steinem said, "men exercise power over, and Kay was a great example of how women wield power." Katharine had used her power to reform the culture of her company, and in doing so had given the nation a new view of women and what they could accomplish.

CHAPTER FIVE

CLAIMING HER COMPANY

"To make a living is no longer enough. Work also has to make a life."

—Peter Drucker

Beset by her fears and insecurities, feeling the pressure of those who would have her fail, and both undermined and underestimated by the men in charge, Katharine stayed motivated by a mission: to build an outstanding company. She was guided by her father's memory. "He and I both assumed I would always be in journalism," she told an interviewer. He had taught her an overriding value: maintain the public trust. He had famously turned down a million-dollar profit from Andrew Mellon, who wanted to buy the *Post* when it was still losing money. "You haven't enough money to buy the independent sort of newspaper I am trying to build," he politely told Mellon. Now it was Katharine's turn to carry his values forward. She also thought about her children. She had secured the company for them, and she began to believe she could leave them something more than she had found. In this way, the job had become her higher calling, providing a place in life with a simple, noble purpose. She wrote to a friend that it had become the focus of her love. For the sake of her company she could endure all the rest.

If she curled up inside at a remark she made that seemed foolish or uninformed, she nevertheless spoke up. Those around her, so comfortable with collegiality, expressing opinions, and operating in the pressure-cooker world of the news, had no concept of the tortures she went through to earn the place she had taken.

Part of her progress depended on a striking lack of narcissism. She focused on her performance, on the impression she left with people, and on the effect of her decisions, but always in relation to the business. She appeared to have no interest in creating a personal throne but rather in finding her seat in the overall business plan. Because she cared more about the greater good of the company, rather than her personal needs, she grew more quickly. She realized that some employees welcomed her, some resented her, but most were "not bothering about me at all." She never saw herself as the center of any universe, which, after years in Phil's shadow, is not surprising. But by not expecting the company to revolve around her, Katharine was able to make more clear-eyed decisions. As leadership author and management consultant Jim Collins explains, the greatest leaders "channel their ego needs away from themselves and into the larger goal of building a great company. It's not that [these] leaders have no ego or self-interest. Indeed, they are incredibly ambitious—*but their ambition is first and foremost for the institution, not themselves.*" Collins's ideal came to life under Katharine's leadership of the *Post*.

Katharine's selfless, laserlike focus on the company quickly became a critical ingredient in her early leadership actions. She wanted to learn about everything. One day she asked President Johnson's aide Walt Rostow to explain the multilateral nuclear force and ended up with a two-hour explanation. "It was like taking the cork out of Niagara Falls," she told an interviewer. She pushed herself to understand everything from liquidity to the Green Bay Packers. She fell back on the journalist's questions: "Who did what, when, why, where, and how?" Her inquisitive instinct intimidated some, aggravated others, and cost her endless self-recrimination. But how was she to learn if not by questioning? Her approach differed little from men with her drive and purpose. Ben Bradlee, when he first started as assistant managing editor at the *Post,* described his approach this way, "In the city room at night I bugged everyone for answers to a thousand questions." Her father had been the same way, roaming the creaky old *Post* building, asking questions of employees, occasionally shooting craps with them and soaking up what he needed to know. Katharine shared the same intense curiosity and drive for knowledge as she took charge.

For Katharine, one of the most difficult places to develop her authority was with *Newsweek.* Robin Webb, Phil's lover, had come from *Newsweek,* which made it feel like somewhat hostile territory. Some of the magazine's staff had set Phil up with Webb and helped facilitate the affair. Katharine could easily have avoided that part of the operation, leaving it to others or selling it off. But she was determined to keep her personal feelings out of her professional decisions, and she acted accordingly only days after Phil's death.

As she headed off to Europe to rendezvous with her mother, Katharine wrote letters to two *Newsweek* reporters—Ben Bradlee and Arnaud de Borchgrave. Both men had been "Phil" people, loyal to their boss, especially since Phil had bought *Newsweek* partly at the urging of Bradlee. She told them that she wanted to move forward and forget the past. It was an early and unexpected overture signaling the priorities and character of their new CEO.

After she returned and took over as president, Katharine traveled to New York every week, sitting in on *Newsweek* editorial meetings and conferences on the cover story. She bought a co-op apartment at the United Nations Plaza, where her friend Truman Capote lived, signaling her intention to be a presence at the magazine. Her attention did little to ease fears among the staff. Katharine was getting offers to buy all or part of her company, and *Newsweek* seemed the most at risk. Rumors kept popping up in the media. An offer of $100 million had been made by Samuel Newhouse, more than ten times what Phil had paid. Why didn't she let it go?

Katharine explained in her autobiography that selling "wasn't right." She saw the magazine as an institution; it had been around since 1933. She felt the weight of that legacy and, most urgently, of protecting the people who labored for the magazine. They deserved stability. They deserved the continuity that the previous owners had provided in order to create a news outlet that the public enjoyed and trusted. Despite her personal history with some of the staff, despite that Katharine had often felt ostracized by them, she put her values above her personal feelings. *Newsweek* stayed in the company.

Building Her Team

As she learned more about the various parts of the company, Katharine sought out the advice of friends and those she trusted. They served her well by being honest, but they also surprised her. She had so idolized Phil, so believed in his talent and brilliance, that she cast that belief over the paper. She assumed it was brilliant too and must have been outstanding just as Phil had been outstanding. But it wasn't.

Her dear friend James "Scotty" Reston, the *New York Times* reporter who came to be known as the greatest journalist of his time, made the point to Katharine in a way she couldn't ignore. In a chat with her at Glen Welby he asked, "Don't you want to leave a better paper for the next generation than the one you inherited?" Other friends echoed Reston's comment. Richard Clurman of *Time* told her, "Kay, don't confuse the paper with the radiance of Phil. The *Post* is not a good paper." Walter Lippmann, who had been advising her with such respect, thought the paper was "sluggish and not very adventurous." The critics had become a chorus.

Katharine listened and began making her own assessment of the operation. A year after Phil's death she had developed opinions about the product she was showing the public and the culture that produced it. The young woman who had written energetic letters advising her parents in the early years of Meyer ownership of the *Post* resurfaced as a mature woman who could act on her instincts. While Katharine had found it hard to be decisive up to this point because of her lack of knowledge, she still recognized the perils of uncertainty in the paper's management. She observed a "great deal of indecision among the executives." The brightest reporters were leaving for lack of incentive. The foreign staff was pitifully small, and first-rate talent was buried out of sight. In Phil's time, one journalist described the atmosphere as "cold, impersonal; no one cared whether you lived or died." Katharine cared a great deal.

Ever since her short stint in the chaotic circulation department shortly after her marriage to Phil, Katharine had been a stickler for strong organization and order. These seemed to be lacking overall. Excitement and energy, or "adrenaline," as Katharine called it, was also in short supply. She heard the rumor that a dead cat could be swung around the city room after 9:00 p.m. and not hit anyone. That wasn't the kind of paper she intended to run.

Recognizing the problem and changing it were two very different tasks. Even as Katharine became more convinced that the paper had problems, the solutions seemed out of reach. Shifting the paper's culture, its point of view, and its cohesion meant changing the people in charge. The two men in question were not only Katharine's colleagues but also her friends: managing editor Al Friendly and editorial page editor Russ Wiggins.

The most immediate problem lay with Al Friendly, who had authority over the entire news operation. Friendly's domain extended from the hiring of reporters to personnel administration and production coordination, from the moment a newsworthy event occurred to its retelling in the newspaper. Phil Graham had said that newspapers wrote the "first rough draft of history"—a lofty description for an unruly, often chaotic process. Friendly's job required him to organize a disparate team and a nightmare of details. But Friendly wasn't a detail person. Most of the administrative maze he left to his assistant, Ben Gilbert.

Friendly had been with the paper for a quarter century when Katharine took over. He had been a pillar in its development and one of the men who held the place together during Phil's worst days. He hung on when people were capriciously fired and rehired, when a bureau might be created or dismantled without warning, and when the newsroom was in "a defensive crouch," as Ben Bradlee described it, in anticipation of Phil's next assault. Katharine also had a personal relationship with Friendly. He and his wife, Jean, were two of Katharine's closest friends. Jean had played with Katharine when they were little children in the neighborhood at Connecticut Avenue and Kalorama Street in Washington, D.C. Al had been one of Eugene Meyer's favorites when Katharine's father hired him in 1939. They had shared in the happiness and tragedy of her life as dear friends do. How could she betray that friendship by pushing Friendly out?

Part of the answer came from Friendly himself. Ten years into the job of managing editor he had grown hard of hearing, making his job difficult both for him and those around him. He had also started taking a month off for vacation twice during the year. One month was normal, but Phil had given him an extra month for "travel and contemplation." He had bought a house on the coast in Turkey, taking him completely out of touch. Leaving the operation in subordinates' hands for such extended periods added to the newsroom malaise. If the managing editor didn't have the energy to be there on top of things, why would anyone else?

Perhaps Friendly, aging and tired, had begun to trade too heavily on his friendship with Katharine. His main motivation for staying on seemed to be to wait out the three years until he became president of the American Society of News Editors. It was an honor he coveted, but a purpose too narrow to animate his leadership. As her doubts about the paper's management grew during the 1964 election year, Katharine tried speaking to Friendly about investing more energy in the news side. He didn't take her seriously. No doubt he believed that the paper owed him a great deal. No doubt he counted on Katharine preserving his role because he had been Phil's choice, a presumed allegiance that blinded him to her transforming role.

Some signs of Katharine's transformation were subtle, such as changing the way she signed her name, from "Mrs. Philip Graham" to "Katharine Graham." Others were more obvious, such as her pointed questions to Friendly about the paper's direction, its future, and their shared vision. Friendly, however, couldn't adjust his view of the old Katharine. He also seemed to have lost track of the greater mission of the paper. What he failed to realize was that Katharine had not.

Even as she puzzled over the Friendly problem, Katharine had her eye on new talent. In an astonishing move, she landed on the idea, in early 1965, of promoting Ben Bradlee from his post as head of *Newsweek*'s Washington bureau. From a personal perspective, Bradlee was the enemy. He hadn't only been loyal to Phil, he had gone further than many others in Washington had dared during Phil's affair with Webb. Bradlee and his wife had Phil and Webb over for a dinner that made the gossip rounds. Katharine had heard that Bradlee had been quoted as saying that "there was nothing wrong with Phil Graham that a quick divorce would not cure." And after Phil's death, although Bradlee returned from a trip to Europe to attend the funeral, he did not pay his respects at the Graham home afterward. Word filtered back to him that Katharine had noticed.

Rather than thinking of him for a promotion, it seemed more likely that Phil's widow would fire him from his job out of spite. Instead, Katharine arranged a lunch with Bradlee to discuss his future. "The past is behind us," she had written to him the previous year. She meant it, yet her ability to overcome her feelings is surprising. If she felt pangs of resentment toward Bradlee, she tucked them away under her CEO's hat. Bradlee said, "It was ballsy of her to call me."

Katharine had just returned from a six-week around-the-world tour with *Newsweek*'s editor, Oz Elliott, who had been accompanied by his wife. She had had time to discuss Bradlee with Elliott. She had also gained enough confidence to strike out on her own in a search for talent. The CEO Bradlee met with in the spring of 1965 wasn't the same woman whom he had seen at Phil's funeral twenty months before. She had changed during the 1964 presidential election year, when President Johnson and the Republican nominee, Barry Goldwater, treated her as a person with power. Johnson had courted her avidly, hoping she would break tradition and endorse him. She didn't, but the entreaties and attention of a president were heady fare.

A few days after his reelection, Johnson invited Katharine to a dinner in honor of his wedding anniversary. Johnson went off to bed around midnight, which was the signal for guests to leave. As Katharine was saying good night to his wife, Johnson called for her and his friend and lawyer Abe Fortas to come into his bedroom. LBJ was furious over a *Post* headline about Commissioner Tobriner appointing a new police chief for Washington. Johnson had wanted Tobriner to inform him before going public. "We had supported Tobriner's appointment," Katharine said later, "so somehow it became my fault. [Johnson] just started dressing me down . . . yelling at me." As Johnson raged on, he also began to undress. "I was pretty new at this sort of thing, and I just could not believe that I was there in the bedroom, being dressed down by the president as he was getting undressed." When he got down to his underwear, he ordered Katharine to turn around. He was in his pajamas and in bed before he told them they could go. The episode was an unforgettable part of Katharine's initiation into Phil's world.

Overseas, in the first months of 1965, she interviewed the president of Egypt, Gamal Abdel Nasser, met with a population minister in India, with Prime Minister Sato of Japan, and lunched with General Westmoreland as part of a tour of Vietnam. She worked hard and loved it. She returned feeling that she had "more energy and enthusiasm for my job than ever." It was at this high-water mark that she arranged to see Bradlee. It was also the first time in her life that she had invited a man to lunch.

Katharine took care to maintain her role as the one in charge. Since men normally picked up the check, she invited Bradlee to the F Street Club, a regular rendezvous for the Washington establishment just blocks from the White House, where only she could sign for the bill. Having never arranged such a meeting before, she prepared well. She knew a great deal about Bradlee before they ever sat down—his personal situation as a remarried father with a blended family of six children and his professional credentials. Bradlee shone in his job for *Newsweek*. He had refused more than one promotion to the New York office in favor of staying in Washington. He wanted to provide the continuity that a newsmagazine needs, and he liked running his own show. He had a reputation for hiring the best young talent, for publishing solid, straightforward reporting and doing it with a style that combined professional standards and irreverence. Katharine, so worried about the propriety of her lunch arrangements, was about to get a taste of the Bradlee vernacular.

Bradlee thought the lunch started off on "the starchy side." But when Katharine asked him if he might want to return to the *Post*, where he had spent two and a half years as a city desk reporter in 1949, Bradlee couldn't contain himself. He loved the immediacy of a daily paper and thought the *Post* had fabulous potential to "right wrong" and expose the workings of government. "If Al Friendly's job ever opened up," Bradlee told Katharine, "I'd give my left one for it."

If Katharine found the language shocking, she didn't let on. The substance of Bradlee's answer put her more off balance than its delivery. She hadn't mentioned Friendly's job to Bradlee. Yet, as the idea bubbled in her mind, it grew in attraction, and Bradlee wanted the job with an intensity that suggested the kind of leader he would be. Once he blurted out his intentions at lunch, he spent the following weeks pressing Katharine for an answer every time he got the chance. Dogged, determined, forthright, with a rough kind of charm and relentless energy—that was Bradlee. "I turned her on by seeing the vision," Bradlee said later. Despite his often annoying persistence, she began to see him as a partner for the big changes ahead.

Over the next few months, she met with Bradlee and conferred with others about his ability. Meanwhile, some influential people were pushing for his hire. Walter Lippmann was a family friend of the Bradlees, and fully supported bringing him on. *Post* chairman Fritz Beebe and *Newsweek* editor Oz Elliot were on board. But when Katharine brought the idea of bringing Bradlee on as assistant managing editor to Wiggins and Friendly they objected. They were shaken up by the threat that Bradlee represented. Wiggins wanted Bradlee to work his way up the ladder, perhaps starting as a political reporter. Friendly didn't want any pressure to move out before he felt ready. Bradlee had already taken the opportunity of a private chat to tell Friendly that if he came in, he would want to take over the top job within a year. Friendly told him to back off and not be in such a hurry. Katharine listened to everyone, then made her own decision.

Four months after their lunch, Katharine brought Bradlee onto the staff as deputy assistant managing editor, but her plan was awkward and ill formed. Everyone knew that Bradlee would inherit Friendly's job eventually, but when? They also knew that Wiggins and Friendly didn't agree with the decision. Katharine ignored the questions and uncertainty. She let the issue slide, with no real notion of how it would get resolved. She wanted it to disappear without pain or confrontation. She learned the hard way that those hopes were naïve.

From his first day on the job Bradlee acted like a man in a hurry. He was supposed to start September 1, 1965, but he skipped taking vacation and showed up for work August 2. Even before he started, he had been quizzing a couple of friends who were outstanding *Post* reporters about who on the staff needed to be replaced. Once on board, he worked endless hours, going home for dinner and time with his kids only to return to watch the presses churn out the paper overnight. Meanwhile, Friendly kept to his routines, going to Turkey in the fall for a month.

When Friendly returned, he told Katharine that he had made a date to have lunch with Walter Lippmann, as she had suggested months before. Lippmann, knowing that Katharine hoped to move Bradlee into the top spot, called Katharine to ask "how far she wanted him to go," in the talk with Friendly. According to Katharine's account, she told him to go as far as he felt he could. She said later that she only meant that she wanted Lippmann to discuss what was wrong with the paper and how to fix it, but the ambiguity of her statement supported the tacit understanding that she and Lippmann shared about removing Friendly. Lippmann took the opening. He suggested to Friendly that he step down and go back to writing. Lippmann called to tell Katharine the news. Shortly after, a crestfallen Friendly arrived in her office. He wanted to know if Lippmann had been carrying her message. Did she want him to step down? She said she did. "I wish you had told me yourself," Friendly replied.

In her autobiography, Katharine admits to the failure of "courage" this incident revealed. She hadn't been able to confront her old friend, but she also wouldn't give up on the organizational change she wanted to achieve. "As much as I loved Al," she told an interviewer, "I could see management decisions in the city room not being made. But it was extremely difficult . . . Al was hurt." Lippmann handled the dirty work, and many in Washington viewed the demotion of Friendly as evidence that Katharine was at best disloyal and at worst heartless.

There is a disingenuous quality to Katharine's version of the Friendly ouster in her autobiography. Her own words mask the leadership that lay behind her decision, perhaps in an attempt to make amends years later for a situation she handled badly. In her version, Katharine denies that she sent Lippmann on a mission to oust Friendly. Yet, it seems likely that she intended Lippmann to pressure Friendly in some way to move on. Lippmann, after all, was a close friend and advocate for Bradlee. If Katharine had simply wanted someone to discuss ways the paper could improve, why hadn't she picked a more neutral surrogate to talk to Friendly, such as Scotty Reston? And why hadn't she joined the discussion? It's not surprising that Katharine's account of the Friendly affair paints her actions as someone who tried to protect and support her friends. But by doing so, she masks the sound business instincts for which she deserves credit.

Resetting the tone and direction by changing managing editors and bringing in her handpicked person were great business decisions. If Katharine had allowed her personal relationship with Friendly to override her strategy to move the company forward, she would have been an ineffectual figurehead. Using Lippmann as a buffer helped her launch these improvements. The change was "her first act of independence," David Halberstam wrote, "and she . . . moved very quickly and decisively once she had made up her mind." She had also acted badly toward her friend. Both were true, and while many tongues wagged about her insensitivity to Friendly, others wagged about Katharine taking charge.

The move was based on "a shrewd judgment that the paper needed a major infusion of new managerial vigor," according to *Post* chronicler Chalmers Roberts. As company chairman Fritz Beebe put it, Katharine wanted "to rule, not merely reign, but she wants to do it with the help of a lot of other people." It was an astute observation that Katharine's style would be different, but not necessarily less effective, from that of her husband or any other publisher. Beebe could see, before many others, that she was building a team. For an excellent paper, she wanted an outstanding staff, and she threw aside compromise even at the expense of her feelings or those of people she cared about. Robert Samuelson, a nationally syndicated economics reporter who has admired and closely followed Katharine's career, observed, "You don't get second chances to make critical decisions. She made the right ones when the time came, and it set a tone. She wasn't sentimental when decisions had to be made." The Friendly matter had been painful, but necessary. Happily for all concerned, Friendly enjoyed his return to reporting, going overseas as a roving reporter. Bradlee gave his pieces excellent play, and in 1967 Friendly won a Pulitzer Prize for his coverage of the Six Days' War in Israel. In an admission of his culpability in the ouster, Friendly wrote to Katharine that he regretted that he "hadn't the wit to have initiated it myself." The old friends resumed their relationship over time, and the *Post* began the transition to greatness that Katharine had envisioned.

Bringing on her first high-level hire had an unexpected consequence for Katharine. She had put one foot in front of the other, listened, learned, and then taken action. She anticipated changing the paper, making it better and, she hoped, more profitable. She had said that she hired Bradlee "for his ability as a talent finder, because I essentially think that is what any business is all about." She had acted on that belief, bringing in her own high-powered talent. What she didn't anticipate was that the act of hiring him would change her view of herself. She began to see herself as a leader, or at least a partner in leadership with Bradlee.

Discovering Her Leadership

Before hiring Bradlee, Katharine felt that the management already in place at the *Post* was made up of "the leaders and teachers and I was the follower." In her autobiography, however, there is a tangible change in the narrative as she moves into the post-Bradlee period. Her tone as narrator is more confident. Her story contains fewer apologies and self-blame and more recognition of the responsibility of others in unfolding events. Of Bradlee she wrote, "He excited people under him, eventually corrected whatever mistakes he made, and moved on." It seems a description of who she was becoming, or at least who she hoped to be. Her father had taught her "that organizations don't get built up overnight," and so she proceeded with a long view both of her development and that of her paper.

Working with Bradlee gave Katharine her first chance to test her leadership style. She had trusted her instincts, and they proved right. Two years after hiring him she told an interviewer, "I think I have a feeling for first-rateness in people." As her hire, unlike anyone else at the paper, Bradlee's loyalty was to her. As he explained it, they were both outsiders, which gave them a special bond and the freedom to demand change. Bradlee said that "what makes a good editor is a good owner," and Katharine met his standard by trusting his judgment. Before he started, he asked her to freeze five open positions so he could fill them with his selections. She did, and within months Bradlee brought in some of the greatest talent in journalism: political reporter David Broder, whom Bradlee wooed away from the *New York Times;* tough-talking former marine Richard Harwood, of the *Louisville Courier Journal and Times;* the elegant writer Ward Just from *Newsweek;* Don Oberdorfer for foreign affairs; and Stanley Karnow, the China expert, to open a bureau in Hong Kong.

Katharine also made Bradlee believe that the business was a public service. To fulfill that mission, she took chances, not only on Bradlee, but also on his ideas. Bradlee's mind churned with new plans, and he involved Katharine at every step. She enjoyed staying close, visiting the newsroom every day and joining Bradlee for impromptu Saturday lunches with stray reporters. Politicians or important international visitors, such as Israeli defense minister Moishe Dayan, sometimes joined them. Bradlee joked with Katharine, saying she had "round heels for the reporters," meaning that she loved the newsroom side of the paper. She joked back, teasing him about being too eager and biting off too much. As the newsroom staff changed, Katharine joined in the excitement they brought to the paper. She had a focused mission, and she could see it being fulfilled. By 1966 she had a sense of her leadership style, telling an interviewer for *Time* magazine, "I don't tell people what to do all the time. I'm interested in finding people, developing them, giving them leeway and backing them up." One way she used her position and power to support her reporters was by hosting lunches that were like "mini-Chautauquas," according to former *Post* journalist Peggy Engel. The lunches were often held in Katharine's private dining room with uniformed waiters and elegant service. "You'd be summoned to a lunch and be thrilled to be asked," Engel recalled.

Once Katharine invited a psychologist from the National Institutes of Health to discuss personality disorders with her health reporters. "It was such a brave topic to explore publicly with her employees," Engel said. "Mrs. Graham asked very brave and pointed questions. We all thought how amazing it was that she was turning her tragedy into something useful for reporters, and she showed intense curiosity in the true spirit of a newswoman." Katharine had begun to find ways to merge her passion for journalism with her position as the head of a growing business. She was showing, as her friend Warren Buffett put it, that she understood "the two most basic rules of business: First, surround yourself with talented people and then nourish them with responsibilities and your gratitude; second, consistently deliver a superior, ever-improving product to your customer." Her approach touched off newfound success. The *Washington Post* had grown in substance and stature, as had its owner. The changes, however, cost money, and the business side of the *Post* was Katharine's Achilles heel. She had far less confidence in her business knowledge than in her knowledge of journalism. The managers on the financial side of the company ignored her, to her fury and frustration. John Sweeterman, who kept the purse strings tight in his grasp, seemed to take every opportunity to belittle his boss. One incident involved Molly Parker, who had been switchboard operator at the *Post* for fifty years. She knew the Meyer and Graham families well and had often taken calls from the Graham children. On the afternoon of Phil's suicide, Katharine's first call had been to the *Post* switchboard, where she told Parker the horrible news and asked for help. When Parker retired, Katharine invited her for dinner at her home and gave her a small diamond pin in recognition of her service. Sweeterman, claiming that Katharine's action set an intolerable employee relations' precedent, reduced his boss to tears with his angry tirade. Sweeterman, however, had resuscitated the paper into a profitable enterprise after it had been losing more than $1 million a year for twenty years. His success gave him some cover for his arrogance. For him, Phil had been the ideal hands-off boss.

Katharine's questioning approach, her tendency to ask opinions from people outside the paper rather than relying on what Sweeterman called "good judgment," led him to be contemptuous and condescending. He succeeded in slowing Katharine's ability to understand the business of the paper. She attacked that problem, however, with the hiring of Bradlee, with help from Fritz Beebe, and with her dogged determination to master the financial side of her business. "One of the things I learned," Katharine told reporter Judy Woodruff years later, "is that you simply had to be profitable as a business in order to have the funds to invest in the business of editorial, and therefore it was up to me to make sure we had a business that was profitable." Sweeterman's chokehold on the money only increased Katharine's determination.

When Bradlee went in to push for his first budget, he showed up unprepared for the onslaught he received from Sweeterman. The money manager went through the numbers line by line right down to the money for stationery. Bradlee didn't have the answers. He came out of the meeting defeated and chastened. His boss, however, equated editorial content with the paper's survival. That was how her father had kept the paper going in 1933, when it was at the bottom of five newspapers in town and had a circulation of 50,000. "His own dedication to quality editorial products," Katharine said, "certainly affected me." Katharine gave Bradlee her full backing, and the next budget year he went to Sweeterman armed for every question. The editorial budget soared and continued to rise by half a million dollars or more each year. Between 1966 and 1969, about fifty jobs were added in the newsroom, and Bradlee's budget shot from $2.25 million to nearly $7.3 million. Katharine said that during those years she and Bradlee "grew to trust each other." Their shared vision and their relationship of trust and respect changed the culture of the paper as well as the product that the public saw. In 1966, a report in *Time* magazine gave Katharine credit for "financing an uninhibited hiring spree [that] pumped new life into the paper." Sweeterman came around as Katharine began to prove that it took money to run a great newspaper.

Katharine's father once said, "A newspaper shall be prepared to meet the sacrifice of its material fortunes if such course be necessary for the public good." His daughter had been true to that value. As James MacGregor Burns writes in the classic *Leadership*, she had girded herself with moral purpose and become a "tiny principality of power." Her leadership had built a paper that not only served the public but also set a course for future profitability. From this foundation, and under Katharine's continuing commitment to her father's vision, the *Post* redefined America's standards of professional journalism and the willingness to reveal the facts of a story, without regard to consequences. Katharine had claimed her company, and had begun to reclaim her talent and passion for journalism.

CHAPTER SIX

A DESIRE TO PLEASE

"You can't expect to make friends of everyone. And you can't make everyone happy."

—Gail Evans

Katharine had many battles in her early years at the *Post,* but the most difficult battle was with herself. She fought off a persistent desire to please. "The idea that you might have to make a decision that might displease someone around you," she told an interviewer in 1997, "just really freaked me out, because I wanted everybody to be happy and I wanted everybody to agree with me. And I felt obsessively or compulsively . . . about persuading them that this was the right decision. So I went on and on and on." She consulted and reconsulted; she went outside the company as well as inside for advice; she reopened discussions and reignited debates. To the other executives she came across as indecisive. Their view fit neatly with conventional views of women, and so those who judged her looked no further for an explanation. Despite her apparent indecision, Katharine was making decisions. Her roundabout methods were leading to action. The executives around her may not have liked these methods, or understood them, but the measure was not in the methodology but rather in the results. While Katharine's style rankled, while others could question whether the best decisions were being made, the *Post* was, nevertheless, a company on the move. Gaining the stature of the *New York Times,* achieving unquestioned dominance in the Washington, D.C., market, adding new media properties and building the company's wealth were all on the horizon. Change on a great scale, the kind of change Katharine began to think possible, meant conflict. Dealing with that conflict is the least attractive part of leadership for many people but the most essential. Leadership "is grounded in the seedbed of conflict," wrote historian and leadership scholar James MacGregor Burns. "Conflict is intrinsically compelling; it galvanizes, prods, motivates people." For Katharine, the idea of confrontation, of facing other people's displeasure and criticism, was torturous.

Her executive staff began to grumble about her actions as CEO. But the alternative, keeping the status quo to avoid the displeasure of others, was out of the question. "I quickly learned that things don't stand still," she said. "You have to make decisions." Fighting the paralyzing sense that her decisions might be wrong, Katharine pushed ahead.

Bringing Bradlee on board brought about the first big, dramatic change. He announced by his arrival that Katharine had also arrived at a new level of leadership. Katharine had defied her managing editor and editorial page editor with the hiring of Bradlee. She had moved him into the top spot in a few short months, leaving the newsroom watching warily, with those from the Phil era feeling unsure of their place in the new regime. Bradlee had shuffled the players, bringing in young talent and encouraging them to be innovative, to keep the paper alive and interesting. He systematically pushed out the deadwood. Katharine had hired him for action. She wasn't disappointed. But many *Post* staff had other, more hostile feelings, and Katharine became the focus of their anger.

The Power of Her Press

Hiring and firing weren't the only actions that brought out feelings Katharine hated to confront. Behind the people who found and wrote the news stood the policy of the paper they served. The *Post* had a culture, a sensibility about what made news, what was fit to print, which angles would get played. Here Katharine had definite beliefs, and they differed from those that had dominated when her husband was in charge.

Phil had seen the paper as a vehicle for social change. "He would rather suppress a story and operate behind the scenes than put the story in the paper," said a longtime friend. Phil supported Eisenhower for president in 1952, and as a result he suppressed the barbs of *Post* cartoonist Herblock during the election. Phil advised Lyndon Johnson when he was a senator, even writing speeches for him. He gave John Kennedy political advice and took credit for getting him to put Johnson on the ticket in 1960. He threw his influence into local issues as well.

When Bradlee had first worked for the paper in 1949 he had written a story about discrimination against blacks in city swimming pools. At a pool in Anacostia, a neighborhood overlooking the Capitol, about four hundred blacks and whites had rioted, swinging clubs, sending more than a dozen people to the hospital, and ignoring about twenty mounted police who waded into the melee. Bradlee said he "covered it like Dunkirk" and felt certain that his story would run on page one. Instead, it was buried in the local section, with the story of the riot hidden even farther back in the body of the story. Bradlee and Jack London, who had covered the story with him, were furious. Bradlee discovered later that Phil had cut a deal with Secretary of the Interior Julius Krug and the special counsel to President Truman, Clark Clifford, who controlled government in Washington, D.C. In exchange for holding back the story of the riot, they had agreed to close the Anacostia pool immediately and to integrate all six city pools the following summer. The compromise was "unthinkable" to Bradlee. "I don't think you can pay too great a price for telling the truth. The point was that if we'd put this on page one and called it what it was, you might have had the 1968 riot in 1949 . . . I can't make the judgment, but I'm sure no one else can, either."

Katharine shared her new managing editor's view that the paper should not be a vehicle for policy-making activism. One friend said that Katharine believed in straight news coverage the way other people believe in God. Bradlee also disliked what he viewed as a "liberal" bias in the news. He began to push for change with his staff, but it came slowly. In the fall of 1967, journalist Ben Bagdikian wrote that "too many *Post* news stories are flawed by policy." Comparing the *Post* to its in-town competitor, the *Evening Star*, Bagdikian wrote that the *Star* editors had as strong feelings about issues as the *Post* but "a minimum of these leak into its news stories." Change had to be made at the staff level, and Bradlee's city editor, Ben Gilbert, stood out as part of the old thinking.

Gilbert's leadership style relied on terrorizing his staff, and many had fled the paper. He had also been Phil's sidekick in using the paper for reform. Achieving racial equality in the city had been one of their prime targets. When Bradlee arrived in 1965 racial progress had been made, and the *Post* tended toward downplaying news that contradicted the impression of increasing racial harmony. When whites fled to the suburbs in a quest for better schools, the *Post* didn't cover the trend. Reports of race riots after black and white high school teams battled for the city football championship were "sanitized" in the paper, playing down the violence and animosity. An "unofficial policy of encouraging good things and discouraging bad ones" came across as the paper's overall editorial theme. There was an inappropriate view of the paper as part of the city and national

Agnes Ernst around 1910

Eugene Meyer (right) and Thomas Mann

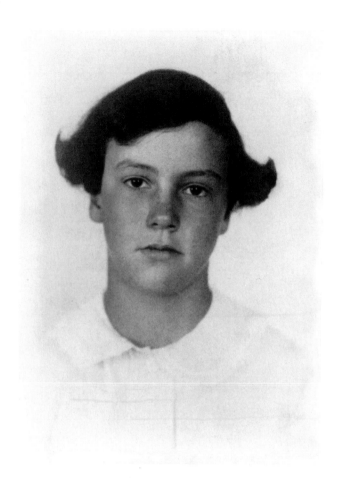

Young Katharine Meyer

Senior class president Katharine Meyer
and secretary Theodora Griffis,
Madeira School, 1934

Phil Graham, 1954

Eugene Meyer and
grandchildren,
Donald on the left
in suspenders

Katharine watching page makeup, 1964

Katharine and Scotty Reston at James Reston Jr.'s wedding, where she first learned about the Pentagon Papers, 1971

Katharine and Ben Bradlee after a federal court agreed that the *Post* could publish the Pentagon Papers, 1971

Katharine with Fritz Beebe (right) and John R. Stern from the American Stock Exchange, who points out the opening transaction on the ticker tape for shares of Class B common stock of the Washington Post Company, 1971

Katharine at her desk during the Watergate investigation, 1973

Katharine, Mary Beckner (right), and an unidentified man taking a break during the Guild strike, 1974

Katharine at an Associated Press board meeting, 1975

Katharine addressing a meeting of her stockholders, 1981

Katharine with Don Graham (left) and Ben Bradlee, 1991

policy-making apparatus. The issue came to a head over the appointment of the mayor of Washington, D.C., by President Johnson.

The president's aides had asked the *Post* to quietly float the name of Walter Washington as the city's next mayor. Washington was Gilbert's best friend. He was furious when he discovered that Bradlee had independently gotten the story and intended to run it. Gilbert knew that Johnson hated leaks, and the story might kill the appointment. He called one of Johnson's top aides, Joe Califano, who in turn called Bradlee and told him that running the story would doom the appointment. LBJ himself called Katharine with the same threat. She said, "It was not . . . the *Post*'s job to make Walter Washington mayor." The story ran. Johnson delayed the appointment a few months. To the relief of much of the staff, Gilbert resigned sometime later. Katharine had set a new tone that embittered some "Phil" people but succeeded in planting her own priorities.

She gave her editors "autonomy" but insisted on standards of journalistic excellence, saying editors needed "liberty, not license." Under Katharine, Bagdikian noted that the "taint of policy in supposedly objective news accounts" was fading. She had succeeded in changing the paper's culture, in creating a new journalistic atmosphere. That atmosphere would be severely tested over the most explosive issue of the late 1960s.

Vietnam, the war that Johnson inherited, had cast an angry black cloud over his administration. Other major national newspapers, like the *New York Times*, had placed a reporter in Vietnam when President Kennedy raised the troop level in 1961. By contrast, the *Post* lagged behind, finally sending a reporter in 1964 whose desultory reporting led to a short tenure. When Bradlee came in mid-1965 he found that "Wiggins [editorial page editor] was a hawk, Kay was a hawk, most of her peers were super hawks, the town was filled with hawks." Bradlee wanted to stay out of politics. By the time he became managing editor, the *New York Times* had three star reporters covering the war. The *Post* finally sent a brilliant reporter, Ward Just. For

Americans wanting hard-hitting news about the conflict that was beginning to tear the nation apart, this was not enough. Even worse, Wiggins, the remaining leader of the old guard, staunchly defended Johnson and the war effort on the *Post*'s editorial page. In the battle for Americans' hearts and minds, Johnson had told one of Wiggins's friends that the *Post* editor was worth two divisions to the White House.

Katharine had visited Vietnam in early 1965 with *Newsweek* editor Oz Elliott. Their official tour showed the war effort to best advantage. Katharine found no reason to argue against Wiggins's position: that it was necessary to stay in southeast Asia and help the South Vietnamese fight the Communists. Thinking and acting otherwise meant bucking the status quo, inviting the anger of LBJ, joining the lonely antiwar voice of her friend Walter Lippmann. In 1967 she wrote a simpering letter to Johnson saying, "These times are so difficult that my heart bleeds for you. . . . The only thanks you ever seem to receive is a deafening chorus of carping criticism. . . . But I want you to know I am among the many people in this country who believe in you and are behind you with trust and devotion." Katharine's desire to please led to meekness, a lack of reflection, a tendency to follow the pack that weakened her leadership when it came to Vietnam.

At her paper, lines were being drawn. The editorial writers called for change in the *Post*'s position on the war. Wiggins wouldn't budge, and for a time Katharine backed him up. In protest, one of the editorial writers, Alan Barth, taped the picture to his door of a South Vietnamese half-track, its tank-styled back end dragging a dead Vietcong body. Then, in 1966, Katharine's eldest son, Don—the Harvard grad, the student with top honors, the editor of the prestigious *Harvard Crimson*—enlisted in the army. He told his mother, "The rich are staying in school and the poor are being drafted. I can't live with that." Meanwhile, Bill, her next eldest son, was becoming an active war resister, soon to be arrested and threatened with jail.

Don's letters home were grim and disillusioned. In the streets of Washington and on television, young people like Katharine's own children, adults including Bradlee's wife, were protesting. In the *Post,* foreign correspondent Ward Just wrote from Vietnam, "This war is not being won, and by any reasonable estimate, it is not going to be won in the foreseeable future. It may be unwinnable." On the editorial page, however, Wiggins carried on with jingoistic fervor. He had told his writers that no one would be forced to write an editorial "contrary to his own beliefs." Since they all opposed the war, none of them wrote about it at all.

For Katharine, the exciting helicopter rides and encouraging meetings with military officers in 1965 during her visit to Vietnam were paling beside the reality of a war that had come too close to her home and heart. Her unquestioning support of Johnson began to waver. Her ties to the man who had been so close to Phil, and had seemed to want a friendship with her, began to fray. Johnson had heard a rumor about Katharine. Supposedly, she had told her editors that the president was trying to influence her by inviting her to the White House, and that they "shouldn't pay any attention to this." Based on the rumor, Johnson turned a cold shoulder to Katharine, a notorious "freeze-out," starting in 1966. It was a long period "of almost non-speak, and bolts of lightning coming out of the White House," according to reporter Chalmers Roberts.

But Katharine was shaking off her dependence on powerful men and her need for the approval of others. For this, at least some credit goes to her friend Truman Capote, who decided to hold a party to introduce her to his friends on November 18, 1966. It was called the "Party of the Century," and Katharine could barely accept her place in it. Modeled on the Ascot scene in *My Fair Lady,* guests were invited to the Grand Ballroom of the Plaza Hotel in New York City. They were to wear only black and white and be disguised by a mask. Women were to carry fans. The event came to be known as the "Black and White Ball." Capote picked 540 carefully selected invitees—

great beauties, actors and actresses, and the rich, powerful, and talented from around the world. Guests included Frank Sinatra; the daughters of presidents Theodore Roosevelt, Harry Truman, and Lyndon Johnson; Lauren Bacall; authors Katherine Anne Porter, Norman Mailer, and Tennessee Williams; and various Vanderbilts, Rothschilds, and Rockefellers. Fashion designer Oscar de la Renta summed up the feelings of many guests when he said, "I knew Truman well, but I didn't really know Kay. It's funny, a lot of people at that ball didn't know who Katharine Graham was."

Katharine didn't stand out in the glittering crowd. Fifty years old, tall and trim from her love of tennis and the discipline of Canadian Air Force exercises, she had simple looks even in her elegant French gown. Her thick hair was characteristically swept back. Her brown eyes could sparkle, but her smile was often taut. She spoke as she had been bred to, but laughed with a rich, throaty abandon. She harbored no illusions about her looks and couldn't understand why Capote was arranging the party for her. "It seems funny," she commented to an unsuspecting hairdresser preparing her for the event, "but I'm the guest of honor." In Katharine's mind, Capote had many more glamorous and interesting friends than she. The simple truth, according to Ben Bradlee, was that "Truman really liked her." One of Capote's biographers speculated that the flamboyant author was trying to make Katharine "her own woman before the entire world." If so, his timing was perfect.

The president kept on snubbing her, but thanks to Capote, Katharine discovered that the most glamorous and interesting people in the world were very much interested in her. LBJ could be pleased with her or not. She began to see that her position, her power, her role as publisher, CEO, and woman in charge gave her authority that didn't rely on anyone's approval. Katharine's friend Arthur Schlesinger Jr., punctuating the glowing effect of the ball, wrote an adoring piece in *Vogue* two months later.

Whether or not she realized it, and whether or not she was willing to admit it, this attention helped remake her self-image. Writing about the transition from obscurity to fame, the playwright and author Eve Ensler said, "The truth is that you are radically changed by it. It was only after I got a bit of it that I realized how profound outside recognition can be in letting one know that she matters." The Black and White Ball cast Katharine as the star on center stage, and she began to act the part.

First on the agenda for action was dealing with the split on her paper over Vietnam, and by early 1967 she had a plan. She wouldn't tell her editor Russ Wiggins to change his point of view. She didn't believe a publisher should do that. Instead she wanted to replace him, especially since Wiggins was scheduled to retire at the end of 1968.

She looked to Phil Geyelin, diplomatic reporter of the *Wall Street Journal,* and a close friend of Bradlee's, to come to the *Post*'s editorial page as a writer. Phil Graham had tried to hire Geyelin twice before. Before accepting the job, Geyelin spent a weekend with Katharine assessing her values and view of his role. "She was uncomfortable with the *Post*'s position on Vietnam," he said later, "and she really did want to turn us around, but she did not want to go to the mat right away." Geyelin came on as an editorial writer, challenging Wiggins, but not forcing his hand. Geyelin believed that the paper and its readers would fare better if he could carry off a gradual shift of political positions. Katharine shared his cautious approach, but the bottom line was clear—the Wiggins-LBJ axis would be ended. Wiggins saw the future and took the opportunity to retire early, in September 1968, accepting an offer from the president to be United States ambassador to the United Nations.

In the midst of shifting the paper's editorial leadership, an incident during the Christmas holiday in 1967 created an even deeper breach between Johnson and Katharine. Johnson had publicly announced that he would attend the funeral of the prime minister of Australia, but privately he had called his former aide, Jack Valenti, to set up a secret meeting with Pope Paul VI. It would be the first time that an incumbent president met with the pope. Valenti, using a pay phone to preserve secrecy, called his Vatican contact, Bishop Marcinkus, saying, "My friend wants to see your friend." After flying to Australia, and on to Thailand to visit the troops, Johnson and Valenti went to the hunting lodge of Italy's president, where they received the call from the Vatican. A helicopter, newly assembled, brought them on a harrowing ride to the pope. "We could have been killed," LBJ said as he got out. "Yes, but the pope would have given last rites," Bishop Marcinkus said as he escorted the president inside.

Johnson had a "pleasant and cordial" meeting with the pope, according to Valenti, where the president asked him to intercede on an exchange of prisoners with North Vietnam. Only Valenti, Marcinkus, and Cardinal Cicognani, the pope's secretary of state, heard the conversation, yet two weeks later, *Newsweek* carried a story on the meeting that claimed the pope had chided LBJ about the war. The article claimed that after sharply questioning why the president didn't suspend bombing in Vietnam, the pope became "visibly upset" when the president said he could not. Quoting a "knowledgeable official in Rome," the article said, "everyone left unhappy." According to Valenti, "Johnson blew his stack." Valenti was angry as well, since he had personal knowledge that the report was false. He called Katharine and said, "I was there. I heard everything. It was a wonderful meeting and your story is wrong." Katharine agreed to call Oz Elliott, her *Newsweek* editor, who told her that his stringer in Rome stood by the account. No retraction was printed. "LBJ never forgave her; he was furious," said Valenti. "It was a melancholy time."

Despite the seriousness of this incident, Katharine did not include it in her memoir. It was, however, a more credible reason for Johnson's notorious "freeze-out" of her than the far more trivial account she relates of his annoyance at her having told editors not to be influenced by her invitations to the White House. Perhaps in retrospect she regretted the incident that angered her friends and cast doubt on *Newsweek*'s accuracy. It had occurred when her mind was on bigger issues, in the midst of a transformation at the *Post*.

Five years after taking over, Katharine had fully changed the old guard of Al Friendly and Russ Wiggins. The news side under Bradlee had charged ahead with new reporters and coverage full of the sizzle that Bradlee demanded. Katharine named him executive editor, reporting to her. By mid-1969, Geyelin, as editorial page editor, had shifted the *Post* solidly against the war.

Katharine knew that she had brought about a mixed victory. She should have been more decisive on Vietnam. The *Post*'s support had consequences for the country. "It gave the war," in the words of historian David Halberstam, "a crucial liberal imprimatur." By influencing the newspapers across the nation, "it helped legitimize the war in much of the interior of the country and removed a potentially powerful network of adversaries." In a cause with much more consequence than the selection of a mayor of Washington, or the integration of public pools, Katharine's failure to insist on maintaining the firewall between policy makers and her paper's autonomy had dire costs.

How much of Katharine's hesitation in questioning Wiggins's ties to the White House or in moving to replace him were related to avoiding the president's displeasure? She had clearly enjoyed her invitations to the White House, the chumminess that began when LBJ first swept her off to his ranch after the 1964 convention. He wasn't just the president, after all, he was in many ways Phil's president. Phil, who took credit for getting Johnson on the ticket; Phil, so like Johnson in his moods and energy and appetites. It's no wonder that Katharine would want to please him, but it was also no excuse when the stakes were so high. In an interview taped for the LBJ library in early 1969, Katharine commented on the *Post*'s coverage of the war, saying, "We supported him [the President] longer than almost any paper in the country." She seemed to be admitting her error at the same time that she was reminding Johnson that she had tried to stay in his good graces. With the perspective of six years, she would write to a friend about Vietnam, "As one who was wrong too long and backed an editor who was wrong even longer." The experience with Johnson further tempered Katharine's instincts to keep everyone happy. In a few years she would face another conflict with the White House, this time bringing the detachment and courage that her role as a leader demanded.

Management 101

In the meantime, Katharine concentrated on her weaknesses: management and finance. She had come into her position feeling so unprepared that she later said, "I literally did not know how to use a secretary, much less how to manage a business. I had no idea what profitability was appropriate, what we should be looking for, what we should be striving for, how we should spend it." To overcome her deficits, she had studied, read, observed the operations of other companies and newspapers, and taken classes on public speaking as well as managing a business. Her increasing confidence showed in her changing style. No longer the meek, often mute matron, she felt free to show her anger, use profanity, tell people off in no uncertain terms.

Katharine took on changing the culture in an unruly company where the *Washington Post* was only one fast-moving part. The weekly newsmagazine *Newsweek* needed her attention as well. As *Newsweek* contributing editor Robert Samuelson noted, "*Newsweek* was number two to a strong number one—*Time*, and the two magazines were so similar, so it was harder [for Katharine] to do well and she tended to focus on the *Post*." Her loyalty in keeping the weekly, however, had paid off as it gained the reputation of the "hot book" by New York advertising executives. Katharine, with Fritz Beebe's help, gave her editor Oz Elliott a great deal of freedom and little oversight of budgets. Soon after Katharine took over, Elliott argued for a bold expansion of *Newsweek*. He won increases in his budget of over $6 million in the 1960s. Circulation grew along with four-color illustrations, new talent, and better salaries. Between 1963 and 1967, five hundred thousand additional readers brought circulation to 2 million readers, a testament to Katharine's support of the magazine.

Business, and the competition for news, was always on her mind. A friend of her son Don, who worked for *Life* magazine, recalled that if he and Katharine heard a bit of gossip at the same time, she rushed to call it in to her magazine before he could get it to his own. Bradlee called her "a barracuda for the news." Then, in 1969, Elliott grew bored and left his job as *Newsweek*'s editor. He returned in 1972, but the break in leadership created some chaos at the magazine, chaos that added to an already tumultuous time in Katharine's life.

At home, her mother had become an alcoholic, overweight, physically unstable, and emotionally unmanageable. Agnes's children arranged for psychiatric intervention, which helped her drinking but not her overbearing disposition. Her intellect intact, she continued, in her last years, to harangue relatives and guests with stories of her exploits. Katharine was in Mt. Kisco on September 1, 1970, when her mother died in bed.

Other family stresses pressed on Katharine's mind in the latter half of the 1960s. Her brother had divorced, and she worried about his use of drugs and alcohol. Her youngest son, left home alone after his brother went off to college, took to partying and smoking marijuana in Katharine's house. She worried that her oldest, Don, had married too young. Then her worries skyrocketed when he returned from Vietnam to join the Washington Metropolitan Police Department in January 1968. He had felt a moral obligation to join the army. Having fulfilled that duty, he took on another—to understand the city where he had spent his life and where he would soon have a seat of enormous power. Again, Don put himself in danger, and again his mother worried while her daughter caused worries of a different kind. Lally's marriage seemed troubled. It would end in 1971. And in the midst of everyone else's problems, Katharine suffered her own trauma, falling down from an unexplained seizure and having to start a drug regimen that often left her faint or with heart palpitations. Her heart also suffered from missing Phil. As she talked about him, an interviewer wrote in 1967, her eyes filled with tears, she puffed harder at her cigarettes, and poured herself a drink.

As Katharine dealt with these problems, the country itself seemed to convulse. The Tet Offensive by the Communists in Vietnam, in January 1968, fueled the American public's doubts about the war. Tet involved surprise coordinated attacks by North Vietnam against American and South Vietnamese forces. Although a military defeat for North Vietnam, the widespread attacks and invasion of the U.S. embassy in Saigon proved an enormous public relations victory for the Communists. The Johnson administration's upbeat reports about the war and false information regarding casualties was undercut as news of the Tet Offensive reached the American public. In the spring, President Johnson abruptly announced that he would not run again. Weeks later, the city of Washington went up in flames when civil rights leader Martin Luther King Jr. was assassinated. Then, in the midst of the Democratic nomination fight, an assassin killed candidate Robert Kennedy, the slain president's brother.

Katharine led her company through the external turbulence and increasingly filled the role of the matriarch for a family in need. In a spectacular feat of multitasking, she became both caretaker and chief executive. At home, love drove her desire to please and to help her family find happiness. She couldn't say the same for her decisions as a CEO. As her confidence in her management skills grew, so did her willingness to act and to withstand the displeasure of those around her.

At times, she had negative overreactions, what she termed applying a "dentist drill . . . instead of considering things coolly and not constantly complaining." One such time grew out of Bradlee's move to radically redesign the staid and conventional "for and about women" section of the paper. Fashion, recipes, and stories of society women showing up at parties "bored the ass off all of us," as Bradlee put it. He wanted "new journalism" profiles, and stories about "the sexual revolution, the drug culture, the women's movement . . . interesting, exciting, different" stories. He came up with the name "Style" for the new section, and he assembled a talented team of journalists to tackle the new mandate.

Katharine joined in the strategy sessions, enjoying the creative give and take but worrying about the consequences. She foresaw that society women, many of them her friends and acquaintances, would resent being shoved off the page. She was right. Country club locker rooms buzzed about the lead story in Style's debut on January 9, 1969, about a woman on the FBI's most wanted list, and about a story on the third day about a train. "You men have gotten hold of my women's section," Katharine shouted, "and there's no food, no fashion, no parties." The change brought Katharine and Bradlee into their first full-fledged fight, the only time Bradlee ever remembers them raising their voices at each other. She had pressured him repeatedly about moving too fast into Style, and after one too many critiques he exploded. "Damn it, Katharine," he yelled, "get your finger out of my eye. Give us six weeks to get it right." Katharine listened, realizing that Bradlee wouldn't drop his normal good temper toward her without good reason. She curtailed her criticism, and by the time six weeks were up, Bradlee had been proved right. Soon newspapers around the country were copying his Style section.

Tensions over growth and change were intense in all parts of the company at the end of the 1960s. There were executives in and out the revolving door. A new managing editor of the *Post*, Eugene Patterson, started work under Bradlee and barely lasted three years, although he maintained a long and close relationship with Katharine. At other times she fired men who had been hired by her father or husband. "All left with handsome severance purses," wrote journalist and author Howard Bray. "Some of them went badly scalded by Kay's tongue." At times she adopted a style that seemed out of character but was instead revealing of her inner contradictions. "She could be brutal and profane in criticizing them, either directly and in front of others or out of the victim's presence," Bray wrote. She could also be "incredibly shy," worried, as she was on one occasion, about how she would look at a social event. Her character was a complicated blend, with attacks on others, sometimes filled with invective, revealing a thin skin. She hated criticism and handled it badly, but she didn't let it affect her actions. Instead, she railed against those she perceived as critical of her. She worked on living up to her own tough standards, a focus that had more to do with pleasing herself than anyone else.

Anyone who knew her understood that Katharine's greatest pleasure came from running her company. Her agonies over setbacks were made up for by her daily excitement over the challenges of business, which were many and varied. In a complicated but gratifying negotiation in 1966, Katharine became a one-third owner of the *International Herald Tribune,* a newspaper of broad influence among European policy makers. With the acquisition, Katharine let important members of the government, the press, and the business world know that "there was another must-read American paper besides the *Times.*" She also opened new bureaus in Tokyo and at the United Nations. In Washington, the company's all-news radio station, WTOP, held its own alongside its sister newspaper, and the television stations were also doing well.

On the financial side, business manager John Sweeterman, who had been Katharine's nemesis, announced his early retirement late in 1968. Despite their rocky relationship, Katharine admits in her autobiography that after he left "problems seemed to arise everywhere." She feared that her lack of ability would sink the company. Fear, however, also seemed to function as a fuel. After Sweeterman left, Katharine not only kept her title as president of the company but also took the title that her father and Phil had claimed—publisher of the

Post. She hired Paul Ignatius to take Sweeterman's place, wanting to replace him after six months, but on the advice of Beebe, letting him linger for two years. She also undertook plans for a new building for the paper, hiring the renowned architect I. M. Pei.

The building and hiring, marketing and acquisitions took money, lots of money, but Katharine had it to spend. Financially, the paper had become enormously successful. Corporate profits before taxes nearly doubled between 1963 and 1969. More than 58 percent of the company's profit came from the newspaper even though it accounted for less than half of all revenues. By 1966, the *Post*'s total advertising was only surpassed by the *New York Times* and the *Los Angeles Times*.

Katharine had a throne, whether she wanted one or not. A close newspaper friend had told Katharine that she had the "great character" the paper needed. He declared, "You'll be a constitutional monarch; no one will be able to push you around." His comment would have great prescience as the new decade of the 1970s began. The White House, in Republican hands since the 1968 election, would try mightily to push around the owner and publisher of the *Washington Post.* Katharine would have the chance to test whether she had fully overcome her desire to please.

CHAPTER SEVEN

WALL STREET AND A WAR

"What leaders have to remember is that somewhere under the somnolent surface is the creature that builds civilizations, the dreamer of dreams, the risk taker."

—John W. Gardner

On June 12, 1971, Katharine arrived at the country wedding of Scotty and Sally Reston's son Jim in Hume, Virginia. She wore a cheerful white-and-red shirtwaist that set off a strong tan. The wedding was a low-key affair. The groom wore a flower lei around his neck; the bride wore a simple dress. Guests sat on folding chairs on the lawn and enjoyed a country band and beer chilled in large metal tubs. With the ceremony delayed by a rainy sky, the guests chatted, and Scotty took Katharine aside to tell her some big news.

The *New York Times* was about to break the story of a forty-seven-volume study of the Vietnam War that would reveal government deceit at the highest levels. It was a history "based solely on documents—checked and rechecked with ant-like diligence," according to Leslie Gelb, the Defense Department official who had supervised the project. Only fifteen sets of the history, which came to be known as "the Pentagon Papers," had been printed. Their disclosure to the *Times* represented a major breach of security.

Katharine had heard the rumor that the *New York Times* had a blockbuster exclusive. Bradlee and the *Post* newsroom had been worried since the spring about getting scooped by the *Times,* but no one could discover what the rival paper was working on. "It was extremely embarrassing to us," said Eugene Patterson, who was assistant managing editor at the time. Katharine had uncovered the mystery, but stuck on the mountain without a private telephone to use she had to wait for the wedding to end before rushing off to call Ben Bradlee. "She must have been dying to tell him," James Reston Jr. said, "but she was too polite to leave before we were married."

The *Post* knew that its New York rival had a swarm of reporters holed up in offices away from the newspaper's main building, and they were working on something big. Bradlee's insides churned over the thought of being beaten by the *Times.* A few days before the story broke, former secretary of defense Robert McNamara sent a cryptic message to friends at the *Post* warning that their rival was about to publish something that would make him look bad. There had been a brief panic in the *Post* newsroom when reporter Chalmers Roberts heard that the *Times* story could have the astonishing impact of ending the war. Katharine's news from the wedding gave the reporters their first hard information about the story that would break the next day. What were the revelations, they all wondered, in a highly classified history of decision making about U.S. involvement in Vietnam?

The secret was revealed on Sunday morning, June 13, 1971. Katharine was at Glen Welby with a houseful of guests, including her friend Chip Bohlen, the former American ambassador to France and the Soviet Union. She had gotten ten copies of the *New York Times* delivered from the nearby town of Warrenton. Everyone pored over the six full pages of stories and formerly top-secret documents that were announced by a four-column headline that spread across the top of the *New York Times*'s front page: "Vietnam Archive: Pentagon Study Traces 3 Decades of Growing U.S. Involvement." The headline dwarfed the picture of President Nixon at his daughter's wedding. In the following days and weeks, as the Nixon administration continued to carry on the war in Vietnam, articles based on the Pentagon Papers would show that Americans had been intentionally and systematically lied to and misled by elected leaders and their appointees.

Back in Washington, the newsroom went through the humiliating scramble of rewriting the *Times* story and running it a day late. For Bradlee and the others, that they had to repeatedly make the notation "according to the *New York Times*," made it seem like there was "blood . . . on every word."

Even as the *Post* worked on its rewrite, reporters were frantically trying to get their own copy of the Pentagon Papers. Katharine had traveled to New York on Monday for a dinner with Abe Rosenthal, managing editor of the *Times*. She had just congratulated him on the previous day's scoop when he learned that the Nixon administration had started the legal machinery churning toward an injunction to stop him from publishing. President Nixon was desperate to stop what he viewed as a major breach of national security and government secrecy. Even though the Pentagon Papers didn't cover Nixon's actions on Vietnam, the White House could ill afford disclosures that stirred up more anger over an increasingly unpopular war. Antiwar demonstrations in the spring of 1971, including the dramatic protests by Vietnam Veterans Against the War, had increased the pressure on the president to resolve the conflict. Yet Nixon refused to set a date for troop withdrawal. In June 1971, as in every previous month that year, over two hundred soldiers had died in the war. Nixon needed to build confidence in presidential leadership; the Pentagon Papers did the opposite, and he wanted to stop the *Times*.

As Rosenthal sat at dinner with Katharine he received a call informing him that the Justice Department was about to restrain further publication of the Pentagon Papers. He hurriedly left the dinner, and Katharine quickly called Bradlee to tell him of the late-breaking developments.

The *Times*'s second story had run on Monday, and a third on Tuesday, and then a federal district court judge enjoined the *Times* from publishing any more stories, the first time in the nation's history that a newspaper had been silenced before publication. Publication, the court said, could cause "great and irreparable harm to the security of the United States." The next day, June 16, was the first on which the *Times* had no Pentagon Papers articles. The *Post* ran its last rewrite from its rival. Katharine, celebrating her fifty-fourth birthday, had dinner with friends, including Bob McNamara, the man who had caused the Pentagon Papers to be written in the first place.

Meanwhile, *Post* national editor Ben Bagdikian had suspected that the brilliant Harvard-trained defense researcher Daniel Ellsberg might be the source of the leak of the secret documents. Bagdikian worked his connections. By Thursday morning, he flew back from Boston with boxes full of the Pentagon Papers taking up the seat next to him. He went straight to Bradlee's house, where a team had been gathered to work around the clock reading, digesting, and writing original stories for their paper. Bradlee didn't want the rest of the *Post* staff to know that the papers were finally at hand. He knew that a battle over publishing was looming and feared a revolt in the newsroom if reporters discovered that the *Post* had the papers and didn't publish them.

Katharine, whose house stood just blocks away from Bradlee's in the Georgetown section of Washington, D.C., was finishing arrangements for a party to be held at her home for Harry Gladstein, a retiring vice president and business manager of the paper. The business staff took off from work for the afternoon affair, and Fritz Beebe had flown down from New York City as well.

The gracious arrangements at the Graham home were in stark

contrast to the sifting, sorting, analyzing, and writing frenzy that occupied the editors and reporters in Bradlee's library. As they pored over forty-four hundred pages of formerly secret documents to tease out the best story for the next day's paper, even more intense and high-stakes decision making was going on among the lawyers stationed in Bradlee's living room.

The injunction against the *Times* set up an immediate legal question: would the *Post* be considered in violation of that injunction if it published the Pentagon Papers? The *Times* could argue that they did not have "willful or knowing" intent to disclose classified documents, which was the legal standard for a violation. Before the *Times* was enjoined, the government had not tried to protect the secret status of the papers, as would be later proved. But if the *Post* published, knowing of the *Times*'s injunction, a court could find that they had knowingly violated the law. Would the *Post* be "disrespecting the court," as Katharine wondered, and inviting government action against the paper? Injunctions, it turned out, were only half the equation. In an irony of timing, the *Post* was in the midst of a major financial reorganization. The legal jeopardy posed by publishing the Pentagon Papers could blow up the carefully laid business plan needed to correct the company's financial troubles.

Going Public

Fritz Beebe had come up with the idea of taking the Post Company public. He had explained to Katharine that if she died, inheritance taxes would be so enormous that Donald Graham, the heir apparent, might have to sell the paper. Going public would avoid that tax burden and allow the succession plan to go smoothly. That was a future problem, but the financial crunch was not. The company's finances needed immediate attention. In 1955, 711 employees had received nearly a half million dollars' worth of nonvoting stock, thanks to Eugene and Agnes and with Phil's blessing. As these employees retired and sold their stock, which had originally been worth little, back to the company, cash reserves dwindled. Al Friendly, and others nearing retirement, were cashing in $1 million and more of the paper's stock. These large depletions of the company's resources had put liquidity at risk. Either money needed to be raised from new investors or the Jacksonville television station, a thriving profit center, would have to be sold. Raising money on Wall Street seemed the best option, and others in the industry had shown that the idea could work.

It wasn't until the 1960s that some newspapers, closely held by the families that controlled them, decided to raise money with public offerings. Dow Jones, owner of the *Wall Street Journal,* started the trend in 1963; the *New York Times* had gone public in 1967. Certain obligations came along with raising money through stock offerings, and as Katharine considered the idea she had misgivings. Katharine hated the idea of disclosing company finances, including her own salary, to the public. "Do I really have to make my salary public?" she asked her friend Otis Chandler, who had taken the company that owned the *Los Angeles Times* public. Being known for her wealth had already complicated her life. When she met with men professionally who made sexual advances she thought, "You'd really like to f——k a tycoon, wouldn't you?" She didn't welcome further promotion as a woman of wealth and power.

In addition, as a privately held company, management set the share price. This fit Katharine's needs and those of her family but had employees complaining that their shares were not getting fair value. On Wall Street, the market would set the price. Katharine feared that Wall Street priorities, focused so heavily on the bottom line, would harm the newspaper's fundamental public mission. She didn't like the thought of outside investors and stock market analysts pressuring her about how the company was run and how much profit should be made. She knew they would demand more scrutiny of budgets, tightening of expenses, better productivity, at least 15 percent profit or more a year, and while she agreed with a more aggressive approach to managing the company, she feared that the mission of public service would get subverted. To her, the whole idea felt like strangers taking over her life. But going public had one overwhelming benefit—it would raise the $35 million that her cash-strapped enterprise needed without requiring Katharine to sell off parts of the company.

Despite feeling that she didn't understand the issue as well as she would have liked, Katharine chose to follow her instincts and go forward, not back. She agreed to a scheme of two-class ownership that would leave the family in control of the company. Class A shares, which the family would hold, would have most of the voting rights, including decisive votes for the majority of the nine-member board of directors. Class B shares would go to the public with few voting rights attached; 1.3 million shares of the class B stock would be sold, raising $35.1 million. The stock plan gave Katharine the ability to "perpetuate the family control in spite of death or taxes," as George Gillespie III, Katharine's personal counsel, explained. With serendipity that recalled Katharine's roots, the company handling the stock offering was Lazard Frères, where her grandfather had been a partner in the 1890s. Ironically, her father had rejected the expectation that he also join the eminent financial firm, instead setting his own course that led to purchasing the *Post*. A half century later, his daughter led into the world of Wall Street the company that Lazard Frères was shepherding.

Once she got over her initial reluctance, Katharine viewed the new ownership structure as welcome pressure on management to be more disciplined and more profitable. As always, she included herself in the challenge. She knew that the additional scrutiny by outside investors would force her to ratchet up her business knowledge. What she didn't know was that the decision to go public would jeopardize her company in a completely unexpected and dramatic way.

Post stock went on sale with the clanging of Wall Street's opening bell on June 15, 1971. Katharine bought the first share for $24.75 in a ceremony on the floor of the American Stock Exchange. With her stock going on sale at the same time that her paper was deciding whether to defy the government and publish the Pentagon Papers, all of the pieces were in place for a high-stakes game of principle versus profits. It would be the most severe test yet of Katharine's values and leadership.

"The Guts of a Cat Burglar"

As the legal battle raged at Ben Bradlee's house over whether to publish the Pentagon Papers, reporters, led by Chalmers Roberts and Murrey Marder, raced to finish their stories for publication the next day, Friday, June 18. Katharine knew of the turmoil at Bradlee's house, but she didn't realize that a freight train, in the form of the final decision, was heading right at her. She had gone ahead with the retirement party for Gladstein, pleased that her paper had finally gotten in a position to compete again with the *Times*. She stood on her back porch casually greeting guests when the *Post*'s managing editor, Eugene Patterson, confronted her. "I don't envy you," he said, "you're really going to have to make the decision . . . I think the immortal soul of the *Washington Post* is at stake. If we don't print it, it's really going to be terrible because the government knows we have the Papers, and we'll be used as evidence against the *Times*." The *Post*, Patterson went on, would be seen as the paper that supported the government by withholding the papers voluntarily, while the *Times* would be the paper in defiance of the government. "God, do you think it's coming to that?" Katharine asked, looking stunned. Patterson said he did.

The fevered argument at Bradlee's house seemed to be going in circles as they explored every possible contingency. Perhaps they could delay publication just one day, Bradlee offered. A "chicken-shit argument," one of the reporters replied. Murrey Marder said simply that he couldn't work for a paper that would withhold the news. Chalmers Roberts, highly respected and known for his traditional views, was set to retire in two weeks. He said that if publication were delayed, he'd be gone the next day and make a public statement of dissent. Ben Bagdikian whispered in Bradlee's ear. "You're going to get a full-scale revolt from the staff," he warned. The time had come to call the boss.

Katharine stood on the lawn talking to her guests about how much Gladstein meant to her and the paper. "You're wanted on the phone," she was told in the middle of her speech. She said that she would finish her speech and be right there, but Beebe wanted her on the phone right away. The deadline for printing in time for the next day's edition loomed, and he didn't want a decision by default. "You're asking me to do something over the phone that the *New York Times* took three months to do," Katharine told Beebe when she got on the phone, but she sat down in her library and listened to the tense men at the other end of the call.

Beebe went first, telling her that the lawyers from the *Post*'s firm of Rogers & Wells believed, as he did, that the *Post* could be seen as breaking the law if they published. They wanted to wait or not publish at all. *Post* President Paul Ignatius stood by Katharine's side as she listened. Brought to the paper by Robert McNamara, he told her he concurred with the lawyers. "Wait a day, wait a day," he kept repeating. Financial considerations were also in play. The stock had been offered two days before. As Beebe had explained to Bagdikian, "I have to worry about stock in a 193-million-dollar corporation. Our contract with the underwriters can be canceled if the corporation has a catastrophic event, and it's been determined by the courts that a criminal indictment is a catastrophic event. And if we get convicted we lose all our broadcast properties because a felon may not hold a broadcast license." Beebe also worried about a statement in the original company prospectus that committed the paper to the

"community and national welfare." If publishing the papers was con-
strued as contrary to the national welfare because of the exposure of
government secrets, might the underwriters use that as a reason to
back out?

Everyone understood that the danger to the company could not
be overstated. A decision to publish was a decision to risk everything.

Bradlee and the editors had picked up other extensions in his
house and were beginning to make arguments in favor of going forward. Katharine asked why they couldn't wait a day, but she already
knew the answer. Staff at the *Post* had figured out that Bradlee had
the Pentagon Papers. Any delay would be unacceptable to them.
Besides, two smaller papers, the *Boston Globe* and the *St. Louis Post-
Dispatch*, were known to have gotten their hands on the documents
as well. Already scooped by the *Times*, Katharine could ill afford the
embarrassment of those papers beating her to publication of the documents. Publishing could destroy the paper, she argued with her editors. "There's more than one way to destroy a newspaper," Phil
Geyelin replied.

Geyelin's remark had to be weighed against Beebe's caution.
Beebe was her most trusted business adviser, the one man who had
shown her consistent respect, who had given unstinting support.
There had been no important issue on which the two had disagreed
in the eight years since Katharine took over. His arguments were more
than sound; they were built on a foundation of business expertise that
she did not possess. Finally she asked him whether he would go ahead
and publish. Beebe replied, "I guess I wouldn't." The journalists argued back. They were demanding that she go ahead. But what if by
following their high-minded arguments for press freedom she ended
up losing the paper that gave them their voice? They could afford to
be concerned with only one side of the enterprise. She could not.

"I guess I wouldn't"—those were Beebe's words. They rang in her
ears. They were enough to hide behind, enough to use as a basis for
caution, for taking this complex issue more slowly, for giving it time

as Katharine desperately wanted to do. She had joined in Beebe's conclusions many times before. But this time, Katharine chose to read between his words, to hear what he didn't say. "I asked about fifty questions," Katharine told an interviewer in September 1971, just months after her decision. She said she wouldn't have agreed to run the story without Beebe's OK, but she read his concurrence from the ambiguity of his statements. Asked directly whether he would publish he had said he would not, but he used tentative words. He had, on the other hand, also agreed with Katharine and Bradlee that "when you have news, you have to print it." Beebe's ambivalence left the door ajar for Katharine to make an independent decision. She did it with fear and tension, and on "viscera," as she told an interviewer years later. As the men hung on the end of handsets throughout Bradlee's house, Katharine swallowed hard and said, "Go ahead, go ahead, go ahead. Let's go. Let's publish."

Second thoughts and frazzled nerves would follow, but at the moment of decision Katharine chose principle over profit and loss. Her decision to publish became the act that finally proved to those who doubted her that she had the iron of a leader, and the willingness to take a risk. Chalmers Roberts wrote in his history of the *Post*, "It is, of course, impossible to be certain, but it is probable that Philip Graham would not have taken the risk that Katharine Graham took. Quite probably James Russell Wiggins [a former *Post* editor] would not have printed the papers even if they had been handed to the *Post* first." Like Roberts, Bradlee had the perspective and insight to recognize Katharine's strength and courage. After her decision, he often said to people, "She has the guts of a cat burglar." His boss loved the image.

Many people had believed that other, more experienced leaders inside the company controlled Katharine's decision making. The events surrounding the Pentagon Papers proved otherwise. At a moment that would have tested the most experienced and stalwart publishers, she had shown independent judgment. And it was sound judgment, rooted in long-ago discussions with her father. Hadn't he taught her that "the newspaper's duty is to its readers and to the public at large, and not to the private interests of its owner"? Hadn't he believed that "in the pursuit of truth, the newspaper shall be prepared to make sacrifice of its material fortunes, if such course be necessary for the public good"? Katharine carried these ideas in her head and heart along with her honest devotion to journalism and journalists. She had been underestimated for a very long time. The events surrounding the Pentagon Papers would change all that.

The *Post* would get out only two issues on the Pentagon Papers before they were enjoined. As she sat in Bradlee's office, Katharine got a call from assistant attorney general William Rehnquist with a formal request for the *Post* to cease publishing the papers. In a few months Nixon would appoint Rehnquist to the Supreme Court, where the case against both the *Times* and the *Post* was headed.

As the case wound its way through the federal courts, Katharine sat in on hearings and anguished over the outcome. The judiciary moved more swiftly than anyone had imagined. On Wednesday, June 30, Katharine stood in the *Post*'s newsroom awaiting the Supreme Court's decision. When it came, Managing Editor Eugene Patterson jumped onto a desk to yell out, "We win, and so does the *New York Times*." The staff applauded, and those who had placed bets on the outcome settled their accounts. Chief Justice Warren Burger announced a six-to-three vote against restraining the publication of the Pentagon Papers. Katharine sent a memo to her staff: "I know I speak for all of us when I say what a great moment this is for the *Washington Post*." Bradlee called everyone "beautiful." The next morning the *Post* printed three articles on the Pentagon Papers.

Wall Street had little reaction to the drama playing out in the courts. *Post* stock opened at $26 per share and stayed level for a short time before beginning to fall. The disappointing performance, however, had nothing to do with political events, but everything to do with the vagaries of financial markets and investor behavior. After the resolution of the crisis over the papers, Katharine would have a very different but demanding challenge in the foreign world of high finance. At least she would go to Wall Street free of the cloud of indictment or government sanction, and as the victor in defense of her company's core mission.

Victory in the courts had given the green light for the papers to be published, but Katharine remained disappointed. The Court opinion, expressed in nine separate essays, had failed in reinforcing the role of a free press. Katharine believed that publication, contrary to administration arguments, was "a contribution to the national interest . . . the obligation of a responsible newspaper." She talked about her deeply held values, arguing that the only way to have "no more Vietnams," as the protesters chanted, was to "open up the system and expose its workings to the light of public scrutiny." Only Justice Hugo Black, in his last opinion for the Court, had said what Katharine believed, that "only a free and unrestrained press can effectively expose deception in government. . . . In revealing the workings of government that led to the Vietnam war, the newspapers nobly did precisely that which the Founders hoped and trusted they would do." Katharine felt she had met her obligation to herself, her paper, and her country. But her country, in the form of the Nixon administration, had no intention of congratulating her.

Katharine had heard rumors that the government might still use federal criminal laws against the paper. Word had also been spread that the Post Company's radio and television licenses might be in danger. The fallout came from the Nixon White House, bitter over their defeat in the courts. As Henry Kissinger later told Katharine, "[Nixon] was convinced that the *Post* had it in for him. . . . He wanted a confrontation with the press. He really hated the press. As soon as there was an unfavorable article about him, he'd send notes around . . . prohibiting you from talking to the *Post* or to this or that reporter." At one point in 1973, Kissinger invited Katharine to a secret lunch, explaining that he would be "looking for a job" if the president found out. Ironically, Katharine had supported Nixon's reelection, although the paper continued its policy of nonendorsement.

Nixon had such a blind hatred for the press that Katharine's personal support, or even the paper's endorsement, would have meant little to him. Reporter Ken Clawson had quoted Deputy Attorney General Richard Kleindienst as saying, "The president is going to pick up a stick and start fighting back . . . the big issue of the 1972 campaign may not be Vietnam or the economic situation, but whether an arrogant press is free to undermine the security of this country without check." Even though Katharine and her editors agreed not to quote diplomatic or military cables in full or include the names of CIA agents in the interests of national security, Kleindienst wanted her to turn over all the documents—or else. She refused, and she told some friends in the administration about the threats. Word of her worries filtered back to Attorney General John Mitchell, who called the *Post*'s publisher to reassure her that "Kleindienst couldn't have done a thing like that." Mitchell's reassurance, however, rang hollow in light of the history of the Nixon administration's relationship with the media.

Nixon had been conducting an assault on the press for over two years, using Vice President Agnew as his stalking horse. Historian Arthur Schlesinger described Agnew as going around the country on a "jihad against disloyal newspapers and newspapermen." He called television newsmen "a small and unelected elite" who abused their influence over the public. He said that networks should not be allowed to "wield a free hand in selecting, presenting, and interpreting the great issues of the nation." He turned his fire at the *Post*, which stood out as a media conglomerate. In 1971, the company was full owner of the *Washington Post* newspaper, two magazines, including *Newsweek*, three television stations, two AM radio stations, one FM radio station, and was part owner of the *Los Angeles Times–Washington Post* news service, the *International Herald Tribune* in Paris, a paper company in Canada that provided newsprint, a terminal and warehousing business for newsprint storage in Alexandria, Virginia, and *Book World,* the book review supplement on Sundays. Agnew said that the Post Company news outlets were "all grinding out the same editorial line . . . hearkening to the same master," Katharine Graham. The charge was absurd and infuriated Katharine, who prided herself on the independence of her news outlets.

The day after the vice president attacked her, Katharine responded in the *New York Times.* "It is long-standing policy of the Post Company to enlist in each of its enterprises the best professional journalists we can find and give them a maximum of freedom in which to work. Each branch is operated autonomously. They compete vigorously. . . . We think that the result is journalism of a high caliber." Katharine's defense did little to stop Agnew, whose remarks played well at Republican gatherings. Meanwhile, Nixon ordered wiretaps on the telephones of journalists, threatened networks for liberal bias and lied repeatedly about White House activities. He avoided the press, giving fewer press conferences than any president since Hoover.

Attorney General John Mitchell added to the poisoned relationship between the press and the administration by his assaults on civil liberties. Mitchell jumped at the chance to prosecute war protesters and newspapers, but he refused to convene a grand jury investigation after National Guardsmen shot four students to death at Kent State University during a protest rally in 1970.

The administration also chafed at the national prominence the hated *Washington Post* had achieved by fighting the government instead of caving in. Katharine and her paper had become, in her words, "major players." They were finally mentioned in the same breath with the *New York Times.* Katharine felt a new sense of self-confidence, as people do when their risks are rewarded. She called the fight over the papers "another extraordinary learning experience for me." What she discovered about her resolve, about her relationships with her staff and the public, and about withstanding criticism and attacks would serve her well as battles with the White House escalated.

The sniping and tense relations, the attempts by Nixon to limit reporters' access to his staff or to control which reporters covered his events would soon be understood in a larger, more sinister context. Nixon's obsession with secrecy, his suspicions about the sinister motives of those outside his circle of power and influence, would lead to one of the greatest crises in American political history. It would test the sense of confidence "forged forever between the Grahams and the newsroom," as Bradlee wrote later. Once again, Katharine would be center stage as the drama between the Nixon administration and the fourth estate reached its climax.

CHAPTER EIGHT

A BUSINESSWOMAN TAKES ON THE PRESIDENT

"Having strong beliefs, being able to stick with them through popular and unpopular times, is the most important characteristic of a great leader."

—Rudy Giuliani

Katharine had taken her company public, but the $26 per share price at which the stock had opened in June of 1971 had dropped and seemed stuck in a disappointing limbo by the fall. Katharine decided to travel to New York to gain the confidence of Lazard Frères and the analysts who could get her the money her company needed. She was nervous and tense. These men were experts in finance, in managing a business to maximize profits. They were unlikely to share her investment philosophy. She also knew that they distrusted her liberal paper and distrusted her even more. Was she savvy enough, tough enough, to meet their expectations? "If you were a woman in those days at the head of an organization," Katharine recalled years later, "people were entirely unused to you and didn't know what to make of you. I had to care about what Wall Street thought about us for the first time."

Beebe's plan for stock ownership had worked, but only so far. "We were lucky . . . we had been able to take some chances like the Pentagon Papers, which was a risk," Katharine said, "because we were a two-share company and the family had the controlling shares." Family control, however, didn't solve the problem of the company's stock price.

Wall Street wanted certitude. These men wanted to see what they called "depth of management," not just a superstar like Ben Bradlee who might leave at any time with no replacement in sight. They had other ideas that were foreign to the paper. They thought about a "farm system," smaller papers bought by the Post Company and used to train promising young executives at those sites. "The market wanted not just profitability but a guarantee of the future, it wanted insurance on its investments," David Halberstam wrote. Katharine's job came down to convincing these financial skeptics that she had the answers, she had the resolve, and she had the strategic vision that would deliver a great paper with great profits.

She had never liked public speaking but hated begging for money even more. "Because I still had vast problems with self-confidence in public situations, I feared dealing with the industry and with Wall Street, especially the excruciating ordeal of speaking to financial analysts." The company's future, however, depended on her performance. She had shown over the last eight years that she could endure the slights, the harassment, the put-downs and doubters for the sake of her company, and so she went to see the men with the money.

As usual, she prepared and prepared some more. Post Company executives had complained about going over her speeches with her forty times or more, seeing the rehearsals as signs of insecurity. Few people, including those who wrote feature-length magazine biographies, saw this kind of behavior as anything other than obsessive. They thought she acted this way out of insecurity, but that was only part of the truth. Katharine had the attributes of a perfectionist, a style of behavior with positive and negative aspects. Her desire to overprepare, to agonize over perceived mistakes, and to consult many resources caused discomfort for her and other people. But this behavior also reflected her deepest needs for fulfillment. In his famous formulation, psychologist Abraham Maslow wrote that people must be what they can be. "This is the need we may call self-actualization . . . man's desire for fulfillment [to become] everything that one is capable of becoming." Maslow believed that striving for perfection through self-actualization showed an absence of neurosis, not the opposite. Katharine's work had become her life's fulfillment. She could not do without it, and she would not let herself fail.

She brought discipline to the success she was after. Passion for her enterprise made her a more successful business owner than her father or her husband. Eugene had paid out overly generous raises and bonuses and lost hundreds of thousands of dollars as publisher. Her husband had brilliantly expanded the company but neglected future profitability and cash flow. Katharine did better. She treated the company with the sensibilities of a founder, in the way that founders see their business as their child. She spoke of it in almost human terms, as "peculiar and charismatic," as if it had a life and soul, which to her it did.

Katharine began her speech in New York with a flood of words, fighting her inner terror with well-prepared remarks. She had a reputation for directness that went back to her college days, so she told the financiers that she hated being there and "huckstering her paper and her stock." But she had overcome her resistance for a purpose, and it was that purpose that they must understand.

Coming through the management fires of the 1960s had crystallized her beliefs about the company, both what it stood for and how it should perform as a business. She spoke with straightforward conviction about what she had learned firsthand—quality and profits, excellence and profits, an outstanding paper and profits must go hand in hand. "One hears a certain amount of conversation about whether our commitment to journalistic excellence and integrity is consistent

with our commitment to profitability," she told the assembled analysts. "I can assure you that it is. In fact, you cannot have one without
the other. And as you improve the one, you can always improve the
other." She won the day and a three-point stock jump a few days
later.

Wall Street had its way with her as well. The Post Company
bought a paper in Trenton, New Jersey, as a place to try out and train
up-and-coming editors and managers. Budgets were tightened, scru-
tinized, justified, and tightened some more. Katharine felt the pressure and acted on it with a string of hirings and firings that some
people saw as tough, others as capricious. She went through four
presidents or publishers in short order, and a number of lower-level
managers. The tide of firings left an angry wake. "She turned on
people who helped her," said one fired executive.

Former executives with a reason to be negative were happy to give
interviewers the most unsavory perspective on their boss's decision
making. But as Frank Waldrop, the last editor of the *Times-Herald,*
put it, "She always had a damn good instinct for control. When she
found herself in control, she had the temperament and determination to do it . . . the first thing you saw was a lot of guys out the window and down the street."

As CEO, Katharine wanted people who were decisive, like
Bradlee; she looked for the toughness that she herself was developing, and she wanted people with vision. When top executives, like
Post Company president Paul Ignatius, disappointed her, she showed
the resolve she sought, giving him a $150,000 severance package as
he was shown the door. Ignatius's successor, John Prescott, had good
business sense, but, like Ignatius, lacked toughness and was soon
"promoted" out of his job.

Sometimes her treatment of those who fell out of favor betrayed a
harsh side of her personality. When *Newsweek* editor Oz Elliott disappointed his boss in Washington, she took to running him down in
public. In unfortunate displays of indiscretion that were often vulgar,

Katharine did this with others as well. "This bastard is f———g things up," she said, referring to a high company official. The public tongue-lashings and gossip left her targets angry and bitter. Her behavior smacked of payback, if not to those who were the target, perhaps to those who had targeted her in the past. From a management perspective, it was undisciplined and suggested her own insecurity, yet over time and combined with her growing power, it gave her a kind of protection. People were loath to cross or disappoint her, and those who were loyal were fiercely so. "You get the feeling that if she loses faith in you she'll cut your balls off or your ovaries or whatever," was the way reporter Bob Woodward put it.

Bradlee was the one person with unquestioned staying power, even after he divorced his wife for a younger woman reporter on his staff named Sally Quinn. "If Ben needed his Sally to be a good editor, as Grant needed his liquor to be a good general, then so be it," Katharine had said. In light of her own marriage, her dispensation showed the depth of her belief in Bradlee and his value to her enterprise. If he was her Grant, she was his Lincoln, a leader relieved to find an inspirational general unafraid to use his troops.

Bradlee had two approaches that would prove key to the *Post*'s spectacular success in the first half of the 1970s. He shared Katharine's belief that the newspaper should observe government from a healthy distance, avoiding the temptations of becoming so cozy with policy makers that journalistic and editorial decisions were affected. Katharine had recognized this weakness in her late husband. Phil loved being an insider, the friend to presidents and politicians. He became too "fascinated with power, to the destruction of the good of the paper, I believe," Katharine told author Laurence Leamer. Bradlee cared about "impact," about the great story that would hold readers' attention. He shrugged off an offer to join the ultimate venue for press hobnobbing with politicians—the Gridiron Club. He had developed a close friendship with President Kennedy, a relationship he viewed as strictly personal. Running the presses, rather than making policy, is what excited Bradlee. He and his boss shared a singular passion for reporting news. Bradlee had also been an inspired choice for editor because he believed in talent. "I devote a lot of time to horseflesh," he said. Katharine had shown her respect for his hiring talents by freezing positions so that he could have a solid impact on personnel as soon as he became editor. He hired experienced reporters who had, in his words, "real firepower," and he preferred new recruits from the Ivy League colleges. Like his boss, he wanted a paper on a fast track. He liked creative tension, a culture that made reporters hungry and determined to impress him.

Hire great talent, report great stories. That was key to making the *Post* a great paper. In his book *Good to Great,* Jim Collins writes that successful executives "*first* got the right people on the bus (and the wrong people off the bus) and *then* figured out where to drive it. They said, in essence, 'Look, I don't really know where we should take this bus. But I know this much: If we get the right people on the bus . . . and the wrong people off the bus, then we'll figure out how to take it someplace great.'" That was the formula Katharine was after. Her determination to shake up the status quo in her company, to rattle the vested interests and demonstrate her independence turned the *Post* into a newspaper ready to handle its greatest challenge: a ferocious and frightening battle with the President of the United States.

"White House Horrors"

Katharine often went to Glen Welby for summer weekends, but she was never far out of touch. As a routine part of his job, the *Post*'s managing editor, Howard Simons, called her on Saturday morning with an update on the stories that had come in the night before. On June 17, 1972, he had two strange stories to tell—a car had crashed in one side and out the other of a house where two people were making love on the couch, and five well-dressed men carrying a lot of cash and sophisticated equipment had broken into the headquarters of the Democratic National Committee in the Watergate apartment complex. Katharine shared a laugh with Simons. She didn't suspect that the strange break-in would become a turning point in the nation's history and would make her a legend. The Watergate burglary story had obvious political ramifications in a presidential election year. The next day's paper carried the details, although they seemed to belong more in the realm of pulp fiction than of fact. In the early morning hours on Saturday, a sharp-eyed security guard had noticed that a locked entry door from the garage to a stairwell in the posh Watergate complex had been taped to keep it open. He removed the tape, but he returned ten minutes later to find it taped again, along with other doors inside. The guard called the District police, who surprised the burglars in a small office of the Democratic headquarters. The five saboteurs had highly sensitive bugging devices, lock picks, door jimmies, $2,300 in cash, a walkie-talkie, a short-wave receiver to pick up police calls, forty rolls of unexposed film, two 35-millimeter cameras, and three pen-sized teargas guns. They all wore Playtex rubber surgical gloves. They were hustled off to jail, their elaborate planning quickly denounced by White House spokesman Ronald Ziegler as a "third-rate burglary attempt." He warned against anyone trying to "stretch this beyond what it is."

The White House staff had reason to worry about suspicion falling on the president or his campaign. Some of the burglars had known connections to the Committee to Reelect the President or to consultants to the White House. Yet suspicions about White House involvement didn't seem to fit the circumstances. The president was nineteen points ahead of any of his potential Democratic challengers, with the Democratic Convention still a month away. He and his campaign had little reason to risk an illegal activity to secure his return to office. Instead, with four of the suspects being from Miami and having ties to anti-Castro activities as well as the CIA, the idea formed that the caper was inspired by anti-Communists. Inside the

Post newsroom the competing theories were discussed. Dirty tricks by the president's committee? Maybe, mused Howard Simons, or maybe it was "crazy Cubans."

Two young reporters, Bob Woodward and Carl Bernstein, were assigned to dig into the Watergate burglary. The already antagonistic relationship between the Nixon White House and the paper made the *Post* team cautious. Katharine approved of the strict rules the editors enforced for all Watergate stories. "First, every bit of information attributed to an unnamed source had to be supported by at least one other independent source," she recalled. "Second, nothing reported by another media would be repeated in the *Post* unless it could be independently verified. Third, every word of every story had to be read by at least one of three senior editors before it went into print." These were extraordinary standards meant to withstand an extraordinary assault. That assault came quickly. Because the story broke in the summer before the campaign, the White House tried to portray the *Post* as having a vendetta against the president and trying to influence the election. Republican National Committee Chairman Senator Robert Dole told the media that Katharine had said she hated Nixon, a charge she resented and vigorously denied. When she coincidentally ran into Dole on an airplane and confronted him with the misstatement, he brushed it off casually as something he had been told to read. Politics as it's usually played, he implied. But for Katharine, the suggestion that her personal bias tainted the paper was not casual. She fiercely protected the *Post*'s reputation during the long months of attacks that accompanied the Watergate investigations.

After the initial disclosures, the story slowed, but Woodward and Bernstein were doggedly pursuing their sources. Just before the election, a burst of sensational stories hit the pages of the *Post*. The FBI knew that the break-in was part of "a massive campaign of political spying and sabotage," directed by people in the White House and the president's reelection committee. Other stories focused on top White

House aides and their role in the break-in and a secret campaign cash fund. The White House mounted a furious counteroffensive, accusing the paper of "using innuendo, third-person hearsay, unsubstantiated charges, anonymous sources and huge scare headlines." The *Post* was accused of being partners with Nixon's Democratic opponent George McGovern in a campaign to oust the president. Other news outlets seemed to agree. Of twenty-two hundred regular reporters working in Washington, no more than fourteen were covering Watergate. Many leaned ideologically toward the president, and Katharine began getting a cold reception at industry events.

The *Post* had taken the lead in breaking the story and following up in the initial months, before government investigations confirmed suspicions and began pointing toward the White House. In the first six months of the scandal the *Post* published nearly two hundred news articles about Watergate. The *New York Times* printed less than half that number. The *Post* stories made it to the front page and revealed investigative details that pointed to White House involvement. In Washington, readers rushed to get the *Post* each morning to see what new revelation might be splashed on the front page. Other papers showed more reticence about playing the story and failed to break new ground as Woodward and Bernstein did. The *Post* team, with Katharine's support, had taken the lead. Other newspapers would catch up over time, and provide excellent reporting as well, but Katharine and the *Post* were the main focus of an increasingly frantic White House.

Toward the end of September, administration venom gave the newsroom some gallows humor at their boss's expense. Bernstein had called Attorney General John Mitchell late one evening to get his comment on a story: the attorney general had controlled secret Republican funds that were used to gather information about the Democrats. Mitchell shot back with a personal and crude reaction. "All that crap, you're putting it in the paper? It's all been denied. Katie Graham is gonna get her tit caught in a big fat wringer if that's pub-

lished. Good Christ. That's the most sickening thing I ever heard."
Only the words "her tit" were left out of the next day's story.
Katharine dropped by Bernstein's desk in the morning. "Any more
messages for me?" she asked.

One message that worried her came in the form of a disturbing
vacuum. Her paper seemed to be alone on the story, especially in the
months after Nixon won reelection and the Watergate revelations
seemed to dry up. Those who had said that the *Post* had a vendetta
against Nixon seemed to be vindicated by the lack of new revelations.
At times her nerve seemed to be deserting her. She saw herself as
"wading little by little into a stream . . . you were in up to your waist
having gotten yourself in gradually. I couldn't say 'This is getting too
dangerous.' Having put them [editors] in you stuck with them." As
historian Arthur Schlesinger Jr. wrote, "Another publisher than
Katharine Graham might have succumbed to pressure and taken her
reporters and editorial writers off the story." Instead, Katharine
waded farther ahead, sticking to her credo of support at all costs for
her newsroom.

Later she wrote that she endured "an unbelievable two years of
pressured existence—the first in particular when one never dreamt
it would all come out. . . . It was painfully obvious they were out to
destroy us . . . there was a blood chilling moment when Henry
Kissinger said to me, looking at me with incredulity, 'Don't you believe we are going to get re-elected?'" Kissinger repeated his warning
on other occasions, as did other administration insiders. A good
friend who was in a position to know told her she shouldn't go anywhere alone and cautioned that her conversations were bugged.

As CEO, Katharine understood the implication of these threats.
"I lay awake many nights worrying, though not about my personal
safety," she wrote later. She might lose national advertisers, the stock
price could be affected. Ironically, The Washington Post Company
made its first appearance on the Fortune 500 list of companies, at
number 478, during the year that the Watergate story broke. Kath-

arine became only the second woman to head a company on the list. That distinction didn't mitigate the fact that one of the most lucrative parts of her enterprise was vulnerable because of Watergate: the television stations.

In September 1972, Nixon had started planning an attack on the company's television licenses. The plot was revealed when the tapes of Nixon's Oval Office conversations were disclosed. "The main thing is the *Post* is going to have damnable, damnable problems out of this one," Nixon told his chief of staff, H. R. Haldeman. "They have a television station . . . they're going to have to get it renewed . . . the game has to be played awfully rough." Katharine heard about the threat to the stations when she received a telegram as she was dining in Japan with a friend, Kiichi Miyazawa, who would later become prime minister. He remembered her fearless response after reading the telegram: "Well, if he dares to do that, just let him do it." Nixon did dare, and Katharine met him head on.

The license challenges came shortly after the election. Three were filed challenging the Post Company's ownership of Jacksonville's WJXT, and one was filed against Miami's WPLG. The Post Company had paid $2,470,000 for WJXT in 1953 and $20,000,000 for WPLG in 1969. Of the thirty television stations in Florida in 1973, only the two stations owned by the Post were challenged.

Ties were easily made between the groups challenging the licenses and Nixon or his reelection campaign. The challenges were "a part of a White House-inspired effort . . . in retaliation for [the *Post's*] White House coverage," Katharine wrote in an affidavit to the Federal Communications Commission. The quality of the stations added to the argument that the challenges were politically motivated. Katharine had made as strong a commitment to quality television as she had to print journalism. As a result, the two stations being challenged were widely considered among the top ten local television stations in the country.

Meanwhile, Wall Street was reacting. The stock price slipped from $38 a share down to $16 on news of the license challenges. As the company's value sank, legal fees rose to over a million dollars for the defense of the television licenses alone. As one of the lawyers working for the Post Company in Florida wrote, with the net worth of her company on the line, "there was every reason to figure out ways to trim the sails and to accommodate." Instead, "Katharine Graham was at her combative best during the challenge. She wanted to hear no talk of compromise." She put more resources into the stations, pressing them to do better in every area from news to editorial. She had, in the words of journalist Richard Reeves, "bet the company on journalism," even though it meant pleading "for Wall Street's forgiveness for her own brave brand of Americanism."

Back in Washington, however, Katharine had concerns about the Watergate story. As expected, Nixon won in a landslide reelection, even as the Watergate saga escalated. The burglars went on trial and were convicted or pleaded guilty by February 1973. During the trial Katharine had a nervous lunch with Woodward, during which she voiced some of her anxieties. "When are we going to find all the truth?" she asked Woodward. He replied, "Never," because he believed that Nixon and his people were "good at choking off information." "Never?" Katharine asked. "Don't tell me never." Woodward wrote later, "her face said, do better." He left lunch "a motivated employee." Katharine had stayed out of the way of her editors and reporters, but her company was on the line, and she expected to have her faith in them rewarded. A few months later, as she traveled in the Far East, she got the call she had hoped for.

The White House connection to Watergate had been leaking out through the trial of the Watergate burglars, and through investigative reporting by the *Post* and the *New York Times*. Woodward had come up with an unnamed source, dubbed "Deep Throat," after a popular pornographic movie star. The *Post*'s source remained invisible but active, giving the paper a continuing edge in coverage. The pressure was increasing on the White House when one of the burglars, James

McCord, disclosed in a letter to the trial judge that some of the burglars had received hush money and higher-ups were involved.

Howard Simons called Katharine overseas. The months of lonely reporting, of enduring the doubters, threats, and innuendo finally seemed worth the price. Katharine had been vindicated for being the kind of publisher who stood by her staff. As the White House lies withered under the light of congressional investigation and judicial pressure, the *Post*, for the first time, shone brighter than its great rival the *New York Times*.

Ben Bradlee described the month of October 1973 as a newspaper career all by itself. As Nixon furiously fought to maintain the secrecy of his White House tapes, his vice president was under siege. Stories of bribery and corruption had been leaking out about Agnew since the summer, with *Post* reporter Richard Cohen taking the lead for his paper. Agnew's lawyers accused the Justice Department of leaking information and subpoenaed the notes of reporters who were covering his case, including Cohen's. The *Post*'s lawyers came up with a novel defense. They argued that Cohen's notes belonged to the paper, specifically to the owner, Katharine Graham. Lawyers Edward Bennett Williams and Joe Califano reasoned that a judge might throw a reporter into jail for refusing to give up the notes, but they said, "Let's see if he has the balls to put Kay Graham in the clink." Around the newsroom the legal tactic was referred to as the "Gray-haired Widow Defense," and Katharine made it clear that she was perfectly prepared to go to jail. She gave the court an affidavit asserting "ultimate responsibility for the custody" of the notes. Before the theory had a chance to be tested, Agnew resigned.

Nixon quickly appointed House Minority Leader Gerald R. Ford of Michigan as an above-reproach replacement for Agnew, then the president began an all-out assault on the investigation against him. He fired Special Prosecutor Archibald Cox and abolished his office. The House of Representatives began calling for impeachment, with the battle focused on getting Nixon's tapes. When Nixon's tapes were finally revealed, they proved the incredible extent of White House corruption. Nixon had tried to cover up the crimes of Watergate, misusing the FBI, the CIA, the IRS, and other government agencies.

On August 9, 1974, the solemn crowd that had been gathering all week in front of the White House swelled through Lafayette Park and blocked traffic on Pennsylvania Avenue. They were waiting for the historic moment when President Richard M. Nixon announced his resignation. Attorney General John Mitchell, who went to jail for his part in the Watergate scandal, called the events the "White House horrors."

That night, Katharine and some of her staff went to dinner in Georgetown. Haynes Johnson, who had run many features on Watergate in the Outlook section of the paper, remembered it as an "amazing, wild, wild night . . . with crowds gathered in the streets." As they sat in the restaurant having dinner, Johnson began to raise his glass for a toast but felt Katharine give him a swift kick under the table. "We don't want anyone to see we're celebrating," she whispered. "She wanted to protect the image of the paper," Johnson explained, "and she was right." For Katharine, and the staff of the *Washington Post*, Nixon's resignation marked a new era. Katharine would not rest on her laurels, however, or lose sight of maintaining the integrity of her paper.

Transformation Again

For the *Post*, many honors followed from Watergate, including a Pulitzer Prize for the newspaper. Woodward and Bernstein wrote a book, *All the President's Men*, which was turned into a major motion picture. Their names, along with Ben Bradlee, became known throughout the country, particularly among aspiring young reporters and journalism students.

Katharine, swept up in the surge of attention, became a sought-after speaker and interviewee. She won two of the most important awards in journalism, although she commented in her autobiography that she thought others at the paper were more deserving. She had landed in the one place she did not want to be—the limelight. For her, fame presented more problems than rewards. She had a determined humility and loathing of hubris that were tested by Watergate's aftermath. As all the lofty accolades showered down on her, she kept her mind focused on fundamental values. The press had to be wary of becoming a "party to events, too much an actor in the drama . . . it's not the business of the press to uphold institutions, to reform them, or to make policy. Our job is to relate what's happening, as fairly and completely as we can—whether or not that is what people want to hear and what officials want the people to hear." That was the philosophy that underpinned her hiring and firing, her building of the kind of team that made the Watergate reporting possible. In May 1974, the slick city magazine, *The Washingtonian,* titled an article, "Investigative Reporter as Star: Has Success Spoiled Bob Woodward and Carl Bernstein?" The article captured the worries Katharine had about her stars, and the rest of her team as well. She was determined to keep herself and others on course.

After Nixon's resignation she wrote a letter to Woodward and Bernstein. She lauded them for "an extraordinary, gutsy, hard, brilliant piece of journalism." She also complimented them with a warning: "We've all kept the demon pomposity in moderate if far from complete control. The sound of our own voices, while listened to by us with some awe and even some admiration, is receding—and if it isn't, there are all sorts of stark realities before us to restore balance and defy hubris." She saw little time for looking back, still concerned with the future of her newspaper and those she depended on to continue its rise to prominence. Her single-minded focus on the fortunes of her business became intertwined with perceptions of her character.

People often described Katharine as arrogant and aloof. Her style in social settings could be off-putting, but that style was a social construct. She had a particular way of dealing with her social world and relationships, partly a product of being highborn, partly a result of the insecurities that plagued her despite her rise to power. Colleague and friend Sally Quinn said, "It was protective coloring to be imperious, she was unaware of it and surprised by it." Life had taught Katharine that "sometimes the gods give us too much and then exact a price." She had paid the price for wealth and privilege as a child with bitter feelings that came from her mother's criticism, and she had paid dearly for her love of Phil. Even as the powerful head of a growing company, she could still be hurt in very personal ways. In 1978, after being interviewed by a reporter for the *Washington Star*, a harsh and lengthy article was written about Katharine and her life. Quinn and Katharine were sitting in the lounge waiting to board the Concorde aircraft when Katharine starting reading the piece. "She burst into tears," Quinn remembered. The next year, a biography of Katharine was published that alleged that the leadership of the *Post*, including Phil, Katharine, and Bradlee, had inappropriate connections with the government, particularly the CIA. Katharine, furious over what she deemed false allegations that questioned her commitment to journalistic independence, called the publisher. Subsequently, twenty thousand copies of the book were removed from stores. Criticism, whatever the source, was deeply painful, and so Katharine treated her relationships cautiously and her business even more so.

She held the interests of the *Post* above her own. When actor Robert Redford was producing the movie about Watergate, her main worry was about its portrayal of the press, not how she would be portrayed. In an understandable aside, she admitted in her autobiography that being left out altogether did hurt her feelings. As the prizes poured in, however, she often said that Bradlee or others deserved them more than she did. In her autobiography she gives herself little credit for the Watergate reporting. Her role was "peripheral . . . behind-the-scenes . . . a devil's advocate." She won't even credit her own courage, saying that "courage applies when one has a choice," as if she had none.

Katharine did have choices throughout the two-year ordeal of the Watergate imbroglio. She could have insisted, especially when the *Post* was alone on the story and little new information was coming out, that continued investigation was a poor use of resources. When her television licenses were threatened and her stock price sank, she could have pressured Bradlee to back off. She wouldn't have been the first publisher to put profits over performance, especially when the continued existence of her company was at stake. Instead, she kept her fears mostly to herself, suffering long nights of doubt in private. Unlike Richard Nixon, whose insecurities became the nation's grief, Katharine kept her insecurities in check in favor of trust. When she sought reassurance from Bradlee or others, she accepted their analysis of the situation. The reserve of confidence created between Katharine and her staff by the Pentagon Papers served her well during Watergate. She had shown courage and independence then, and Watergate built on that experience. Roger Wilkins, who wrote many editorials on Watergate for the *Post*, shared his perspective on the sweep of Katharine's control leading up to the greatest moment in the paper's history. "You hired Benny and the rest, who made the tough decisions," he wrote his boss. "More than anybody else around here, you had to take the heat for what the fifth floor [newsroom] was doing. None of us has much of an inkling of what it took for you to hang tough, but whatever the cost, you did it." She told Bradlee, "I know I'm No. 1 because you are No. 1. You know that I know that I am No. 1 because you are No. 1." Katharine had been tough at a moment of great vulnerability, and she brought herself closer to her staff as a result.

Katharine described Watergate as "an unprecedented effort to subvert the political process." She would use its lessons to drive home the need for a free and vigilant press. She used her expanded pulpit to remind the nation of founding principles. In her acceptance address for the Lovejoy Award at Colby College she said the press "is *not* a fourth branch of government, the press plays an essential role in 'obliging the government to control itself.' And if we do not serve in this way, the rest of the rights guaranteed by our Constitution cannot be sustained." Her paper would fulfill the promise of the Constitution as her father had envisioned it. To that end, with that mission always in mind, she focused on building the resources to support the newspaper that had gained its place as one of the greatest in the nation.

CHAPTER NINE

BUILDING A FINANCIAL POWERHOUSE

"Somebody once said that in looking for people to hire, you look for three qualities: integrity, intelligence, and energy. And if they don't have the first, the other two will kill you. You think about it; it's true. If you hire somebody without the first, you really want them to be dumb and lazy."

—Warren Buffett

Eugene and Agnes Meyer's ambition and drive for excellence lived on in their daughter Katharine. If she carried one enduring approach to life it was to live up to her mother's credo of Meyer exceptionalism. Mediocrity was unacceptable. Katharine always aimed higher, perhaps in response to the lingering childhood perception that nothing she did was ever good enough. If this drive was the flip side to her insecurity and self-doubt, it might never be satisfied within her, but the *Post*, nevertheless, kept improving. She would settle for nothing less, and so every success became a plateau. Relaxation was rare. Even dinner parties, legendary for the politicians and diplomats in attendance, found Katharine "onstage, powerful and intimidating," as James

Reston Jr. remembers. Her drive to excel sent her searching for the next mountain to climb.

After Watergate, she smiled at the antique washing machine wringer on her desk, a wry reminder of the attorney general's intemperate remark, and a fitting metaphor for two difficult years. She had been through the wringer in ways that went beyond the harassment and threats of the administration. In October 1972 as a flood of pre-election Watergate related stories hit the paper, the controversial new *Post* headquarters building was dedicated. It had cost $25 million, but architectural disputes left Katharine with an undistinguished, some said "ugly," structure that soon proved too small. Six months later, as Nixon's lies began to catch up with him, Katharine's friend, colleague, and mentor Fritz Beebe died. They had shared a decade of transition and growth. She would miss his measured perspective and respect for her leadership.

In the aftermath of Watergate, she became a media star, but the spotlight failed to offer what she craved. She seemed to sit on a throne of thorns, not laurels, uncomfortable unless she had something to strive for. She had bought a 250-acre estate on Martha's Vineyard in Cape Cod, but her job and company were uppermost in her mind.

Her paper had won the grand prize of journalism, the Pulitzer, for its Watergate coverage. Looking ahead, Katharine wanted the grand prize for business. "I want to win a Pulitzer Prize for management," she told security analysts in New York in 1975. At the beginning of the year, her company had $287 million in revenues, an increase of $110 million from four years earlier when the Post Company had gone public. Profits had risen as well to $28 million. *Newsweek* magazine, five television stations, two radio stations, and just less than 50 percent ownership of a Canadian paper mill were part of the company portfolio.

The numbers were good, but they were not holding steady. The first half of 1975 saw a sharp 22 percent decline in profits; almost double the rest of the industry. In the late 1960s, before she went public, pretax profit margins had gone as high as 15 percent. A recession and inflation had driven up costs in the early 1970s, and the profit margin shrank to 9 percent. Katharine wanted to bring it to 15 percent by 1977. Other big papers were demanding even more—20 and 25 percent. She still held excellence and profitability as intertwined goals. She wouldn't sacrifice the paper's quality, but she was determined to succeed on the business side. She would do it by hiring executives who could deliver and firing them if they could not. She had been getting advice from her friend and former defense secretary Bob McNamara. He knew how hard it was to hire the best people. An executive who kept one out of three new hires was doing exceptionally well, he told Katharine. What to do with the other two? Get rid of them quickly, he advised her, so the operation didn't suffer.

Katharine had a quick learning curve. Between 1972 and 1975 she hired and fired three business managers. She had decided that they weren't getting her where she wanted to go. She demanded five-year plans to assess markets and look for new investments. She built up the executive staff and started monthly performance reviews. "Discipline was the objective," she told *Business Week* magazine. As both chairman of the Post Company and publisher of the *Post* newspaper, Katharine ran an unorthodox ship. "It's a messy organization chart," she confessed to an interviewer, "but it works." Her confidence would prove to be well placed.

Her ambitious goal required managerial confidence. She said that Wall Street saw her as only after "prizes and ego trips; that how the stock does doesn't matter to me." She was out to prove them wrong, but she felt heat from inside the company as well. "I get a lot of flak at the *Post* . . . when I talk about profitability . . . they think I'm some heartless bitch," she told a reporter for the *Washingtonian*. "It costs plenty to put two people on a story for sixteen months, and profit making *is* my priority. If it weren't, I goddamn well shouldn't be here." Katharine the businesswoman had taken over.

She had coined her mantra in a speech at the Salzburg Institute. She told the assembled business and political leaders that during Watergate the investment community viewed her as a "crazy liberal woman," only interested in journalism. "To convince them otherwise— that I cared about profits—I invented a saying that has since become a bromide. I told them quality and profitability go hand in hand." To that end, her strategy revolved around keeping editorial budgets mostly intact but cutting production costs. The biggest obstacle to her plan lay in the myriad of union contracts that governed employee relations at the *Post.* Successfully tackling that issue, complex and drenched in counterproductive precedents, might have been impossible if Katharine hadn't formed a bond with the financier Warren Buffett.

Buffettology

Leaders make their own luck. After Fritz Beebe died in the spring of 1973, Katharine lost an important mentor. Around that same time a little known financier from the Midwest named Warren Buffett began buying thousands of shares of Katharine's company. The Dow had dropped that spring by more than one hundred points, and the share price of the Post Company had dipped fifteen dollars from a high of thirty-eight dollars the previous December. By June, Buffett owned more than 450,000 shares of the Post Company, an investment worth more than $10 million. He had studied the company and its owner. He bought in for Katharine's leadership qualities as much as anything, and the success of their relationship grew from her willingness to "buy in" to what Buffett had to offer.

Warren Buffett liked to say that he first became connected to the

Washington Post as a thirteen-year-old delivery boy for the paper when his father served in Congress. He also had a family interest in journalism that went back to his grandfather's ownership of the *Cuming County Democrat* in West Point, Nebraska. In 1969, Buffett bought the *Omaha Sun* and a group of weekly papers. Like Katharine, he had a heart for journalism.

His general interest in newspapers, however, wasn't the only reason that drew Buffett to the *Post*. He had first met the publisher of the *Post* in 1971 when he asked her to consider buying *The New Yorker* magazine, in which Buffett owned stock. Katharine wasn't interested, but Buffett became interested in her and her paper. He recognized a quality in her that he compared to Walt Disney and his successful franchise. He wrote her that there was an "extra dimension" to the sizable commitment he had made to her company. While he felt the stock was undervalued relative to its worth, he valued what Katharine valued—that the Post Company had become "synonymous for quality in communications." Comparing Katharine to Walt Disney he wrote, "Anything that didn't reflect his best efforts—anything that might leave the customer feeling short-changed—just wasn't acceptable. . . . He melded energetic creativity with a discipline regarding profitability, and achieved something unique in entertainment." Certainly the owner of the *Post* felt flattered; most important, she felt understood.

Despite warnings from advisers inside and outside the company that Buffett's acquisition of stock could signal a hostile takeover, Katharine decided to keep an open mind. She met him on a trip to California and found in him the central qualities that she liked and admired: brains and humor. Their relationship, with its twin pillars of economic interest and genuine friendship, gave Katharine an incalculable advantage as she tackled the financial world.

Great teachers are a great gift, but their influence is limited unless students are ready and willing to learn. The most important part of

Buffett's influence was Katharine's use of it. She had found someone who would teach her the complexities of the business world but would never patronize or treat her harshly. She couldn't tolerate "sharp rebukes," but she welcomed constructive criticism. Buffett recognized her insecurity, especially relative to other major newspaper publishers. He remembers walking into her office in 1973 and seeing a piece of paper with a note to herself: "assets on the left, liabilities on the right," but unlike her mother, Phil, or other executives in the company, he never used her relative lack of knowledge to belittle her. Instead, he helped build her confidence by building her knowledge. He demystified the terms of art of the business world and used examples from actual companies by producing financial statements and annual reports. Katharine found that with Buffett she could laugh and learn, her favorite combination. He came to Washington about once a month, and he kept a change of clothes in Katharine's guest room. Buffett was married, and their friendship created uncomfortable rumors of an intimate relationship. When asked, Katharine observed with annoyance that other people relied on Buffett, but "if I used him it was sort of frowned on." Katharine's friend Margaret Carlson, a *Time* correspondent, observed that "Kay and Warren Buffett had lots of fun, and he had a great sense of humor with her." A friend of both speculated that Katharine would have married Buffett if she didn't have to live in Omaha. Regardless of the truth of their private lives, they had created a great friendship in addition to a great business relationship.

Some executives inside the company resented Buffett's influence, feeling that Katharine spoke of his advice too often. Some went further, implying that she was his puppet. "All successful men I know have a couple of people they listen to," remarked Carlson. "Bill Gates has his dad and Steve Balmer. But for women, such advisers are seen as a crutch." Katharine had followed her instincts about Buffett, despite the doubters. She had shown the wisdom, as great leaders do, to use the best human resources she could find to build her knowledge and ability to lead.

With Buffett's help she began to feel that her own business instincts were valid, that in a crucial way this man whom she trusted so implicitly was a mirror for qualities in herself that she simply hadn't recognized. She accumulated a store of "Buffettisms," the examples and quips her friend used to educate her. She asked him to serve on her board, and he readily agreed, solidifying a business relationship that would last through Katharine's tenure as CEO and beyond.

Buffett's effect on her life, she wrote in her autobiography, was "central to everything that followed." That statement captured her future strategic decision-making, but it had an emotional component as well. By expanding her business knowledge base with so brilliant a mentor, Katharine felt a new sense of personal power. As her business insight grew, she told her friend, "I might really get to be the most powerful woman in whatever-it-is." By the mid-1970s, most people thought she had attained that power, but their perceptions didn't matter. After more than a decade at the head of her company, Katharine could believe in herself.

"The Battle of Britain"

More than 840 writers and classified and display advertising employees produced the content for the *Post* in the mid-1970s. They were organized in a labor union called the Newspaper Guild, which had staged an unsuccessful strike in 1974. The Guild members had little leverage and less energy when they went on strike. They had no pickets and enlisted no other unions for support, instead counting on the notion that, as they put it, they had "withheld their excellence." It was a weak strategy. Katharine, Bradlee, and other executives and managers wrote copy and handled the calls for classifieds and advertisements during the strike. One caller told Katharine she sounded overqualified. "Either you know a lot about a Mercedes or you're Katharine Graham." She replied, "Right on both counts." The public noticed little difference in the paper during the strike, and management came out of the conflict stronger than before.

The Guild had demanded a top minimum salary of $500 per week for their most experienced members, but the company countered with $470.47. Union members also had grievances about their treatment on the job. Many employees chafed at Bradlee's style, which they felt pitted writers against each other. Katharine was alternately viewed as a benevolent monarch who was unaware of the employees' complaints or a "tough babe" out to make money at any cost. The strike lasted only sixteen days, and it gave Katharine new confidence that she did not have to continue the company's tradition of avoiding a strike no matter what the cost. The Guild action, she said, showed that she was "willing to take a strike if necessary to demonstrate our determination to keep our costs under reasonable control." That determination would be severely tested in the fights ahead with the more militant craft unions.

The printers had long been resisting the new technology that threatened their job security, but they were willing to cut a deal when their contract came up for negotiation in 1974. In exchange for a cash payment of $2.6 million, the printers agreed to end a contractual practice called "reproduce," or "bogus," that amounted to a company-endorsed featherbedding scheme. Under this system there was always a backlog of work that required the *Post* to hire more printers regardless of actual need. Their new six-year contract reduced the number of printers by almost one-third over the first three years. The company also gained the right to introduce new technology but agreed to bonuses for early retirement, lifetime job guarantees, retraining, and the requirement that all new printers become union members. The contract meant a new era for the paper, with greater efficiency and lower production costs.

Katharine had presided over two notable successes in company labor relations, and the business world was paying attention. *Forbes* magazine had previously given her a gentleman's C in profitability but raised her industry rating to a "solid B" after the completion of the Guild and printers' contracts. The expiration of the contract for Local 6 of the Newspaper and Graphic Communications Union, or Pressmen's union, which came on September 30, 1975, would turn Katharine into an A student.

In the ground-floor pressroom, Local 6 workers waited to complete the production process. After the reporters and copy editors, printers and proofreaders, makeup editors and stereotypers finished their complex production work, they created hundreds of heavy metal plates for printing. The pressmen worked in a cavernous factory about half the length of a city block. Nine printing presses churned out the pages for the daily paper from about ten at night until four thirty in the morning. The workers labored through the night so that the paper could get to the dealers for delivery in the early morning hours. Many pressmen found the relentless clamor of the machinery echoing in their heads after they went home. The dust of newsprint and ink mist filled the air. Pressmen complained that the quality of the food in the night-shift cafeteria was downgraded compared to the day shift. Bathrooms were filthy and dysfunctional, the pressroom dirty and neglected. Even the soda machine needed fixing. The pressmen had one thing going for them—provisions in their contract that allowed them to "shoot the angles," or organize their schedules to maximize overtime and bonus pay. They sometimes worked double or even triple shifts, which they called "going to the whips." One-third of the budget allocated to their pay went to overtime. Their average wage, however, still stood far below that of reporters and editors. Combined with tensions over job security, relations with management were near the breaking point.

Like the printers, the pressmen had found ways to slow down the production process in order to send management a message about keeping their jobs. They resented Katharine's new business strategy. "She used to be cooperative, but now she just wants to get rid of bodies," a union official remarked in 1975. "Most of the guys these days wouldn't lift a finger for Mrs. G." The workers had tipped the other way, sabotaging the operations with frustrating regularity.

A mysterious break in the web from the giant paper rolls meant the presses had to be stopped and the web reinserted. A dart could suffice to break a web, delay the run, and leave the dealers who delivered the paper grumbling in the alley as they waited for their bundles. Katharine said that she frequently went to the alley to talk with the dealers and listen to their complaints. She hoped that by hearing their grievances and explaining her side she could keep the dealers from organizing yet another union. She already felt that, thanks to years of concessions by the company, the unions had left the *Post* out of control. Her deals with the Guild and printers had started the process of taking that control back, but the pressmen were a tougher group. She had offered them a 25 percent increase over three years and a $400,000 bonus to divide among the members, but she wanted to get control over setting schedules and the size of work crews. The union leadership had refused her offer.

At the expiration of the pressmen's contract on the last day of September 1975, Katharine had gone home, expecting negotiations to continue. Instead, the 204 pressmen walked off the job at about four-thirty in the morning. They smashed all nine presses, disabled the fire extinguishers, set fire to one of the presses, and gave a severe beating to the pressroom foreman as they stormed out. Mark Meagher, the general manager of the newspaper, called Katharine to say that they had been "Pearl Harbored." By the time she drove herself to the building, police, fire trucks, and television crews jammed the street, and picketers marched and chanted in the chaos.

Katharine had hoped to avoid a strike, at least this time around. Her main rival paper in Washington, the *Star*, had new ownership and was aggressively taking on the *Post*'s dominance. If the *Post* stopped publishing, the *Star* would likely pick up *Post* advertisers and readers. After years of fighting to build circulation and advertising, Katharine dreaded the idea of seeing her gains swept away along with the loss in profitability. "If a paper is struck and the other is publishing," she said, "you lose. Advertisers have to advertise and they'll advertise in the other paper if one is publishing." She had instructed Meagher to avoid a strike, but she had also been preparing for one just in case. She had been so worried about the business difficulties presented by the labor situation that she had consulted Sam Kagel, a friend who negotiated contracts for unions, and the Harvard labor economist John Dunlop. She tried to follow their advice, finally concluding that her main problem lay with her managers. They didn't know what they were doing. Management training was started, but training and the improved management she hoped it would bring didn't solve the immediate problem.

The pressmen held the strike threat over her head like a club. She had wanted to be ready for the worst, and had asked former editor Ken Johnson to organize Project X. The secret effort involved hiring a notorious antiunion company in Oklahoma, Southern Production Program, to train nonunion employees in running the machines that the craft unions controlled. Closer to home, in northern Virginia, the *Post* built their own training school where employees could learn how to set cold type and use scanners. Union members called the efforts "scab schools," and the graduates were about to be put to the test. When Katharine saw the damage in the pressroom she was appalled and furious, but one thought overrode all others—to keep publishing. All of the other workers in the seven craft unions had walked out with the pressmen. If she could find presses, she could publish without them, but she needed copy and that meant keeping reporters on the job. She felt it was "very, very important to keep the Guild in, very important to the quality of the paper." She was hopeful, knowing that many Guild members had weak beliefs about the labor movement. Many reporters hadn't joined the Guild at all. All of them knew that the Communications Center on the fifth floor received dispatches from news services all over the country, along with cables from foreign correspondents, ensuring the *Post* had some copy no matter what the Guild did. In addition, the pressmen had unwittingly handed Katharine a gift with their violent action.

The strikers had alienated the public, and more important, the reporters and editors of the paper. The pressmen were also hurt by the makeup of their membership; they were all white males, and the suggestion of racism further undermined their cause. Several floors and a world of class difference separated the reporters and editors from the men who ran the presses. Upstairs a new culture of pride had grown in the post-Watergate era. "The accolades had rubbed off on everybody," the Guild's international president said. Downstairs, the post-Watergate culture seemed to target production costs in favor of administration and advertising. Upstairs, the right and obligation to publish was the core mission. Downstairs, the drive to publish translated to leverage for the workers' demands. The president of the pressmen's union, Jim Dugan, said, "I didn't even know who Ben Bradlee was . . . Bradlee works at the *Washington Post*. I work in a factory." The alienation between the production workers and the Guild offered Katharine an opportunity. As the more than eight hundred Guild members arrived at the building, they were shown the wreckage in the pressroom. Guild members voted against joining the picket line, despite encouragement from the union's leadership. Five days after the strike began, a *Post* article said that for the Guild members, the strike was, "a strange and troubling labor dispute."

Katharine had gone to her rival Joe Allbritton, who had taken over the *Star*, and asked him to print the *Post*. Such solidarity would have meant a strike at the *Star* as well, something Allbritton couldn't afford. He refused to cooperate. He also refused to suspend publication to support the *Post*. Furious, Katharine threw some "pungent language" at Allbritton and moved on.

She agreed to an ingenious and risky plan for publishing. After six small newspapers around Washington, and as far away as Lorain, Ohio, agreed to print the paper, a helicopter airlifted copy from the roof of the *Post* building to avoid the strikers. To produce the paper, everyone went to work, with nearly two hundred people literally living in the building. The executive dining room became an all-night cafeteria, with catered dinners for the whole staff. Those who braved the pickets risked being beaten, getting their tires slashed, and enduring the taunts and threats of the strikers. At one point shots were fired into the office windows. Katharine was burned in effigy. The vice president of the union, Charles Davis, carried a sign reading, "Phil shot the wrong Graham." "Oh God, not that," was Katharine's response.

In the early days of the strike, as she worked around the clock, Katharine felt drained and fearful. "The strike was by far the worst thing that ever happened to me," she said. Coming from the woman who had nearly witnessed her husband's suicide, the comment revealed the depth of her emotion and ambivalence. These feelings grew from the sympathy she had shown for labor during her student years in Chicago. After college she had worked the docks in San Francisco as a journalist, socializing with union leaders. As late as the 1970s, *Post* reporter Haynes Johnson remembers her speaking of her admiration for Harry Bridges, the radical leader of the longshoremen in San Francisco whom she had known decades earlier. In those days she called herself a "bleeding heart liberal." She couldn't forget that her father had been an honorary member of the pressmen's union and that he had chosen to give them *Post* stock, making them part of the company. Because of her labor sympathies, the strike presented a stark and wrenching choice: abandon any shred of support for organized labor or save her company. She feared that a wrong decision might take the paper down. Buffett said that "during that period I watched Kay suffer, tormented by the thought that she was destroying what her family had spent more than forty years building. Some of her most trusted advisers urged her to cave. But with her knees knocking louder than ever before, she persevered." With the *Washington Star* pouring resources into competing with her and the pressmen trying to shut down her paper, Katharine felt she was "between the rock and the hard place." The other publishers weren't trying to make things easier. They wanted her to break the union and set a precedent, warning her at every chance about the dangers of giving in. Her response was to fight her way out, responding to crisis with action and expecting those loyal to her to do the same. Bradlee said, "Her spine stiffened every day." Soon she was being called "the iron lady."

Working alongside her, those employees who had crossed the picket line formed a bond of solidarity around keeping the paper alive. They often found their boss working next to them, unconcerned about dirtying her designer dresses. Her son Don was also on hand. He had worked in virtually every part of the newspaper and by the time of the strike was assistant general manager. The strike became a stark lesson in leadership for the young man destined to inherit his mother's role.

Katharine took part in the most menial and difficult jobs. One of the more miserable jobs involved stuffing newspapers in bags and labeling them, which meant hands that were quickly covered in paste and ink. The work took place through the night into the early morning hours. She led by example, and with an unassuming vulnerability. A supervisor in the classified department remembered training Katharine one night during the strike. "I said to Mrs. Graham, 'I'm so nervous I don't know what I'm doing.'" Her boss replied, "It's okay, I'm nervous too." She didn't fear showing her vulnerability, a human touch that encouraged many of the workers on hand during the tense days of the strike.

Only one day of publication was missed. On October 3, the front page headline read, "Post Publishes Curtailed Edition Despite Strike; Small Edition Printed in Pressmen's Strike." A few days after the strike began, Katharine addressed the New Jersey chapter of a journalists' organization. "Just a few days ago the first of the damaged presses [started again] manned by a crew of advertising salesmen and one woman," she told the members of Sigma Delta Chi. "They produced over a hundred thousand copies of a very creditably printed newspaper Monday night and double that output last night." The paper kept growing in size as the presses were repaired and the nonunion team grew more adept.

The pressmen's strategy had been to ruin the machinery so that management's ability to publish would be crippled. They hoped to gain bargaining leverage by cutting into the paper's revenues, and that meant stopping the *Post* from reaching its subscribers. As the paper hit the streets each day, the pressmen watched their leverage dwindle. At the same time, Katharine began to see that she could win, and her anger over the pressmen's actions steeled her resolve. "The wrecking of the equipment was the kind of thing that happens," an executive who was involved at the time said. "But to her it was as if someone had vandalized her house. The real decisions during the strike were hers. She tested the ideas, and then she made them. She was cognizant of every decision." The beating of foreman Jim Hover, who had only come out of his office to see why the presses had slowed, further steeled her resolve. As the tide turned her way, Katharine carefully considered the most fateful decision of all— whether to permanently replace the strikers.

Negotiations with the pressmen were leading nowhere. A final offer by the *Post* had been made on December 4, requiring the union to give management control over scheduling the pressmen. It was the sorest point, since senior pressmen could often double their pay by cleverly using the overtime and penalty clauses of the existing contract. Some pressmen had worked the angles to get in shifts at the *Post* and the *Star*, getting full pay at both. Katharine's hard-nosed negotiator, Larry Wallace, was out to end these practices, and he wasn't backing down. The proposal he put forward went to the extreme in management's favor, making many regular employees part of what the *Post* called a "floating group." "A floater would have to be on twenty-four hours' notice, every day" or end up with no shifts to work, a Guild member explained in a leaflet. Salary increases were not the issue in the strike but rather "the survival of the pressmen's union." The pressmen, as hardened in their position as Wallace was in his, voted down the company's final offer.

Standing in the newsroom six days later, her hands trembling, Katharine explained to those who had stood with her that the company had offered all they could. Replacing the strikers, she went on, "is unquestionably legal. What has been infinitely harder for me to decide is whether we are acting in a way that is humanly right. I have thought about this long and hard, and I have concluded that we are." She had been accused by one of her own journalists, Nicholas Von Hoffman, of waltzing the paper "back to the industrial warfare of the nineteenth century." Her voice cracking, she insisted that her company was not and never had been antiunion. She denounced as a "lie" the idea that she had set out to bust the union, but she explained, "Responsible union members do not set fires or beat fellow workers or make midnight phone calls threatening to kill the wives and infants of their fellow workers." She had reached the point where she could not stomach the idea of allowing the strikers back in her building. She told George Meany, president of the AFL-CIO, that if the strikers had accepted her final offer she would have "slit her throat." With nonunion workers being hired to run the presses, the strike could not hold. On Monday, February 16, the mailers and printers returned to work, and the pressmen's strike collapsed. One of the striking pressmen committed suicide. A candlelight vigil assembled outside Katharine's house in Georgetown, but for the strikers nothing changed. By May the pickets were gone, and in the next year Local 6 was decertified as the representative for the pressmen at the *Post*.

The violence and intransigence of the strikers coming up against an owner intent on breaking their control had killed the union. Katharine had won a boost in profitability that otherwise might have taken years. But the strike had other, more personal costs, creating a rift in the liberal-labor coalition. To some people Katharine's name became synonymous with "union buster," while others denounced labor violence and took her side. Her former national editor, Ben Bagdikian, wrote a critical piece about the strike in *Washington Monthly* magazine entitled, "Maximizing Profits at the *Washington Post*." In the first edition of her memoir, Katharine calls Bagdikian's article "insane," and quotes a memo to Bradlee calling Bagdikian an "ignorant, biased fool," and laments that "the worst asps in this world are the ones one has clasped to the bosom." These remarks were taken out of the paperback edition of her book without explanation; perhaps she regretted their intemperance. But they reveal the intensity of Katharine's emotions during the strike, and the sensitivity she experienced when criticized. She continued to vigorously deny that she set out to bust the union, but she insisted that the right to manage had been eroded by labor over many years and that she had to turn it around.

The *Post* was making money again, its dominance intact. The strike had cost about $800,000 in the last quarter of 1975, but much of that was covered by insurance. The post-strike gains were "staggering," according to the *Post*'s general manager. With $1.2 million in overtime for the pressmen eliminated, Katharine got the profitability she had hoped for and more. New presses, costing $2.5 million each, could print, cut, and fold sixty-five thousand newspapers per hour. The number of employees in the pressroom went from seventeen per shift to nine. She exceeded her profitability target of 15 percent by five points. Profits rose from around $10 million to almost $30 million in 1979. Most of the savings came from labor costs.

Around Christmas the year of the strike, Katharine told a reporter from *Time* that the conflict with Local 6 had been "sort of like the Battle of Britain." She was given to historical and literary allusions, but this one seemed particularly apt. For the woman who hated confrontation, the reference to the months in which British fighter planes had kept the Nazis at bay did not seem overdrawn. She had felt under siege, defending against an enemy whose tactics she abhorred. In her autobiography she insists that the battle was not about busting the unions but rather about upholding her "obligation to our readers." She had been spurred on by principle, not "moneygrubbing," as some people claimed. If others saw the qualities of a Winston Churchill in her resolve and the rallying of her troops, she would have appreciated the comparison.

Thanks to her discipline, and with Buffett's help, Katharine more than rewarded her mentor's faith in her stewardship of the Post Company. In 1973, rather than buying Post stock, Buffett could have bought into the *New York Times*, Gannett, Knight-Ridder, or Times Mirror. He would have received above-average returns but not the extra $200 million to $300 million in market value that separated the Post from the rest of its competitors. In his annual report to his company in 1985, Buffett wrote that the large gain from the Washington Post Company was due to "the superior nature of the managerial decisions made by Kay as compared to those made by managers of most other media companies." She had followed his advice to buy back Post stock at bargain prices starting in 1975, a brilliant move that was ahead of its time. Buffett encouraged the action as a smart investment as well as one that increased the value of the remaining shares. Katharine had reduced cost and built value, and she wasn't finished. Her father had bought the company for $825,000 in 1933. Under his daughter's leadership it was becoming a multi-billion-dollar media conglomerate.

CHAPTER TEN

A FAMILY BUSINESS

"Enduring great companies preserve their core values and purpose while their business strategies and operating practices endlessly adapt to a changing world."

—Jim Collins

There is a persistently uncomplimentary strain in many of the books and articles that discuss Katharine's evolution as a business leader. Her criticism of other executives was interpreted as insecurity rather than an expression of what she had learned about organizational development and human resource needs. After Fritz Beebe died in 1973, one biographer said that Katharine had to take over the title and responsibilities of chairman that Beebe held or send the message that "she was essentially a figurehead" during Beebe's tenure. A 1978 *Washington Star* exposé described her as a "whining child." This kind of thinking fed the idea that she was manipulated, controlled like a puppet, or incapable of independent decision-making. Despite her demonstrations of remarkable leadership, the negative libels persisted.

Katharine's transition from homemaker to executive, as well as her gender, seemed to be a more powerful lens for others to view her than the decisions she had made to remake the company, publish the Pentagon Papers, persist with the Watergate investigation, or remold company labor relations. She recognized this and remarked in the late 1970s, "If I do something unexpected, male executives tend to react more than normally by asking 'who has gotten to her.' I'm sure I'm too defensive about this—but I try to say very clearly where an idea comes from, even if it has been adopted by me and has become mine." Halfway into her second decade running the company, she was forced to refight battles that had been won many times over.

Her detractors misunderstood her approach to decision making. She wanted information. She wouldn't act without being informed, but as her friend June Bingham said, "Once she understood something she could be strong and stubborn." As she shifted from questions to action, sometimes revisiting decisions as a project moved forward, she invited charges of indecision and poor judgment.

These attacks on her ability fed the emotional insecurities that had plagued her throughout her life. She would never fully exorcise these demons, and they likely accounted for her less admirable moments. She was called "Katharine the Terrible . . . an imperious bitch" by one frequent dinner guest. She bad-mouthed executives who had fallen out of favor. She seemed to have no instinct or desire to hold her tongue. On a trip where the wife of one *Post* executive had been questioning a foreign official, Katharine said to her, "We'll all learn a lot more if you stop talking." Her pettiness seemed to come out around trivial matters—a person's dress or manner. She didn't shrink from being disingenuous. At one cocktail party where she was energetically bad-mouthing a colleague, she turned on her heel as he approached and gave him the warmest welcome. Unlike other famous people of wealth, like the Roosevelts, who were seen as traitors to their class, Katharine seemed most comfortable in the world of privilege that had been her lifetime milieu. She kept the upper-crust tone and regal bearing that suggested boundaries she meant to keep intact. When David Remnick, the editor of *The New Yorker* magazine, was at the *Post*, he said her voice sounded to the young staff "like money." Even her friends found her off-putting at times. "She was unpredictable," Bingham says. "She'd be an effusive friend or cold, busy person granting you a few seconds."

The people who were hurt by her, whether in word or action, seized on her most unattractive traits to define her. Beyond the stress of being CEO, Katharine suffered an emotional toll from these personal assaults. She was constantly recalculating the costs and benefits of leadership.

Katharine had turned sixty years old in the *Post*'s centennial year of 1977. The years had given her insight that is only gained by people who challenge themselves to their limit. "She is more interested in her business and the products they turn out," Warren Buffett told a reporter in 1978, "than in anything else in her life." As Katharine wrote, "To me, involvement with news is absolutely inebriating. It's what makes my life exciting." Her detractors failed to recognize her singular passion, to see an intellect able to learn and change, to understand that she could act with independence yet value advice and counsel. The publisher of the *Post* had core convictions, which she approached with perspective, both of the world and of hard personal experience. Of the press she said, "The real world in which we work is neither evil nor heroic. It is the same environment of conflict, ambiguity and hard choices that mark most enterprises in our time." The end of the 1970s marked a time of hard choices for Katharine, particularly on the business side, where she was concentrating her time. She had also begun to consider the realization of a long-held dream: that, as her father had wished, control of the *Post* would move to the next generation. Her firstborn son, Donald, had long been considered the heir apparent. In 1975, she told an interviewer, "It is logical to expect him to become publisher of the *Post*." In the mix of decision making swirled the choice, both emotional and hard-nosed, of when to anoint a beloved son as the next inheritor.

Success at Succession Planning

In 1954, when Eugene Meyer negotiated the purchase of the *Times-Herald,* his competition in the Washington, D.C., morning market, he said, "The real significance of this event is that it makes the paper safe for Donnie." Meyer's grandson was almost nine years old at the time. His grandfather's steadfast vision had been to own a newspaper that would live on through future generations of the family.

Acquiring the *Times-Herald* gave the *Post* a morning monopoly of readers. At the time of the merger the *Times-Herald* had fifty thousand more readers than the *Post,* better writing, editing, sports coverage, and comics, threatening to put the weaker paper out of business. But its conservative owner, Colonel Robert McCormick, had grown tired of Washington. The $10 million purchase concluded on St. Patrick's Day. Phil, thirty-nine years old and smoking forty Parliament cigarettes a day, did a brilliant job as *Post* publisher of holding on to subscribers and advertisers from his former rival. Circulation doubled, more advertising followed, and the *Post* was set to become the powerhouse of publishing that Meyer foresaw.

It was the last great act by the patriarch, then seventy-eight years old, bald, and frail looking, for the paper he loved. He had bested a rival who menaced his dream. "Meyer had shown himself worthy of McCormick's respect," wrote Frank Waldrop, the *Times-Herald's* last editor. "He had been a tough competitor, he had learned while doing, and shown himself under stress to be a gentleman." Meyer passed on a far stronger paper than the one he had bought in 1933, but he also passed on to his daughter and grandson the style of leadership that Waldrop described.

Katharine carried the idea of family succession around like a sacred icon. Her father, the parent who had always believed in her, the parent who had encouraged her love of journalism, the parent who had invited her to be part of his passionate enterprise as he built the *Post*, had passed on a paper and an imperative. He died in 1959, never to know how well he had taught his daughter. She became the unexpected successor, using her father's commandment to keep the paper in the family as validation for her decision to take over after Phil's death. Holding Donnie's place until he was old enough to take charge gave her a public reason, whatever her private or subconscious reasons, to do the unexpected.

By 1977, however, Katharine had established herself as far more than a placeholder. Don was thirty-two years old, and still his mother held onto the power. Don's father had become publisher at thirty. What was Katharine waiting for? Don seemed ready, but she was not.

There were several global issues to address within the company, including the quality of reporting in the *Post* after Watergate. Katharine sensed a new antagonism from the outside and a dangerous ethic within. "Many people, especially in government and business, assume the press is hostile, uninformed and likely to distort or sensationalize everything. Many reporters and editors, on the other hand, assume that everything secret is scandalous, and every claim of confidentiality is a cover-up." She saw the danger as eager young reporters vied to get on staff and be the next Woodward or Bernstein. Objectivity and fairness were at risk. The paper had become large and bureaucratic. Bradlee no longer had a handle on all the hiring. Katharine called it a self-renewal problem, and she recognized the difficulties of that problem better than anyone. She had turned increasingly to the business of the company as a whole, insisting on a profit litmus test for any acquisitions. The *Post* more than met the test, showing post-strike profits almost double the previous average in 1976. The next year, profits increased 45 percent, the next, 25 percent. A chart of operating revenue through the mid-1980s showed the dramatic effect of Katharine's business decisions, including ending any effective union control over production of the *Post*. From 1964, when Katharine took control, until 1976, the line is on a slow ascent, but from 1976 forward it looks like the final push to the peak of Mt. Everest.

Like other media companies, Katharine looked to expand and broaden the company, but she was cautious. New enterprises within the company's portfolio had to meet the profitability litmus test. As David Halberstam points out, her father would have never bought the *Post* under the profitability criteria his daughter put in place. In 1933, the paper was on the auction block unable to meet its debts. Meyer poured millions into what many people thought was a losing proposition. But founders are not inheritors. Meyer's mission grew from a dream and a plan—to serve the public through generations of family commitment. As inheritor, Katharine's first mission was to stay true to her father's wishes.

Katharine never lost sight of her role as protector of a legacy, at times feeling the constraint this imposed. When she became the first woman director of the Associated Press in 1974, she said, "I really am rather pleased about the A.P. I don't know quite why except we inheritors like to do something on our own." The comment suggests a wistful sense that she might have preferred to be an adventurer like her father, gambling with the future. Instead, she accepted the role of protecting what he had entrusted to her. Under Phil's leadership the company had moved into television broadcasting. He had also negotiated the purchase of *Newsweek* at an incredible bargain and established the highly successful *Los Angeles Times–Washington Post* News Service just two years before his death.

Katharine also looked to expand. Like other newspaper owners, she was interested in other big city papers but found them overpriced. She began to look at smaller papers, and her management team became interested in the afternoon paper in Trenton, New Jersey, the *Trenton Times*. She proceeded more on faith than reason. "An impulse buy," one *Post* editor called it. A preoffer market survey had missed the fact that the *Trenton Times* faced a competing paper in the morning market. *Post* management had firsthand experience with the fact that morning papers were becoming dominant over their afternoon rivals. Nevertheless, with the influence of Wall Street's admonition to create a farm team at smaller papers as impetus, Katharine made an offer of $16 million. Only later did she discover that the family selling the paper would have taken $12 million. A team was dispatched from Washington to run the new acquisition, leading to a big city sensibility in a small city market. The *Trenton Times* newsroom became known as "*Washington Post* North." Katharine poured money in for new equipment only to watch circulation and advertising nose-dive. The acquisition became a glaring disaster, magnified because anything Katharine did after Watergate was subject to the public microscope. Seeing "no solution and no way out," Katharine dubbed the venture her "Vietnam."

The allusion was overdrawn, but it revealed the publisher's competitive edge. She hated to lose, and the *Times* was going down in defeat. Having lost too much ground in circulation and advertising, it was sold in 1981 to the former owner of the *Washington Star,* Joe Allbritton, who had refused to stand by Katharine during the bitter pressmen's strike. Expansion in the print media offered continuing problems. Katharine bought a small daily in Everett, Washington, for $25 million. With a great deal of difficulty it turned a modest profit over time. She was outbid for dailies in Des Moines and Wilmington by the growing empire of Gannett Corporation, which would start the first national newspaper, *USA Today,* in the 1980s. An attempt to buy the stylish *New York* magazine ended in an embarrassing defeat. Don Graham was particularly interested in the magazine, and its editor, Clay Felker, had become friends with Katharine. She assembled a high-powered team, including the investment banker Felix Rohatyn, to broker the deal. Negotiations centered on buying the controlling shares of stock from one of the magazine's board members. Katharine waited for the man to call like a "jilted dance-hall dolly." In the end, the magazine went to Rupert Murdoch, the Australian who was building a transcontinental media empire.

Broadcast media proved more lucrative than print. A radio and television station had been added in Miami in 1969; the TV station was renamed WPLG in Phil Graham's honor. Another television station was bought in Hartford, Connecticut, for $34 million, and was renamed WFLB for Fritz Beebe. The returns on these ventures far exceeded expectations and buoyed the company during the worst days of the strike and beyond. To avoid issues that were arising about cross-ownership of media in the same market, Katharine decided to trade her Washington, D.C., television station for one in Detroit. It was her first solo negotiation. As in Trenton, the local media characterized the deal as a take-over by outsiders. It took years to make it a success, and Katharine blamed herself for the problems.

She wasn't the first media CEO to fail with new ventures. Time Inc. tried *Cable-TV Week* magazine without success and later bought the *Washington Star*, which went out of business in 1981. There were others as well who, like Katharine, ventured and lost. In her case, however, her bottom line grew steadily, investors were pleased, and she began to consider the inevitable transition of power.

In 1978, the *Post* was still the money machine of the company, the "cornerstone," Katharine called it. If the time had come for Don to take over, she could hardly give him a better start. During a staff meeting on January 10, 1979, Katharine announced that Don Graham was "ready and I am ready" to take over as publisher of the *Post*. "My mother has given me everything but an easy act to follow," he responded. He struck people as distant and thoughtful, and his actions bore this out. He was a teetotaler, devoted to his young family, uninterested in the Washington social scene.

When Don arrived for work at the *Post*, he started at the bottom, learning about every aspect of the paper he would one day control.

He reported on city stories, ran the sports section for a time, worked on the business side learning promotion and advertising. During the strike he became assistant general manager. He didn't have his father's highs or lows or his mother's insecurity. He had been carefully groomed for a role he was ready to accept.

Katharine was lucky in her oldest son. More than 70 percent of family-owned businesses fail in the transition from founder to the next generation, and an even greater percentage when passed to the next. Lack of an appropriate successor is the main reason. Family infighting is often the culprit, but only Lally, Katharine's eldest and her only daughter, made any protest about Don's succession. She ended up writing for the paper, after threatening to write for the rival *Washington Times*, and made foreign affairs her specialty. The two younger brothers had other pursuits beyond the world of newspapers and seemed content with their mother's choice. As Don noted later, his uncle and aunts on the Meyer side were supportive of the way Katharine ran the Post Company. "Family issues are complicated in any company," he noted, "but family issues [at the Post] are dwarfed by business issues, as indeed I think they've always been." By keeping the company profitable, Katharine had avoided the attacks that other less well-run family businesses had endured. Through her unwavering focus on the company and its welfare she avoided the fate of Otis Chandler, inheritor of the *Los Angeles Times*, who was forced out of control of his family's business in the 1990s, and the internal family war that broke up the Pulitzer publishing dynasty. She had secured the future for the next generation. Don Graham had seen his mother rise from family tragedy and become a new woman driven by duty and devotion to both her father and son. Don had presumably fulfilled his own dream by becoming publisher of the *Post*, but he also vindicated his mother's courage and acknowledged her faith and love.

Making Space

Mother and son both served on the company board when Don became publisher in 1979. The company had a history of attracting blue-chip board members. Former attorney general Nicholas Katzenbach, former Ford Motor Company president Arjay Miller, former defense secretary Robert McNamara were among the members who met for dinner at Katharine's table on the night before the formal board meeting. Katharine had a fabulous French chef, and the talk ranged from business to politics to Washington gossip. Some said the six yearly dinners were the impetus for joining the board. The company they oversaw was worth $500 million, and had five thousand employees and two thousand shareholders. Katharine spent most of her rigorous daily schedule on her dual role as chairman and CEO of the Post Company. The company matriarch and her son, the new publisher, stayed close collaborators.

From the outset of the transition, Katharine had tried to leave the important decisions at the paper for Don. She had wanted to change the leadership of the editorial page, feeling that Phil Geyelin had lost clarity and foresight. Her choice of replacement was her friend Meg Greenfield, but she didn't take action. She knew Don concurred, and she let him make the change after he became publisher. She had learned from hiring Bradlee: the people you pick have a loyalty and closeness that is difficult to replicate in those already in place when you take over.

Don had other big decisions to make. He added new bureaus in the United States and overseas in New Delhi and West Africa. Style Plus was added to the Style section, and the Sunday book review returned to its separate tabloid section. He worried that Time Life Inc., which had bought the *Star*, would close in on the *Post*'s dominance. But just two years after the transition, the *Washington Star* folded. Don made a deal that included payment for the *Star*'s building and printing presses, but also included circulation and advertising at no additional cost. Some of the *Star*'s best talent came to the *Post*, including the Pulitzer Prize–winning editorial writer Mary Mc-Grory, whom Don's father had tried to lure to the *Post* many times. The acquisition created another surge in *Post* stock. The *Star*'s demise, however, didn't mean the end of newspaper competition in the nation's capital. Within a year a new paper hit the streets funded by the Reverend Sun Myung Moon's Unification Church. Identified with the conservative profile of its owner, the *Washington Times*, heavily underwritten by Moon, became the *Post*'s new rival. When asked if his mother was still involved in the "big decisions" at the paper, Don responded, "You bet!" yet she was never heard second-guessing him. That mother and son had formed a collaborative team that seemed to have no rancor was a testament to Katharine's determination to succeed and to her trust. "It was a very classy way to do the turnover," longtime *Post* journalist Haynes Johnson remarked. "She came to the office, but she made the decision to step back. There was no sense of a hovering presence or of the older generation watching over Don's shoulder." If she questioned Don's judgment, she did so privately and deferred with grace. She had put in place a system of values and norms that her son had grown up observing and living. Longtime employees said they stayed on because of the culture, the supportive atmosphere, and the high values and moral standards that had been passed down.

Don also embraced excellence with profitability and relied on Warren Buffett as a mentor in much the way his mother had. Like his mother, he paid close attention to employees, but had a more approachable manner. He would "stop at every desk like a bee chatting with everyone," Tom Sherwood remembered. "Mrs. Graham was more regal." Newsroom employees invariably called her "Mrs. Graham," although she might sign a congratulatory note on an article "Kay" or "Katharine." Rumor held that Don knew the name of every one of his employees, how long they had been at the *Post*, and even the names of their children. By contrast, Katharine visited the news-room almost weekly but had trouble remembering names. Don was keenly aware that he had inherited an extraordinary history of public management, driven by his mother's ownership of the majority of voting stock. That power had given her confidence to make hard de-cisions. "She took shareholder responsibilities just as seriously as you possibly could," he told an interviewer. If there were a Pulitzer Prize for management, Don was ready to award it to his mother on behalf of the shareholders and himself.

Katharine seemed to be looking less for accolades, however, than for continued purpose and challenge. She had a leader's talent for fo-cusing on objectives, and with Don running the paper she put a dif-ferent spotlight on her work for the company.

She had been serving on the board of her alma mater, the Univer-sity of Chicago, and other outside boards. She resigned from these, instead getting active with important trade groups within her indus-try: the Bureau of Advertising, the Associated Press (AP) board, and the American Newspaper Publishers Association (ANPA). In a tell-ing picture, Katharine sits at the head of a boardroom table with the twenty-one white male directors of the AP board on either side of her. She became the first woman director of the group. She also broke the gender barrier at the ANPA, becoming the first woman to chair that association. There wouldn't be another for twenty-seven years. She felt these industry groups would give her perspective on the kinds of problems companies like hers had to face, but she gave the men perspective as well. Al Neuharth, founder of *USA Today*, remem-bers how the men of the ANPA looked on Katharine with "distaste," when she first came to a meeting. The CEO of the Post Company showed them, Neuharth said, that "she was a tough competitor and an unhappy loser and had ways of expressing herself that the guys understood." Katharine could swear like the longshoremen she knew in her youth, a habit that added shock value to the power of her position. If some of her colleagues were thrown off balance, she didn't seem to mind.

Of her role in the company after her transition to CEO in 1979, Katharine wrote with typical self-deprecation. The corporate side was "not well run," she said. The company hadn't grown, "in any sensible or substantive way," despite its profitability. *Newsweek,* where Katharine had hired and fired a merry-go-round of editors, "was in managerial confusion." The next year would throw the editorial side of the business into confusion and worse.

One of Katharine's great worries about the quality of the paper became a nightmarish reality in the fall of 1980. A young Metro staff reporter named Janet Cooke had written a story about an eight-year-old boy named Jimmy. In the story, placed on the front page, Cooke witnesses Jimmy being shot up with heroin by his mother's lover. The story caused an international sensation, although some *Post* reporters had immediate questions about its authenticity. The *Post* editors loved the story, submitting it for the Pulitzer Prize, which Cooke won in April 1981. The *Post* gave front-page coverage to Cooke's triumph, but two days later the story had changed. "The Pulitzer Prize Committee withdrew its feature-writing prize from *Washington Post* reporter Janet Cooke yesterday after she admitted that the award-winning story was a fabrication," the *Post* reported. The incident prompted internal soul-searching at the paper and gave credence to Katharine's fear that reporters would look for "a Watergate under every rock." Her son took the lead, along with Ben Bradlee, in reassuring readers that such an incident wouldn't recur. Katharine was stung by the reaction of her colleagues at other newspapers. They were, she wrote in her autobiography, "self-righteous" in assuming it couldn't happen to them. Her umbrage was prescient. *The New Republic* magazine had titled an article about the Cooke affair "Deep Throat's Children." In the mid-1990s, a writer named Stephen Glass would fool *The New Republic* for several years with invented stories. His transgressions prompted a movie called *Shattered Glass,* a cautionary tale about trampling the ethics of reporting. It seemed to be the unfortunate counterpoint to *All the President's Men,* the Watergate movie about the irreproachable reporting of Woodward and Bernstein.

The Cooke affair was a blow to the excellence Katharine so coveted. Her mantra for reporting, as *Newsweek*'s editor Rick Smith remembered so well, was "Did we get it right? Were we fair? How could we have done it better?" The Cooke disaster seemed to mock her often-repeated guidance. Age and experience hadn't relaxed Katharine's standards. Just the opposite. But her son was in charge now, and she felt he did well with the tough news conference he held about Cooke. Katharine worried about the larger issues. Speaking to the ANPA, she said that the industry should not overcompensate in seeking to avoid other false stories or they would be in danger of not doing the job of a free press.

Corporate Wins and Corporate Woes

Just before the Cooke affair erupted in 1980, Katharine had forced out company president Mark Meagher, who had been instrumental in helping her through the strike. He floated out on a golden parachute worth nearly $1.8 million. Meagher's two predecessors, Larry Israel and Paul Ignatius, had also gotten generous severance packages as they were sent out the door. The Post Company's increasingly large compensation packages for executives, including incentives, followed the trend of other American companies at the time but aggravated already tense relations with members of the Newspaper Guild. Guild members felt they had little opportunity to demonstrate that their work increased profitability and to get the bonuses linked to that goal. Katharine defended her actions saying in 1975, "We do not believe we could in fact attract first-class executives unless we paid salaries and provided incentive bonuses at least roughly comparable to those received by executives in similar-sized companies . . . incentive compensation seems to me an excellent way of recognizing and rewarding good work when a person's contributions to profitability can be readily measured." It was a position shared by many corporations, although often criticized as shortsighted and counterproductive. The economist John Kenneth Galbraith warned against the pay chasm between the lowest paid worker and top executives. Conservative columnist George Will, published on the *Post*'s Op-Ed page, argued that it was "offensive to hear bonuses justified as necessary 'incentives' for executive effort." Even the *Post*'s editorial page railed against "top-heavy compensation packages" and their effect on morale for lower-level managers and workers.

Wage discrepancies, however, were not the only labor-relations issue that called Katharine's managerial judgment into question. Her vice president for labor relations, Larry Wallace, had been a tough and unsympathetic negotiator during the strike. He proved to be an even more intolerant manager of human resources in the years that followed. In 1984, Wallace sent out a nine-page memo on labor relations, advising managers that "the purpose of corrective discipline is to demean the employee, in his eyes, in the eyes of his family and the eyes of his fellow employees—make the demeaning stick with him." The memo went on to advise more severe punishment for union officials, a tactic that violated labor law. Don Graham was publisher at the time but refused to comment on the memo when the Newspaper Guild negotiators brought it to his attention.

Was Katharine aware of Wallace's tactics? It seems likely that she was. Wallace had been hired when she was publisher as the person to help her tame the unions, which she felt were usurping her right to manage. Tom Sherwood, a union negotiator at the time, remembers that Wallace would "snarl and growl" during negotiations. "The Graham family thought they were in a war to keep control of their

growing company," Sherwood said. Katharine had been told and believed that, in Sherwood's words, "she couldn't have a mom and pop
attitude anymore with the Post Company." At times, however, her
instincts were mixed, especially if she could help individual employees in distress. In 1987, Pat Wingert, an education reporter at
Newsweek, had a very premature baby boy, born sixteen weeks early.
As he lay in intensive care, doctors offered little hope of survival for
the child. In the first few days after the birth, Wingert's best friend
got a call from Katharine saying that the company would help in any
way it could. A few weeks later, Wingert was invited to lunch in
Katharine's personal dining room, where they talked "mother-to-
mother about my preemie son's ongoing struggle." Wingert's son survived and thrived. "That baby is now a teenager, and the memory of
that lunch remains one I treasure. Mrs. Graham was a fascinating
and complicated woman. She was also extraordinarily kind." Despite
anecdotes about her personal solicitude to individual employees, she
seemed accepting of maneuvers for greater profitability that came at
employee expense.

Katharine probably agreed with Wallace's harsh personnel mea-
sures as in keeping with larger management objectives. "I'm very
concentrated on good management. It's my consuming ambition,"
she told *Forbes* magazine the same year that Wallace wrote his memo
recommending that employees be "demeaned." Years later, she still
had fierce feelings about running her company. As she interviewed
former Guild member Morton Mintz for her book, she questioned
him aggressively about why the union had tried to interfere with her
"right to manage." "We just wanted fairness," Mintz replied. Fairness
as the union defined it, however, was not something Katharine would
allow to compete with profits.

By 1984, Katharine's company was soaring. She had solved her
long and wearying search for a president of the Post Company by
hiring Dick Simmons in 1981. He helped her with what she considered the main mission of her media company: "the way people com-

municate." They worked well together, making new acquisitions, including the online information service Legi-Slate and the test preparation company Stanley H. Kaplan Company. The latter was destined to become one of the company's main profit centers as the market for tutoring and test readiness heated up along with the record number of students applying to colleges and universities.

Katharine felt her best acquisition with Simmons was the cable systems company Capital Cities Communications. In January 1986, Cap Cities was bought for $350 million, a record amount for the Post Company. Post stock prices were at record levels too: $300 per share in the late 1980s, a price that would triple fifteen years later.

Simmons had been brought in with a compensation package richer than any of the three comparable executives at the *Post*'s main rivals: Times Mirror, Knight Ridder, and the *New York Times*. Two years into his tenure, the company's bottom line seemed to justify his salary. Net income between 1982 and 1983 had risen by 30 percent. Cash and temporary cash investments were up 71 percent from the previous year. "We're not in the slightest embarrassed by our build-up of cash," Simmons told *Forbes* magazine. "Welcome to the wonderful world of media companies, where herds of cash cows produce an extremely rich cream." The company's top executives shared the cream, including Katharine, whose salary rose 13.8 percent between 1982 and 1983 to $514,344, including bonuses.

At sixty-four years old, Katharine still had an unconquerable drive to excel. When things were going well, she felt dissatisfied. She wanted results that were "even better." With her confidence raised by Simmons's management of the company, Katharine became a world traveler. She went to Saudi Arabia, Egypt, Israel, and Libya, meeting with foreign leaders in a tour where she seemed part visiting head of state and part reporter. She traveled to Tokyo in 1986 to launch the Japanese language edition of *Newsweek*. As always, she insisted on a tough schedule. *Newsweek* editor Rick Smith remembers that she seemed jet-lagged on arriving in Tokyo. Looking at her "merciless schedule," he suggested that she might want to skip some of the in-terviews. "A fierce impatient look crossed her face," he recalled. "A long time ago I had to decide whether to be a lady who lunched or a woman who worked," she told him.

For her, the high point of her travels in the 1980s was her inter-view of Soviet president Mikhail Gorbachev in 1988. He had over-seen a new political era in his country that ended the cold war and reduced the threat of nuclear arms. Katharine was excited about the historic opportunity to speak to him. Robert Kaiser, a *Post* foreign correspondent at the time, was along for the trip, part of an entourage of reporters that included Katharine's friend Meg Greenfield, edito-rial page editor of the *Post*. Katharine, true to her reputation for more than thorough preparation, drove the group like "a drill sergeant," ac-cording to Kaiser.

At the interview, Katharine asked the first question, launching a conversation that had the Americans enthralled. After the interview, however, Gorbachev regretted comments in which he named one of his rivals in the Communist Party leadership. He sent an official to ask Katharine to take the offending name out of any story that was written. She listened politely and answered firmly: the paper would not be censored for anyone, including the Soviet president or the U.S. president. When he left the apartment in Moscow where she was staying, the official assured Katharine, "Don't worry, you won't be arrested." She returned to the paper, pleased and triumphant, her re-porter's heart uplifted by her work.

Katharine never strayed far from her reporting roots. Journalist Michael Dobbs remembers an interview at the *Post* with French president François Mitterrand in the 1980s. Dobbs was supposed to write the story, but arrived late because of security procedures. The interivew had already started. "There were all those hotshot journal-ists there, and no one had remembered to turn on the tape recorder or take notes except for Mrs. Graham." Dobbs had to write the story by relying on his boss's notes. "She had been the most diligent of all of us," he said. "She kept good notes."

When she was home, the CEO of the Post Company treated her role as social doyenne as a serious part of her work. The parties in her Georgetown home epitomized what writer Christopher Hitchens called the "permanent, floating evening seminars on high matters of state and policy and gossip." Her dinner parties were legendary for the participants and the potential for networking and information gathering. Sally Quinn called them a "marketplace," where Katharine brought together "world leaders and writers and business people and journalists."

Queen Noor of Jordan remembers Katharine hosting her husband, King Hussein, during "his arduous and often painful struggle to mediate the Arab-Israeli conflict." Microsoft cofounder Bill Gates remembers a dinner in Martha's Vineyard where a leading political figure was monopolizing the conversation. Katharine skillfully cut in to say to Gates, "Bill, I'd be very interested in hearing your thoughts on the technology industry one of these days." She knew how to keep the conversation interesting, making sure her guests were seated with people they could enjoy. "She'd never seat you next to two dogs," remembered Ben Bradlee. In the late 1980s, journalist Margaret Carlson remembers going out with Katharine and other friends and playing a game: If Katharine was having a dinner, whom would we invite? "She liked this sort of mocking of her, but it was also true that nearly anyone we thought of would have come to her house for dinner."

Katharine viewed her relationships as part of an inside-Washington continuum. Acquaintances might become social friends. Social friendships might become more close and meaningful over time, or they might disintegrate under the weight of gossip or an untoward remark. She felt comfortable with people who observed the upper-class social customs she had grown up with and valued, but she could enjoy, and repeat, a vulgar joke punctuated by her legendary raucous laugh. Writer

Nora Ephron said, "It was a deep, warm, throaty, fantastically engaging thing . . . her body absolutely shook with it."

Katharine enjoyed her own parties, always part social and part business in the broad Washington sense. Some people thought she was compromising the objectivity of her newspaper by socializing with those the paper might have to skewer in the future. But she saw herself as keeping the lines of communication open, creating the context for new relationships between journalists and those in power in business and government. "She had a blunt instinct about how to keep a distance from people she had dinner with," former *Post* editor Eugene Patterson said. One example occurred in 1997, when *Post* writer Michael Dobbs broke the story of Secretary of State Madeleine Albright's Jewish heritage. Albright called Katharine to say that she was worried about the story. Katharine replied that she had every confidence in Dobbs. A year after she received the call, long after Dobbs's story had run, Katharine mentioned the Albright call to her reporter. Dobbs said, "I never even knew she got that call. She never interfered in any way." Socializing for Katharine was a way to provide a place for those on all sides of an issue to argue their side; a place to build relationships in a town that runs on them. She was amazed when President Carter didn't even respond to her invitation to a going-away party for Patterson, who was from Carter's home state of Georgia. "He should be here working this room," she told Patterson.

Sitting at her parents' table so many years before, Katharine had learned how to cultivate a venue for conversation. Her "combination of elegance and commitment to bringing people of different worlds together came from the culture of a different generation," her daughter-in-law Mary Graham observed. As Katharine entered the last phase of her life she continued to value and embrace the friends she had gathered over a lifetime in Washington.

Many were people of fame and importance, and she had joined their ranks. She enjoyed people of intellect like herself, people whose bedside tables were also piled with books; people who could turn a breakfast discussion into a marathon that lasted until noon. She also turned a solicitous eye on her guests. *Post* columnist E. J. Dionne remembers attending a Graham dinner where he didn't know many people. She swept over and made some introductions. "She had a gift of making people feel included and comfortable," Dionne recalled, "She was always looking out for the people who were less connected." Introductions, connections, relationships that would help her paper or help those she favored were part of the territory she had claimed in her last years.

In June 1987, Katharine's daughter, Lally, organized a seventieth birthday bash at which Don Graham served as master of ceremonies. Katharine had hoped to avoid hoopla and take a quiet trip with friends. Instead, over six hundred guests filled the cavernous government auditorium in Washington that had been transformed by decorations for the event. The line-up of the rich and powerful rivaled the Black and White Ball that Truman Capote had thrown for his little-known friend more than twenty years before.

Katharine, in a white Oscar de la Renta dress with small polka dots and a four-strand choker of pearls, arrived with Warren Buffett as her escort. She needed no introductions. As *Post* columnist Art Buchwald said, "She had attained godlike status." When he spoke to the guests he quipped, "If there is one thing that brings us all together here tonight, it is fear . . . that if you are not here, you will never be forgiven." It was a lighthearted jibe but held some truth as well. Katharine had power, not just as a result of the prestige and wealth of her company but also through the force of the person she had become. She had earned authority from her accomplishments, and she remained determined to use that authority to accomplish even more. She had no thought of retirement, although she began to think about scaling back her role. She wanted time to reflect on her life, to make sense of those she had loved and lost and of the lifestyle she had chosen.

CHAPTER ELEVEN

THE FATES OF LEADERSHIP

"For success, like happiness, cannot be pursued; it must ensue, and it only does so as the unintended side effect of one's personal dedication to a cause greater than oneself."

—Viktor Frankl

Are leaders born or made? This is one of the most intriguing and enduring questions in the study of leadership. In Katharine's case this question takes on richer meaning because she was twice-born—she had lived one set of experiences before Phil's death and another after. The duality of her experience gives new definition to the nature versus nurture leadership debate.

Katharine had traits and characteristics inherited at birth that she would likely not have understood or used before the rebirth caused by Phil's traumatic death. She became a "born" leader after the events of her life caused her to see the world anew. She did so with all the curiosity, fear, exuberance and awkwardness that characterize birth as a literal and symbolic event.

Katharine's life demonstrated that *born* leaders may never live their leadership but for the experiences in life that *made* them leaders. Her life is a warning against the dangers of viewing leadership as the narrow province of those supposedly born to the task without consideration to the context of their life. Society confers leadership on some but denies it to others based on narrow considerations of personality. Experience, personal development, and the tests of life are too often ignored. Katharine's rebirth as a leader is a testament to the multiplicity of factors that result in leadership. She proved that leaders are both born and made, as well as subject to the fates of leadership.

Cartoonist Herblock, Katharine's great friend, captured the span of her leadership development in a cartoon he drew for her seventieth birthday. In his drawing, toddler Katharine is sitting on the floor building two columns of blocks that say, "Wash Post." An easel has the word *Post* written in a child's hand, and the same word has been cut from a box of Toasties cereal and lies on the floor among scissors and crayons. Her father stands nearby, large cigar in hand, and calls out to her mother, "Agnes, I think Katharine here is trying to tell us something." Eugene didn't buy the *Post* until Katharine was in high school, which reinforces Herblock's point: Katharine was born with leadership traits but was also given the tools to become the paper's leader from an early age. Circumstance did the rest.

Her father identified one of her most important traits when she was young. "Kate's . . . got a hard mind. She'd make a great businessman," he told a friend. Throughout her life, Katharine set that hardness of mind to the task most critical for leaders: personal growth and change. As the last full decade of her life began, she changed once more by choice and design.

A CEO's Flow

On May 9, 1991, Katharine stepped down as CEO of the Post Company. When she took over, nearly thirty years before, the company had revenues of $84 million. She was handing her son leadership of a company worth $1.4 billion. From the time she went public in 1971, Post stock had a gain of 3,315 percent, compared to a 227 percent increase in the Dow. As Warren Buffett said, "This spectacular performance—which far out-stripped those of her testosterone-laden peers—always left Kay amazed, almost disbelieving." She wouldn't squander her success. She wrote that she had seen companies "hurt or even ruined by an owner/CEO not stepping down at the right time," so she determined not to make that mistake. Her own history contributed to her decision as well. "She realized from her stormy takeover after Phil's death that an orderly transition was important to consolidate her gains," friend and colleague Eugene Patterson remarked.

For almost three decades she had been a leader who observed, who learned from what she observed, and who acted on what she learned. Observation, learning, and action: this was the style that set her apart. Most leaders at the end of their careers are aware of the dangers of staying on too long, of stepping down in name but not fact, of interference that causes irreparable dissension. They often act, however, like they will be the exception. Katharine knew better. "It's a pretty hairy existence," she said, "and nobody ever has it made. The minute you think you do—you don't." The drama of her life, as well as her insecurity and self-doubt, had given her a silver lining of humility. The worst could happen to her. It had. She guarded against it at every turn and finally stepped away from a job she loved as the ultimate expression of putting the enterprise above herself. "She believed one person should be in charge, one per generation," said Bradlee. The time had come for the next generation to take over.

Don became president and CEO. Dick Simmons's place went to Alan Spoon as chief operating officer. Ben Bradlee retired as well, and Don put Len Downie in his place. At a meeting of the American Society of Newspaper Editors in 1996, Downie said, "We subscribe to Katharine Graham's often-stated dictum that good journalism produces good profits and vice versa." Katharine's legacy lay not only in the simple act of allowing the next generation to take over but also in forging an enduring vision. She had expressed that vision, and lived it, leaving both a powerful idea and her model of how to realize it. No one doubted that her son would carry her vision forward. Veteran *Post* political reporter Paul Taylor said, "Steadiness, decency, core journalistic values of public service, balance and fairness were the coin of the realm for Katharine and for Don. It wasn't just a business, but a calling to make society better." Don had taken up the day-to-day pressures of that calling, but what would Katharine's future hold?

She had wisely engineered a gradual shift of position. "I think it helps to withdraw from the work force gradually, if you're lucky enough to be able to do so," she told an audience at the Jewish Council for Aging in 1995. "I thought I'd be one of those who would die after I retired. But I did it in stages, retire that is." She went on to explain how she had loved being publisher of the *Post* and taken that role as her identity. It was hard to give up, but when she did she kept an "umbilical cord."

Don took over as publisher in 1979. Katharine was CEO of the company until 1991, and stayed on as chairman of the board after that. Two years later, she took a smaller role as chairman of the three-person executive committee of the Post Company. As her formal role wound down, Margaret Carlson described Katharine as a "professional thinker and adviser . . . always talking about the news and getting awards or giving speeches." She also held on to her passion for protecting and supporting her journalists. In 1992, she heard that security agents in Beijing had searched the office of the *Post* correspondent in China. The reporter's personal papers had been confiscated. It was a Sunday, but Katharine strode up to the doors of the Chinese Embassy to voice her complaint. Dressed in her trademark pearls, she banged on the door until someone answered. Age hadn't diminished her righteous indignation or instinct to take action.

She had spent three decades in the top reaches of corporate life, enjoying not only the tangible privileges of power and wealth but also the intangibles: "the inside seat, the privileged conversations, the ultimate responsibility." Power had fed her curiosity, satisfied her ambition, and given her the freedom to live life as she chose.

Gaining that power, however, had created profound changes in her. Those changes started from the day she addressed the company board right after Phil's death. During that time, she did what many people find impossible: transformed crisis into challenge by taking emotional control of herself. If she had focused on the chaos within her mind and heart after the suicide, she would likely have retreated from public view. Instead, she looked outward to the context of her changed life.

Professor Mihaly Csikszentmihalyi explains that Katharine found the humility to accept the new system in which she found herself and to work within it. Her success grew from this decision. She had what Csikszentmihalyi calls "a hallmark of strong people. . . . The recognition that one's goals may have to be subordinated to a greater entity, and that to succeed one may have to play by a different set of rules from what one would prefer." She was able to do this in the months after Phil's death, setting herself on a course where she gained control over her emotional calamity.

Her early struggles with inner control continued as she became more deeply involved in her work. Her friend former secretary of state Henry Kissinger said, "She tended to look with a certain wonder at the prominence fate had brought her and to treat it as an obligation." She chose that obligation and brought to it the difficult and unremitting labor of mastering her inner life. Paradoxically, from her pain and her efforts to deal with it, Katharine had found the route to happiness.

Professor Csikszentmihalyi has spent years studying the elements that contribute to people achieving happiness, and he has found that they are directly related to the degree of control people have over their inner life. "A person who has achieved control over psychic energy and has invested it in consciously chosen goals," he writes, "cannot help but grow into a more complex being. By stretching skills, by reaching toward higher challenges, such a person becomes an increasingly extraordinary individual." Katharine's intentional efforts to form her life, her active participation in shaping her life, however faltering, were the kind of optimal experiences that Csikszentmihalyi has found lead to a "sense of mastery . . . that comes as close to what is usually meant by happiness as anything else we can conceivably imagine." Katharine had found the "flow experience" in her life by stretching her personal limits and mastering her inner resources. "To love what you do and feel that it matters—how could anything be more fun?" she told friends. She was fascinated by how her life had transformed from tragedy to joy. She decided to tell the story not only of the extraordinary people in her life, notably her parents and Phil, but also to examine her own journey.

Revelation and Reward

Katharine went about the task of writing a book with typical thoroughness and resolve, spending three years interviewing just about everyone she had known without regard to social standing. The interviews were an extraordinary feat, but Katharine understood that we know ourselves largely through the perceptions of other people. In today's business parlance, Katharine did a personal 360, questing for the fullest explanation of her life. Journalists understood her instinct. As syndicated columnist Robert Samuelson said, "She was a very determined lady. She went back and reported her life. I was skeptical about her book, but it was phenomenal."

She took her careful groundwork and began writing on yellow pads in her own hand. She wrote for seven years, suffering the agonies and accidents of every author. One of her researchers dropped a thousand pages of the typed manuscript, which scattered over the floor. She "mapped the heartache of being flawed and human and female," in the words of her friend Margaret Carlson. It was an excruciating effort.

Katharine could have hired a ghostwriter and maintained the fiction of writing the book herself, as many famous people have done. She had never, however, been given to shortcuts. She considered a cowriter, but once reassured by her editor, Robert Gottlieb, that she had a "strong, individual voice," she went ahead on her own. She rediscovered the facility with words that had sparkled in her high school and college newspapers and had impressed her first editors in New York and San Francisco and at her own *Washington Post* so many years before.

Her insecurities as a writer made her an editor's pleasure. "She was never surprised at being asked to cut, expand, rewrite," Gottlieb said, and she never took herself too seriously. She had included a long and boring section in the book on the Brandt Commission, set up in 1977 to examine issues of global development. The commission's report had mixed results, and Katharine's friend and *Post* editor Meg Greenfield wrote in the manuscript margin, "Three sentences will do for this." For Katharine, the Commission had been an important experience in broadening her international perspective, but she took Greenfield's criticism with good humor. Afterward, she told the story with delight and great laughter.

Personal History was published on February 11, 1997. Katharine was stunned by the reaction as the book rose to the best-seller list. "It really never occurred to me in my wildest dreams my book would be a best seller," she told a reporter. Her book was more than a best seller; her story touched people's hearts. "Anytime we went anywhere," her friend Ann Pincus said, "people would come up to her and say how much she had inspired them."

If anything had belonged wholly to Katharine, it was *Personal History.* That she cared about it was evident from the extensive and exhausting book tour she undertook. She used her talks to speak directly to women, to encourage them to be persistent in working toward their goals. Her honesty and introspection caught people off guard, because she had been so famously guarded. "How that pen in the hand of an honest writer went straight to the truth!" her friend Eugene Patterson wrote to her. Why bare her soul to tens of thousands of strangers? Because she was as true to this mission as any other. She, the most avid of readers, schooled in the University of Chicago's great books curriculum, knew that there were no great and false memoirs. Her friend Warren Buffett quipped, "[the book] is very honest. I know if I were writing my autobiography, I'd make myself look like Arnold Schwarzenegger." In *Personal History*, Katharine looked like Katharine, and readers were amazed and delighted.

Characteristically, although she had a right to all the glory, she never failed to thank her researcher, Ev Small, and her editor, Bob Gottlieb. According to Gottlieb, she always "wildly" exaggerated the role of those who helped her. That modesty was evident when she received the Pulitzer Prize for her book in 1998.

On the afternoon when official word was received, Katharine went down to the newsroom. The staff had gathered, and as the *Post*'s veteran reporter and editorial writer David Broder wrote, "When she came out, the applause began—and just did not stop. Without a word being said, all of us realized in the same instant that this was the time we could express our thanks to the woman who had provided us such unstinting support and such unlimited freedom to do our jobs—the greatest gift any publisher could give. As the applause went on, she began to weep, and so did we."

Katharine's autobiography was a gift to herself, as much as to anyone else. She had been the most important audience, needing to understand her life in order to move happily into its next phase. By the book's closing words, Katharine seemed as wise as the collective experiences of her life would suggest. "It's dangerous when you are older to start living in the past. Now that it's out of my system, I intend to live in the present, looking forward to the future." She was eighty years old and had created a storehouse of new enterprises, particularly philanthropic ones.

Philanthropic Leadership

It was in the late 1990s when Katharine took a van ride around Washington with Barbara Ferguson Kamara, the head of the Early Childhood Development Office for the city. Children under the age of five were a prime concern for Kamara, and she was taking Katharine to see their day-care arrangements. They went from the best to the worst, from neighborhoods of wealth to those in poverty, from centers where children wore matching outfits and new shoes to one where the director was washing the dirty clothes of a child who had nothing else to wear. The quality of care for the children varied widely, and Katharine was deeply concerned. "What can we do to improve this?" she asked. That trip led to the development of two day-care centers in southeast Washington, a part of the city described by a *Post* reporter as "slabs of apartments . . . dreary places where children struggle . . . to raise children of their own." Soon she went deeper into the problems of the neighborhood, helping single and unemployed parents to help their children to learn. "With all the wealth and all the power, she could relate to those children on Stanton Road. She was compelled by the disparity in resources," said a school superintendent who worked with her on the project.

Education became an abiding interest as it had been for her mother. She never missed the presentation of the Agnes Meyer Outstanding Teacher award. "She loved the award," said Bradlee. "The whole building came, there was food, it was a party and she would preside." Education, she told an awards audience in 1998, "is the fundamental thing that needs to be maintained and improved." Katharine became a founding member of the D.C. Committee on Public Education but looked for ways to help private efforts as well.

At Gallaudet University, a school for the deaf and hard of hearing in northeast Washington, the staff tells the story of getting a fax from Katharine giving $1 million for a new student center. Her gift was the largest by a living donor that the school had ever received. Katharine didn't want to trumpet her charity, instead asking that the school keep word of the gift on campus. "No measure can be taken of the money Mrs. Graham personally bestowed to help the city's most deprived, and there is no telling how many 'anonymous donor' placards may shield her identity," journalist Ann Gerhart wrote after Katharine's death. Journalist Bob Levey wrote that his boss "was one of the most reliable, generous donors to charity I've ever known. She never sought credit or recognition." Even in her autobiography, she gives little information about her work on behalf of her city.

In August 1981, Katharine asked Levey if he would consider using his column to raise money to send D.C. children to camp. The *Washington Star,* which had just folded, had run such a program for more than thirty years. Levey was new to the paper, but after looking into it, he agreed and got his first contribution, of the millions he would raise over the years, from Katharine.

In her later years, her personal generosity and fund-raising and strategic skills were directed at public education and day care, as well as arts organizations, museums, a shelter for teenage girls, and a senior center. She also served as a board member for a program to prevent teen pregnancy. Joyce Ladner, who chaired the D.C. Campaign to Prevent Teen Pregnancy, recalls a meeting of the board where a group of teenagers came to discuss their life in the District. Afterward, board members introduced themselves, some of them going on far too long. Without ever mentioning her name, Katharine said, "I used to be a reporter and I'm still involved in journalism." She was "gracious and self-effacing," Ladner said, and "she saw the powerful connection between teen pregnancy and poverty, school failure, and lack of opportunity." In typical fashion, Katharine was attacking problems from many angles.

She had diverse interests for her volunteer efforts. Joining with *Vogue* editor Anna Wintour and Diana, Princess of Wales, Katharine helped raise $1 million dollars at a 1996 Washington fund-raiser for breast cancer research. She also cared about politics, speaking out for giving the District of Columbia full political representation. "She stood for full equality when this was a segregated southern town," said D.C. delegate to Congress Eleanor Holmes Norton. "She stood for full democracy and congressional representation." Katharine had been serving on boards and doing charitable work since she was a homemaker in the 1940s. Part of her plan for retirement had been to keep active in "attempts to bring about a better world—to focus on societal problems or participate in solving them." Philanthropy helped fulfill her sense of curiosity, her love of learning, and her desire to give back to the world as her time in it grew shorter. She had given a great deal of thought to aging, and she began to talk publicly about it.

By the 1980s, Katharine was giving as many as twenty speeches a year. She had gone for speech coaching, and her style had become more relaxed and genuine. In a delightful speech on aging in 1985 she told of a trip to Switzerland with her friend Polly Fritchey to take their sons skiing. As the two women hiked over the fresh snow of a small glacier she said to Polly, "I've been thinking about how to grow old gracefully. I've been studying Averell Harriman and Alice Long-worth, who've done it beautifully, and I think I know the answer . . . you have to read a lot and not drink." Polly walked along quietly for a few moments then asked, "When do we have to start?" Katharine had already started, and a major part of her plan was her philanthropic work. In the city she loved she was creating a leadership legacy beyond the company she had grown, a legacy of support and generosity.

"The Perfect Ways of Honour"

Katharine was used to entertaining presidents. After having the Reagans to her house upon their arrival in Washington, she had formed a close friendship with Nancy Reagan. She had been host to Bill and Hillary Clinton, George and Barbara Bush, and on an evening in February 2001, she welcomed nearly one hundred guests to introduce George W. and Laura Bush to Washington's inner circle. When she entertained, she liked to say that she was "turning out the town," and she didn't hold back for President Bush's first Washington dinner. Her billionaire friends came: Warren Buffett, Microsoft founder Bill Gates, AOL's Steve Case, along with the biggest stars of the media and political world past and present. Federal Reserve Board Chairman Alan Greenspan, Henry Kissinger, and Ethel Kennedy joined press stars, including Judy Woodruff, Al Hunt, George Will, and Margaret Carlson. The stage and film director Mike Nichols marveled at Katharine's "gift of personalness," saying she managed to introduce every guest to the new president and his wife.

After the success of her book, Katharine seemed to gain confidence and become more relaxed. Her friend and colleague Sally Quinn said that she "really began to revel in her achievements and the fact that she was so revered." She loved spending time with friends, cooking in their kitchens and trading the latest news or gossip. She had a regular bridge game at the Chevy Chase Women's Club and regular tennis partners on Saturdays. "She was so much *fun*," her friend Ann Pincus remembers. Her friends were used to her "salty" tongue and candid assessments of self-important Washingtonians. She could also be solicitous to the mundane and unsparingly honest in sizing up other people.

One night as she shared a Chinese dinner with friends at the Confucius Café, Robert McNamara came into the restaurant. There were rumors of Katharine's romantic interest in the former defense secretary. But she didn't hold back as she told her dinner companions that McNamara had been too cheap to buy new sheets for his Martha's Vineyard home in the twenty years since his wife died. When Katharine heard the Clintons were coming to visit him on the island, she bought new sheets and gave them to McNamara for his guest room. Margaret Carlson said, "She saw right through McNamara . . . she was an ironic, funny, and snappish old woman."

If Katharine felt her age, she tried not to show it, resenting the way that younger people often treated the elderly. She might look old and suffer from aches and worn-out hips, but her mind and spirit were vital. She agonized over joining her friends who had had face-lifts. Sally Quinn remembers that on the beach in Hawaii a discussion about the issue got so intense the women didn't notice Katharine's purse being stolen. Katharine never had the surgery, instead accepting the fine lines of laughter and concern just as she accepted moving toward the end of her life. She had never been self-conscious about her looks, wearing little makeup or jewelry, yet always looking stylish. She liked de la Renta outfits, buying two or three each year, and then Armani pantsuits after Anna Wintour encouraged her toward the look. Her style of elegant simplicity, evident in her earliest pictures, had altered no more than her values. Her friend Eugene Patterson believed she had changed little from the young woman described in her book: "a conservative capitalist" who believed you had to take care of people. For almost forty years, the company had been her touchstone, and so, after the book's publication in 1997 and her extensive book tour, Katharine came back to the office. She said, "I loved my job, I loved the paper, I loved the whole company." She had reason to be proud and happy, as even her critics admitted.

Morton Mintz came to the paper in December 1958. Active in the Newspaper Guild, he became an internal muckraker, taking higher-ups to task for their treatment of workers and what the union saw as overcompensation of executives. But Mintz was quick to say that where other owners had "acquired," newspapers, Katharine had "built" a newspaper. When Mintz started his job there was one "World" editor to cover all national and foreign coverage. The only foreign correspondent was in London, and the "State" editor handled all Maryland and Virginia news. "Under [Katharine] there was an explosion of staff," Mintz recalled. "A huge national desk, a huge foreign desk, and not all of it paid in dollar terms—how much advertising does a paper get for coverage of Africa? . . . [I]t was gutsy journalism." From a business standpoint, Katharine could have been much more cautious. The *Post* had a monopoly on the afternoon newsstands. Her willingness to spend money grew directly from her conviction that she had a responsibility as an owner to produce an excellent paper.

Mintz also admired Katharine for being the kind of publisher that did not order Bradlee to "get rid of him" for his rabble-rousing activity. He fully expected to be relegated to the worst beats for his complaints about management. Instead, he was allowed to follow groundbreaking stories like the terrible effects of the drug thalidomide on pregnant women and the antitrust suit against IBM. Katharine called Mintz "the thorn in all our sides" and fought what she perceived as efforts to interfere with her right to manage, but she protected the independence of the newsroom above all.

On the management side she had become a recognized powerhouse. *Fortune* magazine had chosen her for its Business Hall of Fame, and the Post Company had been recognized by *Business Month* magazine as one of the five best-managed companies in America. Her status placed her firmly among the elite group of media leaders who gathered every year in Sun Valley, Idaho. Organized by investment banker Herbert Allen, the invitation-only meeting in July 2001 was set to include power players from media, technology, and entertainment companies from coast to coast. It was a "summer camp for Citizen Kanes," and a place where Katharine was a recognized star.

In 2001, the company she built included not only the *Washington Post* newspaper and the national weekly newsmagazine *Newsweek* but also the *Herald* newspaper in Everett, Washington; six television stations around the country; nineteen cable stations; the test preparation and education company Kaplan, Inc.; an electronic information company that included washingtonpost.com on the Internet; a business periodical publisher; the Gazette Newspapers that published in suburban Maryland; the Robinson Terminal Warehouse Co.; and interests in Bowater Mersey Paper Co.; the *International Herald Tribune* newspaper; and the *Los Angeles Times–Washington Post* News Service. In Sun Valley, Katharine would be among friends and peers.

She played bridge with Warren Buffett and Bill Gates on Friday evening. Two generations her junior, Gates always found Katharine warm and open. She could tell a great story, and he enjoyed hearing about her exploits with presidents and publishers. The next day she had lunch with actor Tom Hanks and his wife, actress Rita Wilson. She still walked haltingly, the result of hip surgeries and age. So it happened that later in the day she fell to the ground without warning, hitting her head on the sidewalk and passing out. Her son Don was already at the conference, but much of the family flew to Idaho to be at her side. Three days later, having never regained consciousness, Katharine died just before midnight at St. Alphonsus Regional Medical Center in Boise.

Death had come in the manner Katharine had wished, although her vitality at age eighty-four suggested it had come much too soon. Six years earlier, she had ended a speech with a humorous and poignant story about dying. She told of her ninety-year-old friend Mary Bingham, who had been honored at a civic dinner with much effusive praise. When Mary got up to speak she said that the evening had been so wonderful, she wanted to be taken away on a little pink cloud. She then went into a rousing speech and when she reached the last page, died on the spot. "Very few of us will be that lucky," Katharine told her audience. "I'm on the last page of my speech and I'm still here," she joked. Not many years later, however, she did die quickly, and as she had hoped, "painlessly, with grace, style, and dignity."

At eleven in the morning on Monday, July 23, 2001, Katharine's funeral service was held within the great gothic walls of Washington National Cathedral. The funeral program had a photo of Katharine in the prime of life, wearing her trademark pearls and laughing with the uproarious joy her friends knew so well. Under the photo was the phrase her classmates at the Madeira School had ascribed to her in 1934: "Those about her from her shall read the perfect ways of honour." Their prescient words foreshadowed a life lived with conviction, and nearly four thousand mourners overflowed the cathedral to honor her for it.

World famous cellist Yo-Yo Ma performed "Sarabande" from Bach's *6th Cello Suite* before former senator and Episcopal minister John C. Danforth delivered the homily in his sonorous voice. Katharine's friends and colleagues, including much of the permanent establishment of Washington, joined those who came not because they knew her personally but because of their admiration for her.

Former defense secretary Robert McNamara was a pallbearer along with lawyer Vernon Jordan and with Katharine's brother-in-law, Senator Bob Graham of Florida. Buffett, Gates, Mike Nichols, financier Herbert Allen, and journalists Barbara Walters, Jim Lehrer, Diane Sawyer, and Bob Woodward were among the ushers. Former president Bill Clinton and his wife, Senator Hillary Clinton, sat in the pews along with Federal Reserve Chairman Alan Greenspan, Supreme Court Justices Ruth Bader Ginsburg and Stephen Breyer, U.N. Secretary-General Kofi Annan, and New York Mayor Rudolph Giuliani. Senators arrived in a busload, as did hundreds of workers from the Post Company.

In his eulogy, Ben Bradlee brought the crowd to laughter as he told the story of the paper's decision to publish an article about a U.S. spying operation. President Reagan was so concerned that he called

Katharine at home. She was in the shower when her maid told her Reagan was on the telephone. "My all-time favorite image of the most powerful woman in the world ensued," Bradlee told the mourners. "Kay comes flying out of the shower soaking wet, grabs a towel and starts looking for a pencil and some paper . . . Brenda Starr, girl reporter, is at the scene and ready to go." Throughout her life, Katharine kept the heart of a journalist, but she developed the head of a businesswoman. The combination made her one of the greatest publishers of the last two centuries. "No other news executive displayed greater courage and independence in the face of unremitting pressure from the highest governmental offices, none was more willing to risk losing her entire enterprise because she believed she was acting to fulfill the highest principles of a free press," said journalist Haynes Johnson after her death.

Every verse of "America the Beautiful" echoed through the cathedral as the casket was carried down the aisle. In a private ceremony, Katharine was buried next to her husband in Oak Hill Cemetery. Across the street, her friends gathered for a final party at her house, the kind of get-together she loved. They talked of her restless and unlikely journey to leadership, as she lay buried at the site where her greatest transformation began. Daughter, reporter, wife, mother, friend, publisher, CEO, patriot—and leader. Katharine lives on as an icon representing achievement against the odds, the strength and determination of women, and the idea that a vigorous and free press is essential to our democracy.

ACKNOWLEDGMENTS

Thanks first to Adrian Zackheim, my publisher, and a great admirer of Katharine Graham. He suggested this book and put his faith in me to write it. Thanks also to his team: my able editor Stephanie Land, assistant Sarah Mollo-Christensen, the marketing team of Will Weisser and Jennifer Pare, and the Portfolio copyediting staff for their careful reading of the manuscript.

I'm grateful to the interviewees who gave so generously of their time and memories. Thanks also to librarians Peggy Appleman at the Martin Luther King Library and Martha Andrews and Rebecca Brooks at the Madeira School. Sarah Priestman and Audrey Carter Bredhoff gave wise editorial help, and my sister, Dee Francken, spent many of her precious hours on an early reading of the manuscript. As always, my brother Steve Gerber was unfailingly enthusiastic. Peggy Engel, Marilyn Hannigan, Ilana Bar-Din Giannini, and Laura Liswood gave time and attention to my project beyond what they had to spare. I had wonderful young assistants: Anna Rosengarten, Elicia Nademin, and Ray Blackford. As always, many friends gave me their support in various ways: Pamela Toutant, Robin Gradison, Anne Maher, Cindy Hallberlin, Stefanie Weiss, Marylu Jordan, Lisa Stevenson, Amy Walker, Nance Lucas, Ann Gerhart, Carol Beach,

Lisa and Michael Dobbs, Lynn Petty, Nancy Hadad, Peter Range, Jim Reston, Denise Leary, Jonathon Weisgal, Marie Wilson, Mark Friedman, and Ruthie Beckwith. My thanks as well to the many women I have met as I have traveled the country speaking about women's leadership. Their enthusiasm for more stories about women leaders and their excitement about a leadership book on Katharine Graham inspired me.

I am blessed to have a family loving enough to put up with an author in the house and smart enough to turn to for help. My daughter, Ariel Rubin, gave me wonderful advice on structure and scene-setting. My son, Sam Records, reminded me to keep my expectations and production high. No writer could ask for more than the faith and love given to me by my husband, Tony Records.

NOTES

INTRODUCTION: TWICE-BORN

xiii **"I'd led what I thought of"**: Katharine Graham, transcript, *The Newshour with Jim Lehrer*, PBS, April 14, 1998.

xiv **"I love her"**: Author interview with June Bingham, June 2004.

xv **"Only John Kennedy"**: Arthur Schlesinger Jr., "In Vindicating Herself, She Became a Quiet Revolutionary," *Newsweek*, July 17, 2001.

xvi **Katharine felt "paralyzed"**: Chalmers Roberts, *In The Shadow of Power* (Cabin John, MD: Seven Locks Press, 1989), 365.

xvi **Other publishers told her**: Author interview with Haynes Johnson, December 2004.

xvi **She saw them as "vultures"**: Judith Viorst, "Katharine Graham," *Washingtonian,* September 1967, 33.

xvi **She sat down and straightened**: Osborne Elliott, *The World of Oz* (New York: Viking Press, 1980), 25.

xvii **"There is another generation"**: David Halberstam, *The Powers That Be,* (New York: Knopf, 1979), 722.

xvii **As historian Michael Beschloss**: Meg Greenfield, *Washington* (New York: Public Affairs, 2001), 232.

xvii **As her friend June Bingham**: Author interview with June Bingham, June 2004.

xvii **According to psychologist**: William James, *The Varieties of Religious Experience* (London: Penguin, 2003), 170.

xviii **James believed**: Ibid., 206.

xviii He "experienced his moment of truth": James MacGregor Burns, *Leadership* (New York: Harper & Row, 1978), 107.

xviii "I decided": M. K. Gandhi, *An Autobiography: Or the Story of My Experiments with Truth,* trans. Mahader Desai (Boston: Beacon Press, 1993), 112.

CHAPTER ONE: THE AMBIGUOUS ROOTS
OF LEADERSHIP

2 He had conquered the world: Merlo Pusey, *The Three Careers of Eugene Meyer* (New York: Knopf, 1975).

4 When educated women: William O'Neill, *Everyone Was Brave* (New York: Quadrangle, 1969), 84–90.

4 For Agnes, Katharine wrote: Katharine Graham, "Reflections on an Art Lover," *Washington Post,* May 9, 1993.

5 "She provided a great nurse": Ibid.

5 He wrote that the government: Eugene Meyer, "The Importance of Being Earnest in Saving," *Current Opinion,* January 1921.

6 *Business Week* magazine wrote: *Business Week,* July 1, 1931, 27.

6 "Nobody knew him": Tom Kelly, "The Imperial Post," *Washingtonian,* May 1981, 207.

7 "I'm a 'conscientious'": Katharine Graham, *Personal History* (New York: Knopf, 1997), 21.

7 Katharine shared the assessment: Chalmers Roberts, *The Washington Post* (Boston: Houghton Mifflin, 1977), 366.

8 If, as *Time* magazine reported: *Time,* May 3, 1943, 39.

8 She wrote in her memoir: Agnes Meyer, *Out of These Roots* (New York: Little Brown, 1953).

8 Agnes valued "brilliant eccentrics": Katharine Graham, *Personal History* (New York: Knopf, 1997), 51.

8 After Katharine told her mother: Diane K. Shah, "Pillar of the Post," *National Observer,* March 16, 1976.

8 Agnes said that she and Eugene taught the children: Judith Viorst, "Katharine Graham," *Washingtonian,* September 1967, 34.

8 "In proportion to our lack of experience": Chalmers Roberts, *The Washington Post* (Boston: Houghton Mifflin, 1977), 366.

9 "Katharine had hobnobbed": Author interview with June Bingham, June 2004.

9 Later she told Katharine: Susanna McBee, "Katharine Graham and How She Grew," *McCall's,* September 1971.

10   Agnes quickly interjected: David Remnick, "Citizen Kay," *The New Yorker,* January 20, 1997.

11   "It is a place of rare beauty": *Madeira Alumnae Bulletin,* no. 12 (December 1929).

12   "[T]he pivot of civilization": *Madeira Alumnae Bulletin,* no. 7 (June 1927).

12   Katharine managed As in history: Interview with Martha Andrews, archivist, Madeira School, March 17, 2004.

13   To become independent people: *The Tatler* 28, no. 2 (February 1933), 47.

14   In her end-of-the-school-year report : *The Tatler* 27, no. 4 (June 1934), 13.

15   The graduating class made a prophesy: Madeira School yearbook, 1934.

15   Katharine later said, "Subliminally": *Madeira Today,* Winter 2000, 12.

15   Her writing had snapped with wit: Katharine Graham, *Personal History* (New York: Knopf, 1997), 46.

15   Foreshadowing the self-flagellation: Chalmers Roberts, *The Washington Post* (Boston: Houghton Mifflin, 1977), 365.

15   "Pa started with nothing": Susanna McBee, "Katharine Graham and How She Grew," *McCall's,* September 1971, 78.

15   The fifty-seven-year-old banker: Lisa Gunther and Dina Witter, case study, Harvard Business School, HBS Case 9-801-276, 2001.

16   When a three-star general: "Rise of the *Washington Post,*" *Fortune,* December 1944, 138.

16   Mary Haworth was adviser to the lovelorn: Ibid., 132–39.

16   "The 'human interest'": Katharine Graham, *Personal History* (New York: Knopf, 1997), 69.

17   Her copy, according to another student writer: Elizabeth Pope Frank, "Vassar's Most Powerful Alumna," *Vassar Quarterly* 74, no. 3 (Spring 1978): 6.

17   Her peers found her diffident: Ibid.

17   "It looks quite professional": Katharine Graham, *Personal History* (New York: Knopf, 1997), 74.

18   She took seminars: Laura Bergquist, "Kay Meyer Goes to College," *Ms.,* October 1974, 53.

18   According to a friend: Ibid.

18   Katharine's intensity: Chalmers Roberts, *The Washington Post* (Boston: Houghton Mifflin, 1977), 367.

18   Even drinking bouts: Laura Bergquist, "Kay Meyer Goes to College," *Ms.*, October 1974, 53.

19   "She'll have a lifetime": Ibid.

19   "It is much better sport": Katharine Graham, *Personal History* (New York: Knopf, 1997), 86.

20   She knew that her father: Nicholas Coleridge, *Paper Tigers* (London: Heineman, 1993), 80.

20   "Soon she was our chief outside reporter": Chalmers Roberts, *The Washington Post* (Boston: Houghton Mifflin, 1977), 367.

21   According to a friend: Judith Viorst, "Katharine Graham," *Washingtonian*, September 1967, 35.

22   "If it doesn't work": *Time*, April 24, 1939.

22   Of Lou Gehrig: *Washington Post*, June 23, 1939.

22   Despite her job: Chalmers Roberts, *The Washington Post* (Boston: Houghton Mifflin, 1977), 368.

23   Of San Francisco, Katharine wrote: Katharine Graham, *Personal History* (New York: Knopf, 1997), 102.

23   She would spend the next twenty-three years: David Halberstam, *The Powers That Be* (New York: Dell, 1979), 718.

CHAPTER TWO: PHIL GRAHAM'S WIFE

25   "Victorian values were very dominant": Author interview with June Bingham, June 2004.

25   For Katharine, and so many women of her time: As psychiatrist Anna Fels writes, "A relationship to a man represented the safest source of social approval, necessitating that a woman's personal ambition be subordinated to that of her husband. It was a realistic, if costly, strategy." See Anna Fels, *Necessary Dreams* (New York: Pantheon, 2004).

26   And so, on June 5, 1940: Ibid., 115: "ambitions by proxy."

27   Friends said he helped her: Judith Viorst, "Katharine Graham," *Washingtonian*, September 1967, 82.

28   By the May due date: Katharine Graham, *Personal History* (New York: Knopf, 1997), 137.

29   She had "suggested": Ibid., 138.

29   Her friend June Bingham: Author interview with June Bingham, June 2004.

29   To her, Phil stood: Susanna McBee, "Katharine Graham and How She Grew," *McCall's*, September 1971, 132.

29   **She remembered their early married years:** Katharine Graham, *Personal History* (New York: Knopf, 1997), 140.

30   **She stayed there:** Ibid., 150.

30   **As Katharine put it:** Ibid., 152.

31   **"Phil was very difficult":** Polly Fritchey, "She Moved to an Inner Life," *Newsweek*, July 30, 2001.

31   **From her autobiography it's clear:** Katharine Graham, *Personal History* (New York: Knopf, 1997), 155.

31   **But Bingham recalls:** Author interview with June Bingham, June 2004.

33   **Her pleasure was to:** Jane Howard, "Katharine Graham: The Power That Didn't Corrupt," *Ms.*, October 1974, 47.

33   **She found the inner fortitude:** Ibid., 50.

34   **"Our boys and their friends":** Susan Mary Alsop, "Katharine Graham's Capital Life," *Architectural Digest*, December 1994, 129.

36   **She had clearly educated herself:** Mary Thomas, *Post-War Mothers: Childbirth Letter to Grantly Dick-Read, 1946–56* (Rochester, NY: University of Rochester Press, 1997), 8.

36   **She probably read Dick-Read's book:** Grantly Dick-Read, *Childbirth Without Fear* (New York: Harper & Brothers, 1944), 6.

37   **Evangeline Bruce, a close friend:** David Heymann, *The Georgetown Ladies' Social Club* (New York: Atria Books, 2003), 13.

37   **To her, life "seemed so unglamorous":** Katharine Graham, *Personal History* (New York: Knopf, 1997), 210–11.

38   **Years later she said of this period:** Katharine Graham, transcript, *Larry King Live*, CNN, February 14, 1997.

38   **Similarly, the car manufacturer Volvo:** Margaret Heffernan, "New Order," *Real Business*, February 2003.

38   **Only recently has research begun to prove:** Mariann N. Ruderman, Patricia J. Ohlott, Kate Panzer, Sara N. King, "Benefits of Multiple Roles for Managerial Women," *Academy of Management Journal* 45, no. 2 (2002): 369–86.

38   **For Katharine, this would become apparent:** A study by Wellesley College Center for Women showed that female managers compare their leadership to mothering. Some of the sixty women questioned saw power in their ability to lead warmly, to focus on the positive, and to take care of their subordinates. The women in the study also said they learned leadership from their time at home. Building family loyalty and cooperation, for example, translated to team building. Spending hours with small children developed patience. The mothers had to learn to listen, react wisely, and

observe closely. Sumru Erkut, "Inside Women's Power," Center for Research on Women, Wellesley College, CRW Special Report No. 28, 2001.

38 **If Katharine seemed removed and moody:** Author interview with June Bingham, June 2004.

39 **Somehow Katharine heard:** Author interview with Mary Beckner, March 2004.

39 **Katharine only received:** Chalmers Roberts, *The Washington Post* (Boston: Houghton Mifflin, 1977), 258.

39 **Years later, Katharine's friend Gloria Steinem:** Author interview with Gloria Steinem, January 2005.

40 **He had become:** David Halberstam, *The Powers That Be* (New York: Knopf, 1979), 224.

41 **"With this wild and restless brilliance":** Chalmers Roberts, *The Washington Post* (Boston: Houghton Mifflin, 1977), 361.

41 **He "flooded" the Post":** Ibid., 262–64.

42 **Katharine's friend Evangeline Bruce:** David Heymann, *The Georgetown Ladies' Social Club* (New York: Atria Books, 2003), 13.

42 **A day or two later:** Ibid., 63.

42 **Like many victims:** Katharine Graham, *Personal History* (New York: Knopf, 1997), 213.

42 **"What was not said in those days":** Author interview with June Bingham, June 2004.

42 **He called her "Porky":** Katharine Graham, *Personal History* (New York: Knopf, 1997), 231.

43 **He called her a "Jewish cow":** Carol Felsenthal, *Power, Privilege and the Post* (New York: Seven Stories Press, 1993), 156.

43 **Meanwhile, Phil played the part:** Ibid., 157.

44 **As Katharine wrote:** Katharine Graham, *Personal History* (New York: Knopf, 1997), 306.

45 **"Whatever strength I had":** Harry Jaffe, Capital Comment, *Washingtonian*, February 1997, 7.

46 **Nine years after Phil's death:** Author interview with Haynes Johnson, December 2004.

CHAPTER THREE: THE VAGABOND QUEEN

50 **As Bill George:** Bill George, *Authentic Leadership: Rediscovering the Secrets to Creating Lasting Value* (San Francisco: Jossey-Bass, Inc., 2003).

50 Margaret Heffernan, who has studied : Margaret Heffernan, "New Order," *Real Business,* February 2003.

51 Her father "brought her up": Author interview with June Bingham, June 2004.

51 A new leader's early actions: Michael Watkins, *The First 90 Days: Critical Success Strategies for New Leaders at all Levels* (Boston: Harvard Business School Press, 2003), 5.

51 According to Ben Bradlee: Ben Bradlee, *A Good Life* (New York: Simon & Schuster, 1995), 253.

51 Even her longtime friend: Katharine Graham, *Personal History* (New York: Knopf, 1997), 339.

51 She told friends: Carol Felsenthal, *Power, Privilege and the* Post (New York: Seven Stories Press, 1993), 227.

51 They called her early days: Judith Viorst, " Katharine Graham," *Washingtonian,* 1967, 33.

51 Later she could admit: Nicholas Coleridge, *Paper Tigers* (London: William Heineman, 1993), 81.

52 Katharine had good cause: See Dr. Pauline Rose Clance, *The Imposter Phenomenon* (Atlanta: Peachtree Publishers Ltd., 1985).

52 "And so, while she was demanding": Katharine Graham, transcript, *Larry King Live,* CNN, February 14, 1997.

52 "I thought I was this peasant": Susanna McBee, "Katharine Graham and How She Grew," *McCall's,* September 1971, 130.

52 Early on, Katharine realized: Katharine Graham, *Personal History* (New York: Knopf, 1997), 341.

53 She found Phil's illness: Ibid., 356.

53 "It was tremendously important": Mary Walton, *Washingtonian,* July 2002, 48.

53 "Her working on the paper": Ibid., 48.

54 She felt she had absorbed: Katharine Graham, *Personal History* (New York: Knopf, 1997), 340.

54 "I literally did not know how": Katharine Graham, interview with Judy Woodruff, transcript, "The Editor as Leader—Part 2," American Society of Newspaper Editors, Reston, VA, December 31, 1998.

55 Her realization that she had to lead: Author interview with June Bingham, June 2004.

55 The author and journalist David Halberstam: David Halberstam, *The Powers That Be* (New York: Knopf, 1979), 719.

56   "He was so decent, so wise": Howard Bray, *The Pillars of the* Post (New York: Norton, 1980), 63.

56   Katharine pushed back: Katharine Graham, *Personal History* (New York: Knopf, 1997), 341.

56   Later research would show: Virginia Valian, *Why So Slow?* (Boston: MIT Press, 1998), 127.

57   Katharine called it: Katharine Graham, *Personal History* (New York: Knopf, 1997), 342.

57   She said she was "congealed": Chalmers Roberts, *The Washington Post* (Boston: Houghton Mifflin, 1977), 370.

57   "If you give [people] the truth": Howard Bray, *The Pillars of the* Post, (New York: Norton, 1980), 7.

57   Less than a year after taking over: Pat Munroe and Caryl Rivers, "Kay Graham Talks About Her Job at the Helm of the *Washington Post*," *Editor & Publisher*, May 2, 1964.

59   "She read people very well": Author interview with Eugene Patterson, January 2005.

59   One female CEO: Judy B. Rosener, "Ways Women Lead," *Harvard Business Review*, Nov.–Dec. 1990.

59   She wrote, "When I had to decide something": Katharine Graham, *Personal History* (New York: Knopf, 1997), 346–47.

60   "I was paralyzed with fear at first": Susanna McBee, "Katharine Graham and How She Grew," *McCall's*, September 1971, 130.

63   Asked in an early interview: "A Tradition—A Legacy," *Newsweek*, August 19, 1963, 31.

63   Suddenly thrust into a role: Katharine Graham, *Personal History* (New York: Knopf, 1997), 354.

CHAPTER FOUR: "POWER HAS NO SEX"

65   "There were men everywhere": David Halberstam, *The Powers That Be* (New York: Knopf, 1979), 722.

65   "I think that I would go back": Louis B. Barnes, interview with Donald Graham, September 16, 1997, *HBS Case 9-498-031* (Boston: Harvard Business School Publishing, 1997), 9.

66   Looking back, she wrote: Katharine Graham, *Personal History* (New York: Knopf, 1997), 356.

67 **When he instructed her:** Tape K6312.01, PNO 19, Recordings of Telephone Conversations—JFK Series, December 2, 1963, Recordings and Transcripts of Conversations and Meetings, Lyndon Baines Johnson Library, Austin, Texas.

68 **She sent him a letter:** Katharine Graham, *Personal History* (New York: Knopf, 1997), 359–60.

68 **David Halberstam wrote:** David Halberstam, *The Powers That Be* (New York: Knopf, 1979), 724.

69 **"Oh, shut up, er . . .":** Katharine Graham, *Personal History* (New York: Knopf, 1997), 365.

69 **The women that remained:** Chalmers Roberts, *The Washington Post* (Boston: Houghton Mifflin, 1977), 345.

69 **The company had only male managers:** Katharine Graham, *Personal History* (New York: Knopf, 1997), 417.

70 **As Bass describes:** Bernard M. Bass, "Concepts of Leadership: The Beginnings," in *The Leader's Companion: Insights on Leadership Through the Ages,* ed. J. Thomas Wren (New York: The Free Press, 1995), 49.

70 **women who wanted to lead:** Crystal Hoy, "Women Leaders: The Role of Stereotype Activation and Leadership Self-efficacy," Kravis Leadership Institute *Leadership Review,* Fall 2002; see also Eagly & Johannesen-Schmidt, "The Leadership Styles of Women and Men," *Journal of Social Issues* 57 (2001).

70 **"Be thin, be smart, be gay":** Marya Mannes, *Time,* 1963.

71 **She told** *Editor & Publisher:* Pat Munroe and Caryl Rivers, "Kay Graham Talks About Her Job at the Helm of the *Washington Post,*" *Editor & Publisher,* May 2, 1964.

71 **In explaining her failure:** Carol Felsenthal, *Power, Privilege and the* Post (New York: Seven Stories Press, 1993), 287.

71 **"I was brought up in an era":** Katharine Graham, *Larry King Live,* CNN, February 14, 1997.

71 **Her mother's comment:** Author interview with Eugene Patterson, January 2005.

71 **Frank Waldrop, former editor:** Carol Felsenthal, *Power, Privilege and the* Post (New York: Seven Stories Press, 1993), 230.

72 **At** *Newsweek,* **management continued:** Osborn Elliott, *The World of Oz* (New York: Viking, 1980), 135.

72 **"That would be quite impossible":** Lynn Rosellini, "The Katharine Graham Story," *Washington Star,* November 13, 1978.

72   **"These men seemed to know"**: David Halberstam, *The Powers That Be* (New York: Knopf, 1979), 722.

73   **This weakened her sense of "self-efficacy"**: Albert Bandura, *Self-efficacy: The Exercise of Control* (New York: W. H. Freeman, 1997). See also Crystal Hoyt, "Women Leaders: The Role of Stereotype Activation and Leadership Self-efficacy," *Leadership Review* (Fall 2002).

73   **On one level:** Katharine Graham, *Personal History* (New York: Knopf, 1997), 420.

75   **"We had no funding"**: Author interview with Gloria Steinem, January 2005.

75   **Years later, Katharine told an interviewer:** Katharine Graham on National Public Radio, "Diane Rehm Show," 1997.

76   **She was featured in eleven articles:** Mary Rinkoski, "Magazine Coverage of Katharine Meyer Graham, 1963–1975" (AEJMC conference paper, Miami, Florida, September 2002).

76   **In the *Vogue* article:** Arthur Schlesinger Jr., "Katharine Graham, New Power in the American Press," *Vogue,* Jan. 1, 1967, 152.

76   **In December 1968:** Martin Mayer, "The Lady as Publisher," *Harper's Monthly,* December 1968, 90–100.

78   **In their letter, the women:** Osborn Elliott, *The World of Oz* (New York: Viking, 1980), 146.

78   **Determined and organized:** Ibid., 146.

78   **To one reader who questioned the situation:** Ibid., 147.

78   **Steinem said that Katharine saw:** Author interview with Gloria Steinem, January 2005.

79   **"Gradually I came to realize"**: Katharine Graham, *Personal History* (New York: Knopf, 1997), 371.

81   **As *Post* reporter Sally Quinn put it:** Author interview with Sally Quinn, February 2004.

81   **"If a country club excluded you"**: Author interview with Sally Quinn, February 2004.

82   **"I felt like a surrogate Kay"**: Author interview with Gloria Steinem, January 2005.

83   **With Katharine's support, limited flextime:** Author interview with Peggy Engel, October 2004.

83   **"I introduced Barbara to Kay"**: Author interview with Jack Valenti, January 2005.

83   **"Christ . . . nobody says a thing"**: Lynn Rosellini, "The Katharine Graham Story," *Washington Star,* November 13, 1978.

83   "Women exercise power to": Author interview with Gloria Steinem, January 2005.

CHAPTER FIVE: CLAIMING HER COMPANY

85   "He and I both assumed": Katharine Graham, transcript, *Larry King Live*, CNN, February 14, 1997.

85   "You haven't enough money": Judith Viorst, "Katharine Graham," *Washingtonian*, September 1967, 34.

86   She realized that some employees: Katharine Graham, *Personal History* (New York: Knopf, 1997), 346.

86   "It's not that [these] leaders": Jim Collins, *Good to Great: Why Some Companies Make the Leap and Others Don't* (New York: HarperCollins, 2001), 21.

86   "It was like taking the cork": Judith Viorst, "Katharine Graham," *Washingtonian*, September 1967, 83.

87   "In the city room at night": Ben Bradlee, *A Good Life*, Simon & Schuster, New York, (1995) 283.

88   Richard Clurman of *Time:* Carol Felsenthal, *Power, Privilege and the Post* (New York: Seven Stories Press, 1993), 246.

88   Walter Lippmann, who had been advising her: David Halberstam, *The Powers That Be* (New York: Knopf, 1979), 723.

89   She observed a "great deal": Katharine Graham, *Personal History* (New York: Knopf, 1997), 379.

89   In Phil's time, one journalist described: Judith Viorst, "Katharine Graham," *Washingtonian*, September 1967, 85.

90   newsroom was in "a defensive crouch": Author interview with Ben Bradlee, February 2004.

91   Katharine had heard that Bradlee: David Halberstam, *The Powers That Be* (New York: Knopf, 1979), 725.

92   Bradlee said, "It was ballsy ": Author interview with Ben Bradlee, February 2004.

92   "We had supported Tobriner's appointment": Tom Kelly, "The Imperial Post," *Washingtonian*, May 1981, 209.

93   She returned feeling that she had "more energy": Katharine Graham, *Personal History* (New York: Knopf, 1997), 377.

93   Bradlee thought the lunch started off: Ben Bradlee, *A Good Life* (New York: Simon & Schuster, 1995), 274.

94   "I turned her on by seeing": Author interview with Ben Bradlee, February 2004.

95   **In her autobiography, Katharine admits:** Katharine Graham, *Personal History* (New York: Knopf, 1997), 383.

95   **"As much as I loved Al":** Larry Van Dyne, "The Bottom Line on Katharine Graham," *Washingtonian*, December 1985, 185.

96   **The change was "her first act":** David Halberstam, *The Powers That Be* (New York: Knopf, 1979), 732.

96   **The move was based on "a shrewd judgment:** Chalmers Roberts, *The Washington Post* (Boston: Houghton Mifflin, 1977), 378.

97   **"She made the right ones when the time came":** Author interview with Robert Samuelson, October 2004.

97   **In an admission of his culpability:** Katharine Graham, *Personal History* (New York: Knopf, 1997), 383.

97   **She had said that she hired Bradlee:** Chalmers Roberts, *The Washington Post* (Boston: Houghton Mifflin, 1977), 379.

97   **Before hiring Bradlee:** Katharine Graham, *Personal History* (New York: Knopf, 1997), 386.

98   **Her father had taught her "that":** Katharine Graham interview with Judy Woodruff, "The Editor as Leader—Part 2," American Society of Newspaper Editors, December 31, 1998.

98   **Two years after hiring him:** Judith Viorst, "Katharine Graham," *Washingtonian*, September 1967, 86.

98   **Bradlee said that "what makes":** Author interview with Ben Bradlee, February 2004.

98   **Politicians or important international visitors:** Author interview with Ben Bradlee, February 2004.

99   **"You'd be summoned to a lunch":** Author interview with Peggy Engel, October 2004.

99   **She was showing:** Warren E. Buffett, "Kay Graham's Management Career," http://www.washpostco.com/history-kgraham.htm (2005).

100   **"One of the things I learned":** Katharine Graham, interview with Judy Woodruff, transcript, "The Editor as Leader—Part 2," American Society of Newspaper Editors, Reston, VA, December 31, 1998.

100   **"His own dedication to quality editorial":** Ibid.

CHAPTER SIX: A DESIRE TO PLEASE

103   **"The idea that you might have to make a decision":** Louis B. Barnes, "The Graham Family and the Washington Post Company," Harvard Business School, HBS Case 9-498-031, rev. ed. (July 1, 1998).

104   Leadership "is grounded in the seedbed": James MacGregor Burns, *Leadership* (New York: Harper & Row, 1978), 38.

104   "I quickly learned that things": Mary Rowland, "Mastermind of a Media Empire," *Working Woman,* November 11, 1989, 115.

105   "He would rather suppress": Judith Viorst, "Katharine Graham," *Washingtonian,* September 1967, 85.

105   Bradlee said he "covered it": Tom Kelly, "The Imperial Post," *Washingtonian,* May 1981, 139.

106   Comparing the *Post* to its in-town competitor: Ben Bagdikian, "What Makes a Newspaper Nearly Great?" *Columbia Journalism Review* (Fall 1967):31.

106   An "unofficial policy of encouraging good things": David Halberstam, *The Powers That Be* (New York: Knopf, 1979), 755.

107   Under Katharine, Bagdikian noted: Ben Bagdikian, "What Makes a Newspaper Nearly Great?" *Columbia Journalism Review* (Fall 1967):31.

107   When Bradlee came in mid-1965: David Halberstam, *The Powers That Be* (New York: Knopf, 1979), 741.

108   In 1967 she wrote a simpering letter: David Remnick, "Citizen Kay," *The New Yorker,* Jaunary 20, 1997.

108   He told his mother: Katharine Graham, *Personal History* (New York: Knopf, 1997), 395.

109   It was a long period,: Chalmers Roberts, *The Washington Post* (Boston: Houghton Mifflin, 1977), 392.

110   "It's funny, a lot of people at that ball": *Newsweek,* "The Kay We Loved," U.S. Special Edition: Special Report, July 30, 2001.

110   The simple truth: Author interview with Ben Bradlee, February 2004.

110   One of Capote's biographers: Lynn Rosellini, *Washington Star,* "The Katharine Graham Story," November 13, 1978.

111   Writing about the transition from obscurity: Anna Fels, *Necessary Dreams* (New York: Pantheon, 2004), 35.

111   "She was uncomfortable": Carol Felsenthal, *Power, Privilege and the Post,* Seven Stories Press, New York, (1993), p. 257.

112   Quoting a "knowledgeable official": "Rome Haul," *Newsweek,* January 8, 1968, 40.

112   "LBJ never forgave her": Author interview with Jack Valenti, January 2005.

113   By influencing the newspapers: David Halberstam, *The Powers That Be* (New York: Knopf, 1979), 737.

114   With the perspective of six years: Chalmers Roberts, *The Washington Post* (Boston: Houghton Mifflin, 1977), 386.

114 She had come into her position feeling: "The Editor as Leader—Part 2," transcript, American Society of Newspaper Editors, Reston, VA, December 31, 1998.

114 "*Newsweek* was number two to a strong": Author interview with Robert Samuelson, October 2004.

115 A friend of her son Don: Jane Howard, "Katharine Graham: The Power that Didn't Corrupt," *Ms.*, October 1974.

116 As she talked about him: Judith Viorst, "Katharine Graham," *Washingtonian*, September 1967, 35.

116 At times, she had negative overreactions: Katharine Graham, *Personal History* (New York: Knopf, 1997), 414.

117 He wanted "new journalism": Ben Bradlee, *A Good Life* (New York: Simon & Schuster, 1995), 298.

117 "You men have gotten hold": Carol Felsenthal, *Power, Privilege and the Post* (New York: Seven Stories Press, 1993), 267.

117 "Damn it, Katharine": Ben Bradlee, *A Good Life* (New York: Simon & Schuster, 1995), 300.

118 "She could be brutal ": Howard Bray, *The Pillars of the Post* (New York: Norton, 1980), 63.

118 With the acquisition, Katharine: Chalmers Roberts, *The Washington Post* (Boston: Houghton Mifflin, 1977), 383.

118 Despite their rocky relationship: Katharine Graham, *Personal History* (New York: Knopf, 1997), 413.

CHAPTER SEVEN: WALL STREET AND A WAR

121 It was a history "based": Sanford J. Ungar, *The Papers and the Papers* (New York: Dutton, 1972), 37.

122 "It was extremely embarrassing to us": Author interview with Eugene Patterson, January 2005.

122 "She must have been dying": Author interview with James Reston Jr., September 2004.

126 When she met with men: David Halberstam, *The Powers That Be* (New York: Knopf, 1979), 817.

127 The stock plan gave Katharine: Carol Felsenthal, *Power, Privilege and the Post* (New York: Seven Stories Press, 1993), 298.

128 If we don't print it, it's really going to be: David Halberstam, *The Powers That Be* (New York: Knopf, 1979), 806.

129   Ben Bagdikian whispered in Bradlee's ear: Katharine Graham, *Personal History* (New York: Knopf, 1997), 449.

129   "You're asking me to do something": David Halberstam, *The Powers That Be* (New York: Knopf, 1979), 805.

129   "And if we get convicted we lose": Chalmers Roberts, *The Washington Post* (Boston: Houghton Mifflin, 1977), 418.

130   "There's more than one way": Katharine Graham, *Personal History* (New York: Knopf, 1997), 450.

131   He had . . . also agreed with Katharine: Susanna McBee, "Katharine Graham and How She Grew," *McCall's*, September 1971, 132.

131   She did it with fear and tension: Harry Jaffe, "Capital Comment," *Washingtonian*, February 1997, 12.

131   As the men hung on the end of handsets: Katharine Graham, *Personal History* (New York: Knopf, 1997), 450.

131   Quite probably James Russell Wiggins: Chalmers Roberts, *The Washington Post* (Boston: Houghton Mifflin, 1977), 423.

132   Hadn't he believed that "in the pursuit of truth": Katharine Graham, "On the Centennial of the *Washington Post*," *Washington Post*, December 18, 1977, M3.

133   She talked about her deeply held values: Katharine Graham, *Personal History* (New York: Knopf, 1997), 457.

133   As Henry Kissinger later told Katharine: Ibid., 456.

133   At one point in 1973, Kissinger invited: Scott Shane, "In Call to Kissinger, Reporters Show That Even They Fell Under Super-K's Spell," *New York Times*, October 22, 2004.

134   Reporter Ken Clawson had quoted: Sanford J. Ungar, *The Papers and the Papers* (New York: Dutton, 1972), 309.

134   Historian Arthur Schlesinger described Agnew: Arthur Schlesinger, *The Imperial Presidency* (New York: Popular Library, 1973), 225.

135   Agnew said that the Post Company news outlets: Sanford J. Ungar, *The Papers and the Papers* (New York: Dutton, 1972), 119.

135   "It is long-standing policy of the Post Company": Katharine Graham, *New York Times*, November 21, 1969.

136   It would test the sense of confidence: Ben Bradlee, *A Good Life* (New York: Simon & Schuster, 1995), 323.

CHAPTER EIGHT: A BUSINESSWOMAN TAKES ON THE PRESIDENT

138 **"We were lucky . . . we had been able":** Katharine Graham, interview with Judy Woodruff, transcript, "The Editor as Leader—Part 2," American Society of Newspaper Editors, Reston, VA, December 31, 1998.

138 **"The market wanted not just profitability":** David Halberstam, *The Powers That Be* (New York: Knopf, 1979), 814.

138 **"Because I still had vast problems with self-confidence":** Katharine Graham, *Personal History* (New York: Knopf, 1997), 511.

139 **"This is the need we may call self-actualization":** Abraham H. Maslow, *Motivation and Personality* (New York: Harper & Row, 1954), 22.

139 **She had a reputation for directness:** David Halberstam, *The Powers That Be* (New York: Knopf, 1979), 814.

140 **"I can assure you that it is":** Larry Van Dyne, "The Bottom Line on Katharine Graham," *Washingtonian,* December 1985.

140 **"She turned on people":** Lynn Rosellini, "The Katharine Graham Story," *Washington Star,* November 17, 1978.

140 **But as Frank Waldrop, the last editor:** Laurence Leamer, *Playing for Keeps in Washington* (New York: Dial Press, 1977), 14.

141 **"You get the feeling that if she loses faith":** Ibid., 9.

141 **"If Ben needed his Sally to be a good editor":** David Halberstam, *The Powers That Be* (New York: Knopf, 1979), 817.

142 **"I devote a lot of time to horseflesh":** Laurence Leamer, *Playing for Keeps in Washington* (New York: Dial Press, 1977), 23.

142 **In his book,** *Good to Great,* **Jim Collins writes:** Jim Collins, *Good to Great* (New York: HarperCollins, 2001), 41.

144 **Maybe, mused Howard Simons:** Carl Bernstein and Bob Woodward, *All the President's Men* (New York: Simon & Schuster, 1974), 19.

144 **"Second, nothing reported by another media":** Chalmers Roberts, *The Washington Post* (Boston: Houghton Mifflin, 1977), 434.

145 **The** *New York Times* **printed less than half:** Mark Feldstein, "Watergate Revisited," *American Journalism Review* (August/September 2004).

145 **"All that crap, you're putting it in the paper?":** Carl Bernstein and Bob Woodward, *All the President's Men* (New York: Simon & Schuster, 1974), 105.

146 **She saw herself as "wading little by little":** Nicholas Coleridge, *Paper Tigers* (London: Mandarin, 1993), 93.

146   **"Another publisher than Katharine Graham":** Arthur Schlesinger Jr., *The Imperial Presidency* (New York: Houghton Mifflin, 1973), 265.

146   **Later she wrote that she endured:** Chalmers Roberts, *The Washington Post* (Boston: Houghton Mifflin, 1977), 435.

146   **"I lay awake many nights worrying":** Katharine Graham, *Personal History* (New York: Knopf, 1997), 483.

148   **She put more resources into the stations:** Talbot D'Alemberte, "A Remembrance of Courage," Poynter Online, August 17, 2001, http://poynteronline.org/content/content_view.asp?id=14252.

148   **She had, in the words of journalist Richard Reeves:** Richard Reeves, "Imagine Watergate 2005," Universal Press Syndicate, February 18, 2005.

148   **Woodward wrote later:** Carl Bernstein and Bob Woodward, *All the President's Men* (New York: Simon & Schuster, 1974), 237.

148   **He left lunch, "a motivated employee":** Fred Bruning, "Official Washington's Favored Reporter," *Newsday,* April 29, 2004.

149   **Ben Bradlee described the month of October, 1973:** Ben Bradlee, *A Good Life* (New York: Simon & Schuster, 1995), 370.

149   **She gave the court an affidavit asserting:** Chalmers Roberts, *The Washington Post* (Boston: Houghton Mifflin, 1977), 440.

150   **"She wanted to protect the image":** Author interview with Haynes Johnson, December 2004.

151   **The press had to be wary:** Chalmers Roberts, *The Washington Post* (Boston: Houghton Mifflin, 1977), 442–43.

152   **Colleague and friend Sally Quinn:** Author interview with Sally Quinn, February 2004.

152   **Life had taught Katharine that:** Katharine Graham, *Personal History* (New York: Knopf, 1997), 503.

152   **In 1978, after being interviewed:** Lynn Rosellini, "The Katharine Graham Story," *Washington Star,* November 13, 1978.

152   **"She burst into tears":** Author interview with Sally Quinn, February 2004.

152   **The next year a biography of Katharine:** Deborah Davis, *Katharine the Great* (New York: Harcourt Brace Javonovich, 1979). (After agreeing to a monetary settlement in a case she brought against the publisher, Davis republished the book, with Sheridan Square Press, in 1987.)

152   **She won't even credit her own:** Katharine Graham, *Personal History* (New York: Knopf, 1997), 505.

153 "You hired Benny and the rest": Chalmers Roberts, *The Washington Post* (Boston: Houghton Mifflin, 1977), 435.

153 She told Bradlee, "I know I'm No.1": Ibid., 444.

153 In her acceptance address for the Lovejoy Award: Katharine Graham, "A Vigilant Press" speech, Colby College, Waterville, ME, March 20, 1974.

CHAPTER NINE: BUILDING A FINANCIAL
POWERHOUSE

155 Even dinner parties, legendary for the politicians: Author interview with James Reston Jr., September 2004.

157 A recession and inflation had driven up costs: Kathleen McGinn, Lisa Gunther, Dina Witter, "Katharine Graham," Harvard Business School, HBS Case 9-801-276, December 13, 2001.

157 Get rid of them quickly: Ken Adelman, "So Long, Sweetheart," *Washingtonian,* September 1991, 86.

157 "It's a messy organization chart": "An Organization Woman remakes the *Post,*" *Business Week,* September 9, 1975, 43.

157 "It costs plenty to put two people": Larry Van Dyne, "The Bottom Line on Katharine Graham," *Washingtonian,* December 1985, 188.

158 "To convince them otherwise": Katharine Graham speech, Salzburg Institute, Salzburg, Austria, March 1987.

159 Comparing Katharine to Walt Disney: Katharine Graham, *Personal History* (New York: Knopf, 1997), 512.

160 When asked, Katharine observed: Roger Lowenstein, *Buffett: The Making of an American Capitalist* (New York: Main Street Books, 1996), 188.

160 "Kay and Warren Buffett had lots of fun": Author interview with Margaret Carlson, November 2004.

160 "Bill Gates has his dad": Author interview with Margaret Carlson, November 2004.

161 Buffett's effect on her life: Katharine Graham, *Personal History* (New York: Knopf, 1997), 535.

161 As her business insight grew: Ibid., 534.

162 She replied, "Right on both counts": Jane Howard, "Katharine Graham: The Power That Didn't Corrupt," *Ms.,* October 1974.

162 Katharine was alternately viewed: Chalmers Roberts, *The Washington Post* (Boston: Houghton Mifflin, 1977), 449.

162 The Guild action, she said: Ibid., 449.

164 "Most of the guys these days": "An Organization Woman remakes the *Post*," *Business Week*, September 9, 1975, 45.

165 "If a paper is struck and the other": Shirley Elder, "The Iron Lady Breaks the Pressmen," *Washingtonian*, 55.

165 She felt it was "very, very important": Ibid.

166 "The accolades had rubbed off": Howard Bray, *The Pillars of the* Post, (New York: Norton, 1980), 264.

166 The president of the pressmen's union: Ibid., 263.

166 Five days after the strike began: Robert G. Kaiser, "Members of Guild Uneasy Crossing *Post* Picket Line" *Washington Post*, Oct. 6, 1975.

166 Furious, Katharine threw some "pungent language": Howard Bray, *The Pillars of the* Post (New York: Norton, 1980), 265.

167 "Oh God, not that": "The Right to Manage," *Time*, December 29, 1975, 66.

167 Buffett said that: Warren E. Buffett, "Kay Graham's Management Career," The Washington Post Company, Web site, http://washpostco.com/history-kgraham.htm (2005).

168 With the *Washington Star* pouring resources: Laurence Leamer, *Playing for Keeps in Washington* (New York: Dial Press, 1977), 49.

168 Her boss replied: Author interview with Mary Beckner, March 2004.

169 "They produced over a hundred thousand copies": Tom Kelly, "The Imperial *Post*," *Washingtonian*, May 1981, 216.

169 "But to her it was as if": Laurence Leamer, *Playing for Keeps in Washington* (New York: Dial Press, 1977), 49.

170 Salary increases were not the issue: Howard Bray, *The Pillars of the* Post, (New York: Norton, 1980), 279.

170 Replacing the strikers: "The Right to Manage," *Time*, December 29, 1975, 44.

170 She denounced as a "lie": Howard Bray, *The Pillars of the* Post (New York: Norton, 1980), 278.

170 She told George Meany: "The Right to Manage," *Time*, December 29, 1975, 66.

171 In the first edition of her memoir: Katharine Graham, *Personal History* (New York: Knopf, 1997), 570 *(Hardback)*

172 In her autobiography she insists: Katharine Graham, *Personal History* (New York: Knopf, 1997), 576.

CHAPTER TEN: A FAMILY BUSINESS

173   **After Fritz Beebe died in 1973:** Carol Felsenthal, *Power, Privilege and the Post* (New York: Seven Stories Press, 1993), 320.

173   **A 1978 *Washington Star* exposé:** Lynn Rosellini, "The Katharine Graham Story," *Washington Star*, November 17, 1978.

174   **She recognized this and remarked:** Chalmers Roberts, *The Washington Post* (Boston: Houghton Mifflin, 1977), 464.

174   **She wouldn't act without being informed:** Author interview with June Bingham, June 2004.

174   **She was called "Katharine the Terrible":** Lynn Rosellini, "The Katharine Graham Story," *Washington Star*, November 17, 1978.

174   **Katharine said to her:** David Halberstam, *The Powers That Be* (New York: Knopf, 1979), 816.

175   **"She was unpredictable":** Author interview with June Bingham, June 2004.

175   **Warren Buffett told a reporter:** Lynn Rosellini, "The Katharine Graham Story," *Washington Star*, November 17, 1978.

175   **As Katharine wrote, "To me":** Katharine Graham, *Katharine Graham's Washington* (New York: Vintage Books, 2002), 10.

175   **Of the press she said, "The real world":** Katharine Graham, "The Press and Its Responsibilities" (Speech, Economic Club of Chicago, Chicago, IL, February 10, 1976).

176   **"He had been a tough competitor":** Frank C. Waldrop, *McCormick of Chicago* (Westport, CT: Greenwood Press, 1975).

177   **"Many people, especially in government":** Chalmers Roberts, *The Washington Post* (Boston: Houghton Mifflin, 1977), 455.

178   **When she became the first woman director:** Ibid., 464.

178   **"An impulse buy":** Howard Bray, *The Pillars of the Post* (New York: Norton, 1980), 204.

180   **Katharine waited for the man to call:** Ibid., 218.

180   **"My mother has given me everything":** Katharine Graham, *Personal History* (New York: Knopf, 1997), 589.

181   **"Family issues are complicated in any company":** Louis B. Barnes, "The Graham Family and the Washington Post Company," Harvard Business School, HBS Case 9-498-031, rev. ed., July 1, 1998.

183   **When asked if his mother:** Larry Van Dyne, "The Bottom Line on Katharine Graham," *Washingtonian*, December 1985, 213.

183   **"She came to the office":** Author interview with Haynes Johnson, December 2004.

183   **Longtime employees said they stayed on:** Louis B. Barnes, "The Graham Family and the Washington Post Company," Harvard Business School, HBS Case 9-498-031, rev. ed., July 1, 1998.

183   **"Mrs. Graham was more regal":** Author interview with Tom Sherwood.

183   **Rumor held that Don knew:** Louis B. Barnes, "The Graham Family and the Washington Post Company," Harvard Business School, HBS Case 9-498-031, rev. ed., July 1, 1998.

184   **"She took shareholder responsibilities just as seriously":** Ibid.

184   **The CEO of the Post Company showed them:** Sally Jenkins, "Graham Blazed a Path," *Washington Post*, July 19, 2001.

185   **The company hadn't grown:** Katharine Graham, *Personal History* (New York: Knopf, 1997), 595.

186   **He floated out on a golden parachute:** Morton Mintz, "The $1.8 Million Dollar Man," *Post Unit News*, April 27, 1981.

186   **Katharine defended her actions saying:** Morton Mintz, "The Exchange with Mrs. Graham," *Post Unit News*, August 23, 1982.

187   **In 1984, Wallace sent out a nine-page memo:** Tom Sherwood, "Employee and Union Bashing at the Post?" *Post Unit News*, February 6, 1987.

188   **Katharine had been told and believed:** Author interview with Tom Sherwood, December 2004.

188   **A few weeks later, Wingert was invited:** "What They're Saying: Former Colleagues Remember Katharine Graham," *Newsweek*, July 17, 2001.

188   **"We just wanted fairness":** Author interview with Morton Mintz, December 2004.

188   **He helped her with what she considered:** Katharine Graham, *Personal History* (New York: Knopf, 1997), 602.

190   **Katharine never strayed far:** Author interview with Michael Dobbs, March 4, 2005.

191   **The parties in her Georgetown home epitomized:** Christopher Hitchens, "Georgetown's Last Grande Dame," (London) *Evening Standard*, July 18, 2001.

191   **"She liked this sort of mocking of her":** Author interview with Margaret Carlson, November 2004.

192   **"She had a blunt instinct":** Author interview with Eugene Patterson, January 2005.

192   **One example occurred in 1997:** Author interview with Michael Dobbs, March 4, 2005.

192   Her "combination of elegance": Harry Jaffe, "*Post* Watch" *Washingtonian,* December 2003.

193   "She had a gift of making people feel": Author interview with E. J. Dionne, May 2004.

193   When he spoke to the guests he quipped: C. David Heymann, *The Georgetown Ladies Social Club* (New York: Atria Books, 2003), 342.

CHAPTER ELEVEN: THE FATES OF LEADERSHIP

196   In his drawing, toddler Katharine: Katharine Graham, *Katharine Graham's Washington* (New York: Vintage, 2002), 654.

196   "Kate's . . . got a hard mind": Larry Van Dyne, "The Bottom Line on Katharine Graham," *Washingtonian,* December 1985, 185.

197   As Warren Buffett said: Warren E. Buffett, "Kay Graham's Management Career," The Washington Post Company, Web site, http://www.washpostco.com/history-kgraham.htm (2005).

197   She wrote that she had seen companies: Katharine Graham, *Personal History* (New York: Knopf, 1997), 621.

197   "She realized from her stormy takeover": Author interview with Eugene Patterson, January 2005.

197   "It's a pretty hairy existence": Judith Viorst, "Katharine Graham," *Washingtonian,* September, 1967, 83.

197   "She believed one person": Author interview with Ben Bradlee, February 2004.

198   "Steadiness, decency, core journalistic values": Author interview with Paul Taylor, December 2004.

198   "I thought I'd be one of those who would die": Katharine Graham, "It's Like Going Down Steps," *Vital Speeches of the Day* 61, no. 20 (Aug. 1, 1995): 639.

198   As her formal role wound down: Author interview with Margaret Carlson, November 2004.

198   She had spent three decades in the top reaches: Katharine Graham, *Personal History* (New York: Knopf, 1997), 622.

199   She had what Csikszentmihalyi calls, "a hallmark": Mihaly Csikszentmihalyi, *Flow* (New York: HarperCollins, 1990), 204.

199   Her friend, former secretary of state Henry Kissinger: "The Kay We Loved," *Newsweek,* U.S. Edition Section: Special Report, July 30, 2001.

199   "A person who has achieved control": Mihaly Csikszentmihalyi, *Flow* (New York: HarperCollins, 1990), 6.

200   Katharine's intentional efforts to form her life: Ibid., 4.

200   "She was a very determined lady": Author interview with Robert Samuelson, October 2004.

201   She "mapped the heartache of being flawed": Margaret Carlson, "The Accidental Feminist," *Time,* February 17, 1997.

201   "It really never occurred to me": Antonio L. Sharp, "Former Post Publisher 'Created a Revolution' by Breaking Rules," ASNE Archives, April 2, 2000.

201   "Anytime we went anywhere": Author interview with Ann Pincus, January 2005.

202   "How that pen in the hand of an honest writer": Eugene Patterson to Katharine Graham, 17 February 1997. Personal papers.

202   Her friend Warren Buffett quipped: Warren Buffett, 2001 Berkshire Hathaway Annual Meeting.

202   "As the applause went on": David Broder, "Graham's Courage," *Cincinnati Post,* July 20, 2001.

202   "It's dangerous when you are older": Katharine Graham, *Personal History* (New York: Knopf, 1997), 625.

203   That trip led to the development: Eugene Robinson, "A New Black Dilemma," *Washington Post Magazine,* February 2, 1986.

203   She was compelled by the disparity: Marc Fisher, "Katharine Graham Never Lost Sight of Her City," *Washington Post,* July 18, 2001.

203   "She loved the award": Author interview with Ben Bradlee, February 2004.

203   Education, she told an awards' audience: Martin Weil, "18 Teachers Receive Agnes Meyer Awards," *Washington Post,* April 14, 1998.

204   "No measure can be taken": Ann Gerhart, "Bridging the Divide," *Washington Post,* July 24, 2001.

204   Journalist Bob Levey wrote that his boss: Bob Levey, "Katharine Graham: A Friend to Kids," *Washington Post,* July 23, 2001.

205   "She stood for full democracy": Steve Twomey, "A Pioneer with Courage, Influence and Humility," *Washington Post,* July 18, 2001.

205   Part of her plan for retirement: Katharine Graham, "It's Like Going Down Steps," *Vital Speeches of the Day,* 61, no. 20 (Aug. 1, 1995):639.

206   Her friend and colleague Sally Quinn: Sally Quinn, "Reveling in a Life Lived on Top of the News," *Washington Post,* July 18, 2001.

207   Margaret Carlson said, "She saw right through": Author interview with Margaret Carlson, November 2004.

207   She said, "I loved my job": J. Y. Smith and Noel Epstein, "Katharine Graham Dies at 84," *Washington Post,* July 18, 2001.

208   "A huge national desk, a huge foreign desk": Author interview with Morton Mintz, December 2004.

208   It was a "summer camp": Rick Ellis, "It Ain't Nothing But a Mogul Thing," http://www.allyourtv.com/0304season/news/july/07162003mogulthing.html (accessed July 16, 2003).

210   Not many years later, however: Katharine Graham, "It's Like Going Down Steps," *Vital Speeches of the Day*, 61, no. 20 (Aug. 1, 1995):639.

211   "No other news executive displayed greater courage": Haynes Johnson, "Appreciation: Katharine Graham," *American Journalism Review* (September 2001).

INDEX

Time Life Inc., 182
Times Mirror, 189
Trenton Times, 178–79

Unification Church, 183
United Nations, 111
University of Chicago, 17–19, 202
USA Today, 179, 184

Valenti, Jack, 83, 111–12
Valian, Virginia, 56
Vassar College, Katharine's studies in,
16–17
Vassar Miscellany News, 16–17
Vietnam Veterans Against the War, 123
Vietnam War:
antiwar protests, 123, 135
and Goldwater, 68
media coverage of, 107–8, 109, 111,
112, 113
and Pentagon Papers, 121–25, 133
Tet Offensive, 116
Vogue, 76, 110, 205
Von Hoffman, Nicholas, 170

Waldrop, Frank, 71–72, 140, 176
Walker, John, 44
Wallace, Larry, 169, 170, 187, 188
Wall Street Journal, 126
Walters, Barbara, 210
Washington, Walter, 107
Washington Herald, 62
Washingtonian, The, 151, 157
Washington Monthly, 171
Washington National Cathedral, 210
Washington Post Company / *Washington
Post*:
board meetings of, xvi–xvii, 56, 82, 182,
199
business side of, 99–101, 104, 114, 119,
125–26, 132–33, 137–40, 156–58,
160, 162, 165, 171, 177
compensation packages in, 186–87, 189
competition with, 58, 104, 106, 107,
119, 122, 128, 130, 135, 145, 149,
164–65, 168, 172, 176, 183, 189

corporate culture of, 105, 107, 114,
117, 154, 183
daily circulation of, 58
development of, 99, 101, 104, 117–18,
140–41, 155, 156, 177–80, 182–83,
185, 208
Don as publisher of, 182–84, 186, 197,
198
as family operation, xvii, 21, 35, 39, 45,
51, 85, 126–27, 138, 167, 176, 181
"farm system" for, 138, 140, 179
financial concerns at, 58
as Fortune 500 company, 146–47
Katharine as president/CEO of, xvii,
46–47, 50, 51–58, 60, 63, 103, 140,
157, 182, 185, 198
Katharine as publisher of, 68, 98,
118–19, 156–58
Katharine learns the business, 58–63
Katharine's early days as president/
CEO at, 51–58, 60, 63, 103
Katharine's early jobs at, 15–16, 21–23,
30, 31, 35, 51, 54
Katharine's identification with, 35, 78,
85–86, 97, 118, 139, 151, 152, 156,
188, 198, 207
Katharine's management decisions at,
89–92, 93–100, 128–32, 148, 153,
166–68, 169–72, 177–80
Katharine's retirement as CEO of,
196–200
as male bastion, 69–73, 76–77, 79, 82,
100
media properties of, 35, 41, 43, 58, 79,
88, 104, 118, 129, 133, 134–35, 138,
140, 147, 153, 156, 172, 177, 178,
180, 183, 189, 209
Meyer as owner of, 14, 15–16, 19, 101,
127, 139, 154, 167, 172, 176, 178
neutral position of, 68, 113, 134, 141,
151
new building for, 156
and Pentagon Papers, 122–25, 128–33,
135, 138
Phil as publisher of, xv, 33, 35, 41, 43,
54, 88, 105, 111, 139, 176, 178